T0290673

EMPOWERING RESILIENCE

Improving Health Care Delivery
in War-Impacted African Countries

A Case Study of Liberia

Aaron G. Buseh

University Press of America,® Inc.
Lanham · Boulder · New York · Toronto · Plymouth, UK

Copyright © 2008 by
University Press of America,® Inc.
4501 Forbes Boulevard
Suite 200
Lanham, Maryland 20706
UPA Acquisitions Department (301) 459-3366

Estover Road
Plymouth PL6 7PY
United Kingdom

Library of Congress Control Number: 2007936071
ISBN-13: 978-0-7618-3896-8 (clothbound : alk. paper)
ISBN-10: 0-7618-3896-1 (clothbound : alk. paper)

♾™ The paper used in this publication meets the minimum
requirements of American National Standard for Information
Sciences—Permanence of Paper for Printed Library Materials,
ANSI Z39.48—1984

I dedicate this book to my two youngest brothers, Albert Buseh and Mulbah Buseh. As unscrupulous warring factions were vying for power during the Liberian civil war, my innocent brothers lost their lives in the senseless chaos. The loss to my family of these two vibrant and intelligent young men is profound. And yet their deaths count as just two of the thousands of unspeakable, incomprehensible, and horrific deaths that occurred during the civil conflict. My heart is saddened by the untimely deaths of my brothers, but I am convinced that the loss of their lives, and all the others during the civil war, will not be in vain. I continue to hope that my native land, Liberia, will be able to peacefully reconstruct itself as a viable and productive country that contributes to the economic and social development of the continent of Africa and the global community.

I dedicate this book to all the young people of Liberia and other Sub-Saharan African countries emerging from civil conflicts. If these young people can remember that there are no winners in wars—only suffering, anguish, and despair—they will have the chance to promote lasting peace.

I dedicate this book to all the indigenous and international health care workers who served the people of Liberia during the civil war and its aftermath. I am humbled by their sacrifices and tireless efforts in providing care within a healthcare system plagued by inadequate resources.

CONTENTS

PREFACE

A STORY OF INTERLOCKING CYCLES OF POVERTY AND POOR HEALTH

Today, we are more aware that we live in a global community. Despite our sense of being one world, we are caught in a preoccupation with the differences between peoples. Many of us enjoy access to health care technology and health care outcomes that our ancestors a century ago could not even dream about. In many countries, overall life expectancy has increased, some infectious diseases have been eradicated, and people have the freedom to participate in decisions regarding their health and well-being.

Along with these successes in some communities, are unprecedented deprivations and lack of freedom in other communities. There are many emerging health and social problems, including endemic poverty leading to unfulfilled basic needs critical for survival. While many of these disparities can be observed in both developed and developing countries, due to complex and sometimes difficult to understand cultural factors, sub-Saharan Africa bears the brunt of these social and economic woes that exacerbate health disparities. For instance, recognition of the progress made on the continent of Africa in the area of health care and economic development is overshadowed by the reports of civil wars. In too many communities in sub-Saharan Africa, people are constrained in achieving optimal health and economic stability due to dysfunctional political systems. Corrupt leaders in Africa neglect their public responsibilities to the people, thereby depriving the citizens of Africa of even their most basic human rights. Political stability, especially for countries emerging from civil war, is the prerequisite for the development of critical health care knowledge and the infrastructure necessary to sustain the health and well being of a society.

I am an indigenous Liberian who came to the United States for advanced study in public health. I planned to go back to Liberia when I graduated to help my people to reach for the elusive goal of health that they have longed for and have not been able to achieve. I believed that if I received advanced training in public health, I could pay back that investment tenfold by training my fellow health professionals back in Liberia. During my second year of working on my master's program, civil war broke out in Liberia. Like other families I grew up with, my family had to flee their village and lost loved ones during the war. In the heat of the civil war, intellectuals were being killed, including health care workers, so I had to make a decision as to whether to return or continue my studies in the United States. With an uneasy heart, and grateful for the option, I started doctoral studies in nursing, with an emphasis on global public health. Each year, I closely monitored the civil war in my beloved country, hoping to return someday to the peace I remembered.

Watching my native country self-destruct and virtually collapse, as a nation-state has been an excruciating experience and profoundly frustrating. As a Liberian, I want to send the message to the world that the people of Liberia are humble and hardworking. They want to live in peace and desire self-actualization, as do people in every nation. As a public health professional, I want the information in this book to send the message that it is not merely political issues that have relevance in the rebuilding of Liberia; rather, issues of health and well being must be a central focus of the reconstructive process if the needs of the people are to be served adequately. The country's leaders need to recognize that optimal health is essential to boosting the economy and developing economic stability. The rebirth of Liberia will require popular participation in politics, education, and the economy. This book centers on how efforts should be made in the postwar era to help rebuild the shattered Liberian health care system and improve the overall health status of the people. Because they share a common ground of struggle, it is hoped that these strategies can also be used to revive the health care systems of other sub-Saharan African countries emerging from civil conflicts. Providing health care in profoundly dysfunctional settings is a journey that is not well mapped or understood by the global health care community. In this book, I decided to apply my global public health training in the United States to my indigenous experience of learning about and practicing health care in Liberia and sub-Saharan Africa.

As an assistant professor on the tenure track at the College of Nursing at the University of Wisconsin-Milwaukee, I wrote this book to keep my balance. I teach students who can't imagine carrying water on their heads or working all day in the rice fields with only wild cassava to eat; I work with colleagues who may take for granted the fact that they can see and touch the people they love, while I depend on memories of my family's presence.

I found time to write this book alongside my teaching responsibilities, my research and scholarly activities, and my university and community service because I reside in two worlds: the stimulating atmosphere of a university setting in a developed country, and the village of my heart, Liberia. I am part of an informal network of sub-Saharan Africans residing in the United States. We keep our homelands alive in our imagination through emotional support, as well as the constant collecting and sharing of news media reports related to our countries. I am an African man living in the United States. Although I am warmly welcomed, respected, and appreciated by my students and colleagues, when I leave the refuge of my office and the comfort of the university campus, I may be viewed with suspicion, as are other Black men in America who move through public space.

I teach a health care systems course to students for whom the intricacies of health care delivery to vulnerable populations in the United Sates and globally are difficult to grasp. For many of these young people, 'poor health' is an abstract concept far removed from their experiences; as a result, access to health care is taken for granted. I strive every semester to help students to think locally and globally about health care issues. They come to understand that the inability to address health disparities within a developed country, such as the United States, portends the tolerance of dismal health disparities between developed and developing countries as well as within developing countries. If I can get my health care systems students to feel outrage about the roughly 16 percent of Americans who struggle to access health care without health insurance, it becomes possible to elicit compassion for sub-Saharan Africans in need of health care in conflict-ridden countries such as Sudan, Uganda, Democratic Republic of Congo, and Liberia. Those students, who transcend their innocence and naiveté, to muster the zeal and resolve to use their health care training to address health and social issues here in the United States and around the world, intrigue me.

After a long day at the university, I lay awake at night, remembering my own youthful naiveté as a nurse in Liberia. My first assignment was in the emergency unit of a Lutheran hospital in rural Liberia. I saw cases ranging from infants dying from diarrhea to farmers losing limbs from farming injuries. I remember working the night shift when a young pregnant woman came in. Her name was Lorpu. She did not know her year of birth, which is not unusual for most Liberians, who are delivered in their village by a traditional birth attendant who is unable to read and write, and who does not rely on a calendar to mark the passage of time. Taking into account Lorpu's stunted growth; I guessed she was 14 years old. She was married to a man almost three times her age, a marriage arranged by well-meaning parents who thought this man would provide for Lorpu and their children, as well as the parents in their old age. When Lorpu went into labor, as was the custom, her husband acquiesced in yielding responsibility for the care of Lorpu to women elders.

Lorpu had been in labor for three days, but had not progressed. The traditional midwife of the village kept Lorpu "behind the house," a secluded, women-only area where older village women gathered to support women during a birthing process. The decision to go to a modern health care setting rested in the hands of these elderly women and the traditional midwife. This custom of supporting a woman in extended labor in the hope of a successful delivery has led to the intrauterine death of many fetuses, as well as maternal deaths.

On the fourth day of Lorpu's labor, her mother, Na Korto, and her aunts, along with the traditional midwife, finally decided that Lorpu's pregnancy was too complicated for an at-home delivery. They decided to seek modern medical care for Lorpu from the nearest health center, in the next town and staffed by a physician's assistant and a formally trained midwife. Unfortunately, the physician's assistant and the midwife had not received their salaries in the past six months, and decided therefore to travel to Monrovia, the capital city, to negotiate for their paychecks. A laboratory technician was left in charge of the clinic. He had gained some practical experience from working with the physician assistant. However, he was unable to handle Lorpu's case, so he advised Lorpu's family members to take her to the hospital, which was located 45 miles away.

It was the rainy season and the dirt road from Lorpu's village to the hospital was impassable. Lorpu's parents gathered up all the money they possessed—a few dollars—in order to pay for a "money bus" to transport their daughter to the hospital. Na Korto pawned her last two chickens to Flomo as a security deposit to guarantee that she would pay back his small loan to fund the medical bills. Flomo was one of the elders in the village who had a little shop where he sold simple goods. Na Korto promised to pay him back when she sold her rice at the end of the harvest season.

It was now 5:00 p.m. Besides the lumber trucks transporting timbers for export to the free port, there were only a few transportation vehicles still running at this time. The village chief rounded up four strong men to turn a hammock into a makeshift stretcher for Lorpu. They carried her, moaning in labor, ten miles to the next village, where an open market had been held during the day. Market vendors were loading their goods onto vehicles headed toward a city that was on the same route as the hospital. They convinced a truck driver to leave his goods behind—to be guarded by a market vendor—and make room in the back of his pickup truck for Lorpu, Na Korto, and the traditional midwife to be taken on a bumpy ride to the hospital.

Desperate to make sure her daughter got the care she needed, Na Korto had decided to accompany her daughter to the hospital. It was a difficult decision, as this was a critical point in the rice-farming season and Na Korto played a key role in farming. Traveling to the hospital meant she would miss two or more days of work in the fields. The rice crop had grown to full capacity that year and the yield was predicted to be higher than those of previous years. Na Korto's job was to wake up early in the morning to go on the farm to drive the swarm of birds away from decimating the freshly sprouted rice from their stalks. The financial consequences for being gone at this point would be enormous, but because Na Korto loved and needed her only daughter, she negotiated with her husband for permission to go. As he returned to the farm, her husband reluctantly accepted that this harvest season, in the end, would not yield a bumper crop of rice. They would still be living at a subsistence level, with no cash to spare.

When they arrived at the hospital, the doctor on call scolded Lorpu and her mother, as well as the traditional midwife, for waiting too long to bring her to the hospital. By this time, Lorpu was in shock, hemorrhaging vaginally. There was no fetal tone. The nurse started intravenous fluid while an all-out effort was launched to obtain blood for Lorpu. Na Korto was in the waiting room, distraught over the prospects of her daughter. Lorpu assisted her mother in the rice field, as well as with other activities necessary for sustaining their family's survival. The decrepit refrigerator that served as a blood bank at the hospital was empty. The policy was to ask relatives and friends of a patient for blood for a transfusion. The doctor determined that Lorpu needed an emergency cesarean section to remove the dead fetus. She was rushed into the operating room, but Lorpu died just as the doctor was scrubbing his hands and the operating room staff began to prepare her for surgery. The doctor and the nurse came out together to break the bad news to Na Korto.

The traditional midwife and Na Korto, accepting the tragic fate, used the last of the money for transportation back to the village. With a heavy heart, Na Korto told Lorpu's husband and father the sad news. When the news spread that Lorpu and her baby had died, the people of the village came to console Na Korto, bringing food. The villagers reassured Na Korto and her husband that if their rice yield came up short that year, they could harvest some rice from other villagers' fields.

As a Liberian, I understand that Na Korto may never ask, "Why did Lorpu die?" But as health professionals, that is the very question that we must ask if there is to be a reduction in maternal and infant mortality rates in Liberia and other sub-Saharan African countries. Over 99 percent of maternal deaths globally occur in less developed countries. Lorpu represents the estimated one out of ten maternal deaths in sub-Saharan Africa.

Using my homeland, Liberia, as a focus for this book, I discuss the interrelated factors of health and health care delivery in countries emerging from civil conflicts. *Empowering Resilience: Improving Health Care Delivery in War-Impacted African Countries—A Case Study of Liberia,* is my effort to explain the impact of civil war on the health care system and to provide persuasive reasons why investing in health care in the postwar era is critical to recovery in both Liberia and other sub-Saharan African countries impacted by civil conflicts. This book is a plea to all stakeholders involved in the organization and delivery of health care in Liberia to seize the opportunity to transform the health care system in postwar Liberia and thus transform the country as a whole.

Aaron G. Buseh, Ph.D., MPH, MSN
Associate Professor
University of Wisconsin-Milwaukee
College of Nursing
United States of America

ACKNOWLEDGMENTS

Treading the path of academic and career achievements for me has been a rigorous and sometimes difficult process. Besides the academic rigors of a doctoral program, personal obstacles faced over the years as a Liberian émigré in the United States tested my resolve to complete this book. Writing this book, however, has been a therapeutic process for me and allows me to dream that my beloved country, Liberia, will one day rise up again from the ashes of a failed state to play its important role in sub-Saharan Africa and the international community.

Several individuals have helped shape my life, both in Liberia and in the United States, and as a result are directly or indirectly responsible for me generating this book. I am particularly grateful to my parents for instilling in me the virtues of hard work, discipline, humility, patience, and perseverance. In her reserved, soft-spoken manner, my mother cradled big dreams for her children. Amidst the entrenched poverty and daily uncertainties, my mother gracefully faced the challenges of raising her children in harsh conditions. With quiet dignity, she instilled hope in us that someday we would grow up to be productive people of whom she would be proud. My father, the disciplinarian and organizer, shouldered the responsibility of his family with steadfast pride and dedication. Both of my parents were committed to their family and their community. I hope to honor the legacy of contributing to the greater good of society that both my parents exemplified.

I owe a great deal to all my teachers in Liberia, both in my elementary and secondary schools. Their dedication to learning and teaching inspired me. My professors at Cuttington University in Liberia saw the spark of intellectual curiosity in me, nurtured, and challenged it. They encouraged me to keep expanding my educational pursuits. In the United States, where I pursued my graduate studies, my college professors influenced me greatly with their teaching, and generously served as mentors, advisers, and friends. At the University of Illinois at Chicago, the expansive and innovative approach of the Global Health Leadership Office (GLO) in the College of Nursing was inspiring. Under the leadership of Dr. Beverly McElmurry, the GLO's noble goal of developing programs to reduce the burden of illness and improve health in developing countries expanded my vision of what I, an indigenous Liberian born in a remote village, might contribute to the global health community. The College of Nursing at the University of Wisconsin-Milwaukee is admired nationally and globally for its efforts to improve health outcomes for vulnerable populations. It's collaborative, supportive, and visionary environment has helped me grow as a teacher, scholar, and researcher.

I am grateful to my writing coach, Patricia Lynn Walsh, B.S., M.A., Associate Professor of Professional Communication at Alverno College, for her input and critique of my drafts of each chapter in this book.

I appreciate the students who have been enrolled in my health systems course over the years for getting me to think more broadly, on how health care could be provided to individuals in fragile states. I wish to acknowledge Lori Lierman, R.N., B.S.N., my former student, for her efforts to organize the research information needed to complete this book.

Finally, I would like to recognize the immense suffering that the people of Liberia have endured during the civil war and commend them for their resilience. My plea goes out to all health care professionals in sub-Saharan Africa to unite and use health as a means for solidarity while strengthening the fabric of society.

A poem by the former President of Ghana, Kwame Nkrumah, eloquently and vividly presents one of the themes of this book, in which health care, like other development projects, must be based on a bottom-up approach rather than the usual bureaucratic approaches used in prewar Liberia. President Nkrumah suggests that we:

Go to the people
Live among them
Learn from them
Love them
Serve them
Plan with them
Start with what they know
Build on what they have.[1]

Note

1. Nkrumah, Kwame (1977). *Africa must unite,* p. 55, quoted in *Axioms of Kwame Nkrumah* (Freedom Fighters' Edition), Panaf Books Ltd., 1977, p. 47-48.

CHAPTER 1

INTRODUCTION AND OVERVIEW

We have taken the view that crises are opportunities for important
decision making. Therefore, we are undaunted by these problems.
With the necessary political will at home, and with international
cooperation based on mutual respect, we are confident that we
shall succeed in securing for our children not merely survival but
also protection and development. We must not—dare not—fail
in this.[1]

> —Yoweri K. Museveni, President of the Republic of
> Uganda, in his capacity as Chairman of the then
> Organization of African Unity (OAU), 1990-1991.
> Speech delivered at the World Summit for Children,
> United Nations, New York, September 1990.

Background and Scope

Prior to its civil conflict, Liberia had a fairly functional health care
delivery system for a developing country. For several decades, Liberia
had been making important strides in improving the health and life
expectancy of its population. Despite these remarkable improvements,
enormous health problems still existed. For instance, the country still lagged

far behind neighboring African countries in decreasing its infant, under-age-five, and maternal mortality rates. When Liberia's health care delivery system became paralyzed by war, the morbidity and mortality rate of the general population increased. This is the challenge facing international and Liberian health care policy planners today as the country emerges from protracted civil conflict. In order to create a viable future for the people of Liberia, it is critical to empower local communities with the knowledge and practical support needed to reduce illness and mortality.

Liberia's Civil War

The civil war in Liberia greatly tested the resolve of the Liberian people to function as a successful, independent nation contributing to the global community. Liberia's civil war also tested the capacity of the United Nations (UN) and of the international community to respond to civil crisis. It is estimated that more than half a million people, mostly Liberians, lost their lives because of this 14-year war. During the civil war, all warring factions instigated brutal and widespread killings. The civilian population suffered immeasurable loss. Thousands of people were uprooted and became displaced within Liberia or became refugees in neighboring African countries. The reasons for the war in Liberia are multifaceted: economic greed; intertribal conflicts; corrupt and inept governments; unfair distribution of resources for development initiatives; and a disregard of human rights by each regime. In the midst of all this civil conflict, HIV/AIDS and other emerging diseases were casting their shadow across the West African belt. A dysfunctional health care system during the conflict period made it impossible to address the health care needs of the Liberian people, as done in stable African states.

The economic context was also a factor: the Liberian population consists of a small percentage of wealthy individuals, a majority of poor subsistence farmers, and virtually no middle class to create stability. Even the very history of the country set a backdrop for an imminent civil crisis; former American slaves returned to West Africa in the 1820s, only to disenfranchise indigenous people in the process of founding Liberia. Over time, descendants of these former slaves, Americo-Liberians, became the wealthy ruling class. It was only a matter of time before some sociopolitical crisis would erupt. The catastrophic impact of the civil war in Liberia quickly spilled over into neighboring Sierra Leone, Guinea, and Côte d'Ivoire.

At first, these countries welcomed refugees because of their historically close ties with Liberia and their spirit of generosity, which is common to African cultures. Unfortunately, significant internal political conflicts were on the verge of erupting in each of these countries. The disruptive impact of the Liberian refugees' presence within their borders helped fuel civil crises in Sierra Leone, Guinea, and Côte d'Ivoire. Many West African leaders who were at first reluctant to get involved in the conflict in Liberia soon observed that the war in Liberia was having a devastating effect on the stability of the entire West African belt. Several peace accords were initiated by the Economic Community of West African States (ECOWAS), the African Union (AU), and the UN, but none held because the fighting was out of control; the infrastructure of the country was devastated, and there were so many warring factions that it proved impossible to reach consensus. Compounding these obstacles to peace were indecision and lack of will on a regional and international level about how to implement and sustain the peace accords.

Many individuals in the international community had called for Liberia to be declared a "failed state"[2] at this point because they deemed the country unable to govern itself. Because Liberia is a member of the UN, if it would be declared a failed state, this international body would take over the operation of the country and create an environment for true governance. When the UN deemed it feasible, governance would be handed back to Liberians. While Liberia was not, in the end, declared a failed state, the UN sought to work with ECOWAS, the AU and leaders in the West African region to broker a peace plan.

Finally, a fragile peace was achieved in Liberia in the summer of 2003, when Liberian President Charles Taylor came under immense pressure to step aside from African leaders, the UN, and the United States. A transitional government took power and began to implement the latest peace accord initiated by ECOWAS and the UN. The damage that the protracted civil war in Liberia inflicted on the personal, social, and economic aspects of the Liberian society is harrowing.

Impact of the Civil War on Health and the Health Care Delivery System

Taylor's departure created an opportunity for the international community to begin developing plans on how to rebuild Liberia. During the preceeding 14 years, the civil conflict in Liberia brought all cultural, socioeconomic, educational, and health initiatives to a halt. Without programs in these realms, it is difficult, if not impossible, to provide basic services that ensure a decent quality of life for the general population. Health initiatives, in particular, require a developed infrastructure and trained professionals to implement. War disrupts the delivery of health care services and destroys the health care system in place. For instance, hospitals, clinics, medical training centers, pharmacies, and medical distribution services are quickly looted by opportunists who sell medical equipment and drugs on the black market in other countries. During civil conflicts, doctors and nurses may be targeted for violence or kidnapped to serve the medical needs of various factions participating in the war. Most trained medical professionals in developing countries are women, who are then also vulnerable to sexual assault during war. To escape personal tragedy, many health care professionals flee with their families to other countries, thereby creating a void of trained medical professionals who could have cared for local populations during and after the war. Individuals who sought advanced medical training outside their country with initial goal of returning to help improve health care delivery were unable to return to their homeland during war. Had they been able to return, they would have played a key role in advancing the skills of local health care professionals in their home country.

Unfortunately, the health care delivery system in Liberia was already inadequate and malfunctioning before the war. Enormous health problems existed in the prewar era. For instance, Liberia lagged far behind neighboring African countries in decreasing its infant, under-five, and maternal mortality rates. When Liberia's health care delivery system became paralyzed by war, the morbidity and mortality rate of the general population was increased. Physical and emotional war traumas layered on top of endemic and epidemic diseases create the challenge facing Liberian and international health care policy planners today.

Resiliency and Perseverance of the Liberian People

Liberia can be revived to play its role once again in African and international affairs. My belief is founded in the optimism and resiliency of my people. The majority of the Liberian population have lived in rural areas and engaged in subsistence farming. For fear of their safety, many farmers abandoned their villages and farms and moved to urban centers. Many of these people long to move back to their villages and their communal land as soon as it is safe. In this postwar era, it will therefore be critical for the Liberian Governments and the international community to invest in the agricultural sector, providing the necessary tools and seeds for planting so that sustainable agricultural activities can be reestablished.

One of the many tragedies of the war was that children were traumatized and abused, witnessed atrocities, and were even recruited for warfare and participated in atrocities. All these children lost their childhood. As all who have suffered through war, these children long to return to their former life. In Liberia, this means communal life in a village where everyone knows one another, feels responsible for one another, and assists one another in daily life. Unfortunately, many of these children reached adulthood during the war and missed out on the crucial Liberian socialization process of becoming an integral part of a community. Prior to the war, Liberian children walked for miles on dirt roads, sometimes barefoot, to go to school and upon return worked alongside their parents in the rice fields several hours a day. Parents were devoted to the welfare of their children. It was not unusual to see hundreds of women waiting under the hot sun for health care workers to come by Jeeps to vaccinate their children. Women performed most day-to-day family-sustaining activities communally: rearing children, farming, harvesting rice, fishing, and water and firewood gathering for cooking and household use. Men also worked communally in performing large-scale family-sustaining activities. These include hunting, clearing the forest to prepare fields for rice farming, building fences to keep out animals from the fields, setting fish traps, and building houses. Men also play a role in rearing children, especially mentoring young boys to become responsible and respectful members of the community.

It is the communal nature of the Liberian society that will help heal the country and make it whole again. The Liberian government and the international community need to tap into the power of communal life during the reconstruction era. We must create a forum for allowing people to reclaim their powerful skills of building cohesiveness through self-sustaining community activities. But it is the very essence of community life that was disrupted during the war. People became displaced, young children were recruited to take up arms, and neighbors turned on each other. The communal patterns of living that had been in place for hundreds of years were severely interrupted. Intriguing and pragmatic questions that wait to be answered are: Was this interruption so great that these patterns cannot be restored? How long will it take to restore communities in Liberia? Should restoring local communities to prewar-era status be our goal? Will Liberians remember the good parts of their prewar life enough to work toward restoring those aspects? Will the children who were traumatized and made instruments of war have the courage to return to their communities? Will their communities accept them? Will people who fled to the cities want to return to their rural villages? Will there be enough resources to reestablish sustainable agricultural practices? Will urban people want to work together to build sustainable-development communities within cities and towns?

Given the length and severity of the civil war, we must be realistic about the return of prewar village life. Village life was already changing before the war. In Liberia, like many sub-Saharan African countries, there was a growing rural-to-urban migration. Like any other developing country, Liberia was not immune to the transforming process of industrialization and globalization. As Liberians were becoming literate and educated, the restrictive gender roles in Liberian society were already changing. For example, some women became more economically empowered because they developed the know-how to produce and sell products at the market while retaining control over some of their profits. Literacy programs for the general population also created a means where people became more aware of their rights and how to participate in national and local politics. The progression of modern health care delivery in Liberia also created an excellent opportunity to bridge the gap between village life and urban life. The health care delivery process created a forum for health care professionals to provide health education and health promotion programs that significantly changed people's daily lives.

The rebuilding of a country after civil war must take into account the evolutionary path the country was already on before the conflict. All the forces that were bringing about changes in the society (economics, gender roles, education, literacy, health care, industrialization) must be brought to bear on how people conceptualize the framework for rebuilding war-torn countries. These are powerful forces that are already in motion and out of the control of individuals who are going to be involved in helping structure a new system. It is better to understand how these forces were distorted and disrupted during the war, be aware of, and attempt to predict what shape these forces will take in the future.

The war put Liberia into a position that makes it difficult to provide even the most basic needs for the general population. And yet, many Liberians speak of the future and express optimism about putting their lives back on track. Out of the ashes of a failed state could rise up a sound health care system if the strength and vision of the people are used in designing new programs. If the rebuilding process is done properly, it could be turned into a case study where other African states that have experienced similar conflicts could learn from this new functional system. If nothing good comes of the tragedy and despair of the Liberian people, then their suffering is compounded.

It is harder to rebuild a poor health care delivery system after war than a well-functioning system after war. The people in a country where there was a good health care delivery system have the intangible asset of memory. They remember having confidence in the health care system; they remember getting their medical needs met; they remember trusting medical providers. This collective memory makes it easier to reestablish the interpersonal pathways of health care delivery. In health care delivery, the micro level, which consists of nurses and community health care workers, is essential in rebuilding the national health program that forms the macro level of health care delivery.

Even though health care reform was stalled in Liberia during the war, there is still reason for hope. The dedication shown by health care providers in both the private and public sectors during the civil war is a clear indication that many individuals will be committed to the reconstruction process for the health care system in Liberia. True progress, therefore, will require input from the people at a grassroots level as to how limited health care resources can be most equitably allocated. New and sound health care delivery policies need to be put into place now that the conflict has subsided.

Opportunities for Building Long-Term Organizational Change

A healthy population leads to increased productivity and improvement in the overall economy, which will fund, in part, the perpetuation of the health care-rebuilding process. To enable all Liberians to achieve optimal health in this postwar era, the people will need access to safe drinking water, good nutrition, basic sanitation facilities, immunizations, and primary health care services. A new health care delivery system must be able to tie in primary care with secondary and tertiary levels of care because many serious health care problems cannot be resolved in a primary care setting.

The key to improving the health outcome for the general population will be establishing a comprehensive delivery system for primary health care that ties into secondary and tertiary health care. Primary care is usually the most appropriate entry point for seeking health care. If the primary health care level is well developed, providers will be able to successfully assess, treat, and evaluate conditions that are treatable or determine those that need to be referred to another level. The terms "primary care" and "primary health care" are sometimes confused with each other or are used interchangeably, even though primary care is a subset of primary health care. *Primary health care* (PHC) is an approach to health care delivery that centers on promotion of health and prevention of diseases across the wellness-illness continuum. In contrast, *primary care* focuses on the professional-client dyad—an approach to health care delivery that constitutes the first level of contact by a client with the health care delivery system and first element of a continuing health care process.

The post civil war period is an opportune time for creating a master PHC plan. When peace returns, people at every level of society are ready for change, open to new ideas, excited about the future. Old paradigms are gone; creating room for a new and better paradigm that includes all stakeholders. Resources will start flowing in from the African region, non governmental organizations (NGOs), and the international community. This type of support creates stability for election of new leaders with vision. As the infrastructure is being rebuilt, there is the opportunity to build in design for long-term organizational change.

Although Liberia's brain drain was an adverse effect of the war, Liberian émigrés can be a positive force in postwar reconstruction. During the years of the civil war, thousands of Liberians stuck in exile pursued advanced educations in disciplines that are pertinent to reconstruction. Like most other people who migrate from a developing country to a developed country, Liberians in Western countries found themselves with access to enormous educational opportunities that they could not have dreamed of in their home country. Exile gave them the opportunity to prepare themselves intellectually for contributing to the world. It is generally known that in order for immigrants to become bicultural, they must develop high-level intellectual and social capacities for adaptation. Their host countries are now benefiting from these émigrés achieving their human potential. This intellectual resource could be as valuable an asset to the reconstruction process as the grassroots resource of the local people.

Most Liberians living outside their country longed to return to their homeland in peacetime. It is extremely challenging to take up one's life again in a country that has been ravaged by civil war. It is also an agony to leave behind a life that one has struggled to build over years of time in a host country. The ending of a civil war is like a fork in the road for émigrés.

Each branch of the road creates excruciating dilemmas. Liberian émigrés coped with the protracted civil war in different ways. Some Liberians have assimilated to their new country, married, had children and built their careers and would find it painfully disruptive at this point to move back to Liberia; other Liberians intended all along to return to their homeland and were waiting patiently for an opportune time to do so; finally, there are those Liberians who are torn between their loyalty to Liberia and their identity in their host country.

It would be counterproductive to conceptualize the choice facing émigrés as a dichotomy between choosing either Liberia or their host country, because there are infinite ways that a Liberian émigré can contribute to rebuilding his or her home country. The beckoning question for Liberia and the international community is how to tap into Liberian émigrés in their unique position as a conduit to the enormous resources available in their host countries that would be relevant in the rebuilding process for Liberia. Each Liberian émigré must decide for herself or himself what would be the most useful ways of contributing to Liberia's shattered society. One of the deepest tenets of the Liberian culture is that Liberians cherish the communal process that emphasizes that they are responsible not only for their immediate relatives, but also the community at large. The influx of energy from émigrés contributing to Liberia will bring new zeal and vitality to the reconstruction of their country of origin. One of the coping mechanisms of émigrés is to remember their homeland vividly, while those who were on the ground during the civil war coped by forgetting what it used to be by focusing on survival. In the inspiring tale of regeneration, émigrés hold the collective prewar memory of Liberia intact.

Many exiles chose an area of study they thought they could use to survive in their host countries and also be able to make an important contribution to Liberia when they returned. To many émigrés, a health care discipline was the optimal career choice. This choice will prove to be useful for Liberia because health indicators are dismal and creating relevant health programs could be a unifying force for different warring factions. These émigrés from a developing country have been trained in developed countries where the health care system advocates highly ethical professional standards. These émigrés have absorbed the ideology from their host countries that a good health care system must be built on a strong professional code of ethics for both health care workers and administrators. Even though the health care sectors in developing countries are imperfect, there has been an increasing effort to institute checks and balances aimed at warding off corruption. In many sub-Saharan African countries, there is a corresponding desire for government reforms in creating accountability in all sectors, including the health care system.

Liberian émigrés can help promote this movement for reform. Their experience training and working in developed countries where ethical standards have evolved over a long period of time will help them participate in the reconstruction of the Liberian health care system and the devising of new and culturally relevant ethical standards that meet the current situation of the Liberian population. Liberian émigrés are very much aware of the fact that Liberia has been plagued with rampant corruption, even in the health care system, which might be presumed to be fair.

Institutional Corruption and Bribery: Factors to Consider in the Postwar Era

Corruption is an influential force to consider in the post war era. Corruption is the personal use of public resources. In Liberia, corruption can involve illegally obtaining contracts, tax exemptions, or licenses. Corrupt individuals may hold back public information as a way of wielding power. They can also pay a bribe to get the government to turn a blind eye to illegal activities. Many small corrupt acts and transactions lead to diversion of money for noteworthy projects, as well as stagnation of growth and development at both the national and local levels. As in other African countries, bribery in Liberia is a common form of corruption and is a given for those who want to get something done. Bribery involves using personal financial resources to divert government or organization resources for greater personal gain. If corruption is endemic in a society, positive change and innovation on a national level become difficult to implement. The start-up energy and the effort to launch relevant projects are wasted in attempting to navigate the system.

One sector where corruption has been prevalent is within the formal Liberian administrations. The bureaucratic political structure of the Liberian government creates many layers of institutional corruption. There are numerous government ministries and autonomous agencies, competing amongst themselves, from which anyone seeking to establish or manage a project has to seek approval. In many instances, the need for development is urgent, but the process of gaining approval is laborious, disheartening, and exhausting.

Government ministers and directors in many of these agencies have conflicts of interest. Not only are they running these agencies, they have started their own small businesses to benefit from the lucrative government contracts that are the products of the very agency they lead. In the rebuilding stage, there is going to be a proliferation of contracts to rebuild damaged government ministries, buildings, housing units, roads, and the like. Because of institutional corruption, some of these contracts are likely to be given to themselves, their friends, or organizations they are affiliated with. Depending on the tribal affiliations of the persons granting the contracts, certain tribal groups may be highly favored, which in turn will fuel old tribal hatreds that existed before the war and were inflamed by the war.

Corruption in Liberia could range from major decisions of a government official to management decisions of local projects managers. In Liberia, where corruption has become systemic, rules and decisions become increasingly arbitrary, this makes bribery the norm. Corrupt processes become so entrenched that no one even challenges them anymore.

The electoral processes in sub-Saharan Africa constitute another area where corruption is likely to occur. When elections are held in countries emerging from civil conflicts, failure to pay attention to institutional corruption could influence the electoral process. In Liberia, where the population is emerging from a civil conflict, much conflict and suspicion revolved around alleged election fraud. Trust in the electoral process and election results in Liberia were addressed with international observers including the Carter Center known for its neutral role of observing elections in many countries around the world.

Corruption is not limited only to the Liberian public sector. When private companies or organizations, including NGOs, pay bribes or commit fraud, they contribute to a climate that breeds more corruption. In this postwar era, Western governments, and their agencies including the U.S. Agency for International Development (USAID), will offer lucrative contracts in an effort to help to rebuild the shattered Liberian health care system. Some local business communities in Liberia may try to wield their influence through illegal means when seeking contracts for government-funded or non-government-funded development programs.

In Liberia, there are three layers that make up the retail sector of the economy: the Lebanese who dominate the wholesale and retail operations in the major towns and cities; members of the Mandingo tribe, an ethnic group in Liberia who own small retail businesses in smaller towns and villages; and the indigenous farming families of other ethnic groups who sell their produce and goods in communal markets. Liberia's entire retail economy relies primarily on the first two groups. An empowering rebuilding process for the Liberian people will require reestablishing the communal markets, many of which were destroyed during the war. The communal marketplace system is paramount to distributing economic development opportunities more fairly across the population. It should be noted that the majority of Liberians are living in poverty; before the war, their chance for daily survival was through selling at the marketplace. Effort should be made to create a postwar environment that promotes empower-ment and self-sufficiency among all groups, including the indigenous poor.

Restoring the health care system is profoundly linked to restoring the communal market place. The optimal health care model for reviving the Liberian health care delivery system depends on providing primary health care to the people in their environment with their active participation. Before the war, communal marketplaces were where health care profession-als could set up mobile clinics for prenatal care, infant and childhood immunizations, and treatment of common noncomplicated ailments. These types of community-based programs are known to be cost-effective. This is also an opportune time for mass health education and health promotion programs.

A more equitable distribution of wholesale and retail opportunities would not only provide a venue for cost-efficient health care delivery, which helps to stabilize and expand the economy, but would also reduce opportunities for exploitation. When corruption runs rampant, crime syndicates flourish and potential investors may be discouraged about making any serious investment in Liberia. In every country, including Western developed countries, there is corruption. For instance, in the United States, it is not unusual for pharmaceutical companies to provide perks to members of Congress in an effort to sway them to support legislative proposal that would protect the pharmaceutical companies' business ventures. The ordinary person having a prescription filled may not be aware that the high cost of their prescription pays for these perks. The irony is that many people in the United States are not aware on a daily basis that they live in the midst of corruption, but in a developing country, such as Liberia, corruption is more direct and is more visible at every step of the way, so people know they are living in the midst it.

While many Americans can absorb inflated drug costs, people in a developing country could be shut out of life-sustaining therapeutics because they can't afford the bribe. In the Liberian situation, corruption stems from limited codes of ethics; lack of accountability in government; greedy public officials; leaders who have a lack of commitment to serve the general population; and a destructive policy of paying low wages to trained professionals, which makes bribes tempting. Additionally, the communal way of life for indigenous Liberians includes a system for informal exchanges when someone does someone else a favor. Although exclusive but mutually beneficial ethnics are much stronger in rural areas than in urban settings, tribal favoritism still exists in urban areas. As a result, it is a common practice to appoint an individual that may not be qualified for a given position to an office that requires critical thinking skills.

Dating back to earlier Liberian administrations, those of William Tubman, William Tolbert, and Samuel Doe and, more recently, Charles Taylor, leadership in the country has been, for the most part, based on self-enrichment and ambiguity over ethics of public service. If political leaders and top bureaucrats set an example with high ethical standards, lower-level officials and members of the public might follow. If informal rules come to supersede formal ones, even the most stringent legal principles and procedures lose their authority. Hence, bribery and corruption may become the norm, even in the face of formal rules intended to support clean governance.

To his credit, William Tolbert who ruled during the late 1970s until he was assassinated in 1980 by Samuel Doe established an autonomous agency called the Corruption Bureau. This agency was given the authority to reduce corruption in the government and public at large. With almost two decades of a serious lack of development and economic stagnation and the total modification of people's ways of living, postwar administrations must find the way to indigenize the machinery of government. The moral epicenter that makes for good governance was absent during the civil war and the practice of bribery often became a way of life and necessary for survival in an uncertain environment. A new moral epicenter must be created, one where new leadership will have the opportunity to lead in an environment that is free from fear of making the right decisions and where all involved are held to the highest ethical standard.

In the new Liberian context, these features of corruption discussed above will become critical to the institutional and social dimensions of reducing poverty and enhancing economic development. It is in the rules and practices of governance that the foundations of sustainable economic development and enhancement of health are shaped or undermined. The new Liberian government and international agencies assisting with the rebuilding process in Liberia must understand that rules and practices must be effectively applied and monitored. This postwar era is an opportunity for launching several economic development initiatives. New health and development projects will suffer or be ineffective where the rules of governance allow arbitrary resource allocations and diversion in disregard of the public good and to the exclusive benefit of corrupt Liberian officials, politicians and their collaborators.

Lessons Learned: Creating an Enabling Environment for Health

The end of a war creates a forum for reflection and change. People have time to reflect on their war experience as well as remember life before the war. People are motivated to reclaim their past as well as create a new future. There are lessons to be learned in every direction. In health care, we can learn from analyzing the shortcomings of the prewar health care delivery system, as well as anticipating the new health care needs that have arisen from the war. The World Bank suggests that African countries create an "enabling" environment to improve health care for the people (The World Bank, 1994). Even before the civil conflict, Liberia's efforts to create an enabling environment were impeded by deep-rooted problems in the Liberian health care system. For the Liberian setting and possibly those of many other sub-Saharan African countries, the following major areas by the World Bank must be considered when creating an enabling health environment: (a) absence of economic development opportunities and endemic poverty, (b) absence of mechanisms for achieving those opportunities, (c) efforts required to tap into the few existing opportunities are extremely exhausting and not cost-effective, (d) lack of political commitment, (e) existence of bureaucratic centralized hierarchical structures, (f) lack of international commitment, and (g) general population health and emerging diseases.

Absence of Opportunities and Economic Development

The term "economic development" is used constantly in the international health arena. In the 1950s and 1960s, development was essentially measured in terms of a country's gross national product (GDP), gross domestic product (GDP) and income per capita. The assumption at the time was based on "trickle down economics," which presumes that economic growth in a well-off sector of the population will trickle down to improve personal wealth across the general population, thereby creating opportunities, employment and subsequent reduction of poverty. In the 1980s and 1990s, the definition of development shifted and became broader in its conception to include better quality of life for the population at large. The focus then became about creating opportunities and eliminating inequality, poverty and unemployment (World Bank, World Development Report, 1993).

As in other African countries, before the civil war in Liberia, poverty there was a major factor that precluded people and communities from being developed. Due to the civil war, extreme poverty is now heavily concentrated in the country and must be addressed. Poverty is seen as the deprivation of basic capabilities among a group of people. Poverty robs people of the freedom to obtain optimal nutrition, or to obtain care for treatable conditions, or the opportunity to be clothed or sheltered adequately, or to enjoy clean water or sanitary facilities. Poor individuals mostly lack assets and are often unable to acquire them. Development is therefore often taken to entail methods that enable individuals in poverty to acquire assets and access opportunities. Better financial services, health facilities, education and provision of basic services such as electricity, water and sanitation will be regarded as paramount contributory factors in creating assets and opportunities for Liberians during this postwar era. This means better education, higher standards of health and nutrition, reducing poverty, establishing a cleaner environment, more equality of opportunity, greater individual freedom, and promoting richer cultural life among the people in the villages, towns, and cities. The first goal of UN's Millennium Development Goals also envisions eradicating "poverty and hunger with target for 2015 to reduce the proportion of people living on less than a dollar a day and those suffering from hunger by half" (United Nations, 2006). All the other health-related goals are linked to the poverty goal. It is clear that unless opportunities are created for people to be lifted out of poverty, efforts to achieve optimal health in Liberia and other sub-Saharan African countries emerging from civil conflicts will be futile.

Absence of Mechanisms for Achieving Those Opportunities

In many sectors of Liberian society, Liberians have lacked the basic freedom or mechanism for achieving any opportunities, even at the minimal level. Where income distribution is highly inequitable, mere growth in per capita income will not benefit the majority of society. Development begins with freedom. The freedom to innovate, the freedom to engage in agricultural activities, the freedom to participate in the political process—these were things the majority of Liberians were deprived of for hundreds of years. Opportunities must also be created for the Liberian people to have the freedom to share ideas with people around the world; they must be part of the inclusive information society. An overriding vision for this information society is one that expands political, social, and economic freedom by offering every Liberian, regardless of ethnicity (tribe), educational status, or geographic location, the opportunities to access and utilize information to better his or her life. First, I believe Liberia should focus on creating a domestic policy environment that encourages privatization, competition, and liberalization, but that also protects intellectual property. Government can be equally effective. However, private investment is by far the largest source of funds for the development, deployment, maintenance, and modernization of the health programs and projects. Public policies that do not actively invite such investment simply delay development. Equity and redistribution will need to be incorporated into the new economic plan suggested above.

Efforts required to tap into the few existing opportunities are extremely exhausting and not cost-effective. Because poverty is so entrenched and mechanisms for accessing opportunities are lacking, people spent much of their time attempting to tap into existing opportunities. This process is inefficient and exhausting. For example, a farmer may be successful in growing rice, cocoa, or coffee. But because the roads are poorly built and transportation is unreliable, the crop may become rotten or spoiled before it reaches the market in a larger city. Another example is the fact that many prenatal women may have to walk several miles or kilometers to seek prenatal care at a health post distance away from them. Accessibility—the ability of persons to use services, including factors such as distance, effort, cost, and awareness of services—is a key factor for rural residents. The Liberian government has a responsibility to provide the people with the tools they need to seize the opportunities of optimal health. To use those tools effectively, however, the new government needs to adopt political, legal, and economic policies that make development successful.

Too often, vital resources, sometimes made available with the help of other nations, are lost to the developing countries. Roads that should make market access possible for agricultural entrepreneurs are not completed, succumbing to inadequate financial planning or the diversion of funding. An ambitious plan to provide potable water is canceled when a change of administration alters the political priorities that shape budget decisions. Developing long-term and comprehensive economic development plans will help prevent worthy programs from being eliminated when a new government takes charge. Postwar governments must make better use of resources. Projects must be respectful of local residents' beliefs, values, and environmental interests, as well as the realities of the global health market, while not encumbering postwar administration with overwhelming debt.

Lack of Political Commitment

Because the health care system in Liberia is primarily a government-controlled system, over the years, weak political commitment led to mismanagement of resources. When a health care institution becomes a lower priority in the eyes of the government, the lack of accountability can breed administrative waste and low staff morale. For example, the John F. Kennedy Medical Center, which is the government's largest public hospital in Monrovia and a facility meant to serve a significant proportion of the urban poor, was underfunded because it was not considered a priority. Pharmaceuticals and essential medical supplies are frequently lacking in urban areas and chronically unavailable in rural clinics and health posts. Previous budget allocations for health care were also limited due to the lack of political commitment.

This is not to downplay the remarkable progress Liberia made before the civil war in improving the health care of its people. Although the government of Liberia (GOL) adopted the World Health Organization (WHO) PHC philosophy in the 1980s to promote better health, the government seldom made the institutional and financial changes necessary to implement the programs involved. For example, before the civil war, the government still devoted most of its attention and funding for health to high-priced curative and relatively cost-ineffective services provided through hospitals. Such services not only consumed a large share of the resources of the Liberian Ministry of Health and Social Welfare (MOH&SW), but also tended to benefit only a small proportion of the population. In this postwar era, there will be a need for revitalizing the PHC commitment. Liberia's MOH&SW should organize a health care system based on PHC approaches with well-defined priorities and objectives.

A new, innovative health care delivery system should be designed with health programs for implementation with specific health goals tied to a timeline. Goals must be realistic, benchmarks must be set, and funding should be earmarked to achieve these goals. PHC takes different forms according to the political, economic, social, cultural, and epidemiological realities of each country. However, PHC can only be effective if it is based on individual and community self-reliance and maximum community commitment. It is therefore necessary for MOH & SW officials to improve the mechanisms of community involvement and to delegate responsibilities and resources equitably in terms of population distribution. Practical approaches will have to be created and adapted to the nature of the political structure in this postwar era.

The GOL declared its commitment to the goal of "Health for All" by the year 2000 through its endorsement of the 1978 Alma-Ata Declaration and its signing of the WHO Regional Charter of Health for All in 1980 (WHO Alma-Ata Declaration, 1978). The GOL also decided to establish a National Primary Health Care[3] program to be financed under the National Socioeconomic Development Plan (1981 to 1985) with the assistance of collaborating agencies and governments. Due to serious financial constraints, however, the National PHC Program was not started on a large scale until 1983. The civil conflict also halted many PHC programs. In the immediate postwar era, an analysis should be made to determine which programs should be revitalized and would have greater impact on the health status of the population.

Existence of Bureaucratic Centralized Hierarchical Structures

Another major problem is the hierarchical and centralized structure of the MOH&SW health programs and policies. Although the nation's MOH&SW has been successful in designing and implementing many health programs over the years in local communities, there is still major opposition to the decentralization of authority. The improvement of the health status of the people in Liberia will heavily depend on an overall decentralization process that would encourage local residents and communities to become more responsible and more proactive for their own health.

Lack of International Commitment

To some extent, international donors must take some blame for the many problems cited here. For instance, donor fatigue in the 1980s reduced funding for important programs and affected the overall MOH&SW budget.

Also, some of the donors have been a driving force in the country's health planning, supporting health projects, even when these projects have not truly addressed Liberia's major health problems. The decline of the foreign exchange rate in the 1980s diminished the amount that could be allocated for health. The Liberian government also depended a lot on foreign donors and grants. Inadequate funding for government-owned and government-operated hospitals results in aging or inoperable medical equipment. Devising ways to generate funds from the local economy (e.g., through the profits from natural resources) will help reduce the dependence on donors.

General Population Health and Emerging Diseases

There is also the need to continue to address general health care issues and respond to emerging health conditions. Reviving previous health programs is critical to rapidly extending health care to the people. For example, people would be receptive to the reactivation of familiar maternal and child health care programs started before the war. These programs need to be reactivated so that preventable diseases do not compound public health problems. Also, the government should set up a mechanism for the provision of sanitation and basic primary health care services, because many facilities were destroyed during the war.

The poor management of the national health care delivery system and quality control issues will also need to be addressed in order for long-term sustainability to occur. These factors, if not addressed timely and appropriately, could hamper the potential progress that could be made in reducing the burden of premature mortality and disability. Additionally, the new health care system in Liberia must be prepared to meet the challenges of endemic diseases (e.g., malaria, water-borne illness, and the like) and emerging diseases such as HIV/AIDS, the Ebola virus, the H5N1 Avian Flu, and the resurgence of drug- resistant tuberculosis. Finally, the health care system must also be prepared to provide mental health services for families and individuals who were affected by the war.

Notes

1. Organization of African Unity and the United Nations Children's Fund (1992). *Africa's children, Africa's future: Human investment priorities for the 1990s.* OAU, Addis Ababa: Ethiopia, p. 13.

2.   Failed state is a controversial term that refers to a state in which institutions (health, economic, law and order, etc.), have collapsed or failed to perform due to violence. In many instances warring factions are battling the government forces and other warring factions. As a result, the central government has little control over much of its territory. For more information on the concept of failed state, see Rotberg, R.I. *When states failed: causes and consequences.* Princeton, New Jersey: Princeton University Press, 2004.

3.   The World Health Organization (WHO), in its effort to assist countries in providing health care to all citizens, promoted the framework of Primary health care (PHC) through their Declaration of Alma-Ata (1978). The Alma-Ata document defines primary health care as "essential health care based on practical, scientifically sound and socially acceptable methods and technology made universally accessible to individuals and families in the community through their full participation and at a cost that the community and country can afford to maintain at every stage of their development in the spirit of self-reliance and self-determination. It forms an integral part both of the country's health system, of which it is the central function and main focus, and of the overall social and economic development of the community. It is the first level of contact of individuals, the family and community with the national health system, bringing health care as close as possible to where people live and work, and constitutes the first element of a continuing healthcare process. For more information on the concept of PHC, see World Health Organization. *Alma-Ata primary health care.* Health for All Series, No. 1. Geneva, Switzerland: World Health Organization, 1978.

CHAPTER 2

THE COUNTRY PROFILE:
POLITICAL, ECONOMIC, AND
SOCIAL FACTORS

No you did not die in vain, oh Dead Ones!
This blood is not tepid water.
It waters the roots of our hope, which will bloom at dusk.
It is our hunger and thirst for honor,
those great absolute queens
No, you did not die in vain.
You are the witness to Africa's immortality.
You are the witnesses to the new world which will be tomorrow.
Sleep oh Dead Ones! And let my voice be your
lullaby, my angry voice which is cradled by hope.[1]

—Léopold Sédar Senghor, in *Hosties Noires*, 1948

Overview

One of the major factors that led to the current political instability and unrest in Liberia is the low level of social integration and cohesion among ethnic groups or tribes. The roots of this unrest date long before the country of Liberia was founded by freed American slaves in the 1800s.

Among the indigenous population in the West African belt, there have always been intertribal conflicts, including the practice of slave trade among the different tribes. Besides capturing slaves to perform agricultural activities, one of the goals of the slave trade was expansionism for the tribal leaders. Slaves became a way of building wealth because the product of their labors enriched the tribal chiefs. In addition to the slave trade, the West African belt had been a fertile ground for trading of commercial goods, and Liberia was an important part of that network of trade. European explorers and seafarers interested in buying products such as ivory, gold, and spices frequented this region. Liberia became an important port in international trading because it was strategically located on the European shipping route. A historical practice of slave trade and a role in international trading made this region vulnerable to the European slave trade for several hundred years.

The country of Liberia dates back to the abolition of slavery in the early 19th century. When American slaves were freed, some of them came back to the Western belt of Africa and founded the country of Liberia, deriving its name from the Latin word *liberitas*, which means freedom (Appiah & Gates, 1999). The primary reason for founding Liberia was to provide safe haven for freed slaves of African descent escaping North America (Shick, 1980; Smith, 1987). Today, the descendants of these freed slaves are referred to as Americo-Liberians. From the outset, Liberia struggled to create an environment where the Americo-Liberians and indigenous people could live in unity while sharing resources fairly. The failure of both groups of people to create a unified community over the course of two centuries has had far-reaching consequences, and eventually was one of the factors that led to the civil war that took place in the 1990s.

Despite the abundant availability of natural resources and human capital in comparison to other countries in the region, Liberian governments in the past failed to develop and implement broad-based policies that would lead to sustainable growth and development. Economic growth has been hampered in Liberia because of weak macro-economic policies and lack of serious commitment to social justice. This longstanding maldistribution of resources for development and the lack of economic opportunities, combined with a period of poor governance and social exclusion of the majority of the population, have in essence contributed to the country's long-term economic and social decline, which reached its lowest point during the civil war.

Figure 2-1. Map of Liberia with Neighboring Countries

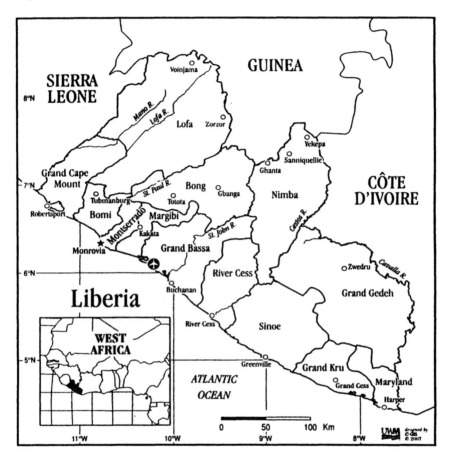

Geography and Land

Liberia (see map Figure 2-1) is located in the bulge of West Africa. Liberia covers an area of about 43,000 square miles, about the size of the U.S. state of Tennessee. It is bounded on the north by Guinea, the south by the Atlantic Ocean, the east by Côte d' Ivoire, and on the northwest by Sierra Leone. Liberia has a coastline of about 350 miles. Monrovia is the county's capital, as well as its largest city, main seaport, and major commercial center. In addition to the capital, other important towns include Buchanan and Harper, which are both seaports. Liberia has mutual socioeconomic and cultural links with its neighboring countries. Because of these close ties, Liberian refugees fleeing the fighting during the civil war were welcomed by these countries.

Liberia is divided into three distinct topographical areas. First, a flat coastal plain with creeks, lagoons, and mangrove swamps; second, plains broken by forested hills that cover most of the country; and third, mountain ranges in the northern highlands. Liberia's six main rivers flow into the Atlantic Ocean. The mountain ranges bordering Guinea and Liberia have high-grade iron ore. Other important minerals include gold, diamond, manganese, silica sand, clay, and bauxite. In the prewar economy, iron, gold and diamonds were mined on a large scale, contributing to a high percentage of export earnings and government revenue. During the civil war, the hard currency (American and European currencies) generated from black-market sales of gems bumped up all warring factions to another level of weaponry, creating the commonly used term "blood diamonds."

Vegetation in much of the country is dense forest growth. The fertility of the soil in Liberia is ideal for timber, a number of tree crops, and rice and cassava production. Although Liberia was originally almost all forest-covered, the expansion of subsistence farming during the last several decades has turned large parts of the country's forest into human-created savannah. The shift from forest to savannah and commonly used "slash-and-burn" farming methods make the country vulnerable to soil erosion and unsuited to sustainable farming. Timber was widely exploited during the war and helped pay for imported weapons. The forested topography hid the warring factions from each other.

The climate in Liberia is tropical and humid, with a heavy rainfall on the coast and some rainfall on the southeastern interior. There are two distinct seasons in Liberia, the dry and rainy seasons, each lasting about six months. During the rainy season, dirt roads are impassable and it is even challenging to drive on paved roads because of floods. Poorly built bridges are dangerously flooded. The lack of passable roads made it difficult for the central government to use its military vehicles to go into the forest to repel the rebels. The inadequacies of government vehicles on rough roads made the government forces vulnerable to surprise attacks.

The topography of the land enabled the civil war to be waged as a guerrilla war, making civilians even more vulnerable. Compared to a conventional war, where two known armed forces are engaged in combat in a militarized zone, a guerrilla war is decentralized, less coordinated, and less controlled. Rebels made decisions for themselves, with gross disregard for ethical standards protecting civilians, including the almost universally respected tenets of the Geneva Convention. A guerrilla war is harder to resolve because so many individuals are making decisions, many of which are counterproductive to their cause.

The guerrilla nature of war often extends the duration of conflict. If they needed to remain under cover, rebels were able to live in the bush for months and eat off the land. Rebels routinely terrorized rural peasant farmers and drove them from their land, lived in their houses, and ate their poultry and livestock. The majority of the Liberian population depends on subsistence farming. The nature of subsistence farming in Liberia is tenuous because it depends on strict adherence to the natural seasonal rhythm of the country's climate. For instance, trees must be felled at a certain time, bush must be cleared, the soil must be hoed by hand at a specified time, and rice seeds must be planted during a certain month. Planting rice during the heavy rainy season will not produce a yield because the seeds will be washed away. When farmers are forced from their farming habitat, the essential farming cycle is broken. If a farm lies fallow, the jungle encroaches and the farm becomes jungle bush again. Rice, which is the staple diet for most Liberians, must be carefully planted and tended in order to have high yields.

Besides planting, farmers must pull weeds from the rice crop; fence the farm fields to keep animals, such as groundhogs from destroying the crops; and keep daily vigil against the swarms of birds that could destroy a crop in a single day. Low crop yield can mean severe hunger and malnutrition for both rural and urban populations. The warring factions that were involved in the civil conflict in Liberia selfishly plundered the farms and drove off the farmers, thus creating Liberia's recent total dependence on food aid from abroad. In the period of reconstruction, it will be critical to revive small-scale agricultural sectors because this will help the recovery spread faster across the population. The achievement of self-sufficiency in food production and the development of small-scale agricultural projects will not only comprehensively improve the economy of the country, but will also uplift the spirit of the Liberian people.

The natural topography of Liberia served as a barrier between the different guerrilla factions during the civil war. The many rivers and the Atlantic Ocean played a role in the war, too; rebels who knew how to make dugout canoes and navigate the rivers were able to be more mobile than the government forces, which lacked boats. From some remote areas of the country, especially in the southeastern region, the rebels would force fishermen to transport their goods and supplies, including their weapons, on the waterways. Even though fish provide a critical protein for Liberians, fishermen eventually gave up fishing out of fear. Fishermen were afraid to bring their fish in from the seas because doing so made them a target for rebels who stole the fish and threatened their lives. Just as the rebels disrupted the agricultural process, they also destroyed the fishing trade.

Population Dynamics

There is a saying that Liberians are fond of repeating: "What an elder sees while sitting, a young person is unable to see even while standing." Prior to the civil war, boys and girls were mentored and supported by the older generation. In turn, the younger generation would care for the elderly people in their villages as a social norm. The cultural mores and traditions that supported a harmonious society for hundreds of years have been tragically disrupted by the civil war. War negatively affects the health and social roles of everyone in a country. The elderly are particularly vulnerable as far as their health because of their frailty and weakened immune systems. Many older Liberians succumbed to the harsh conditions encountered in the refugee camps. The population of elderly mentors has shrunk. The respected social role and status of elderly people became threatened. Many young people exposed to the violence and carnage of war no longer look to the elders for advice. Rather, they look to a new breed of mentors, the rebels who ruthlessly manipulate them with false promises of safety, wealth, and status.

As in other developing countries, Liberia's population consists predominantly of young people. According to recent demographic and health surveys, at the present time, the majority of Liberians are under 18 years of age almost equally divided by gender. Many of the girls in Liberia are of childbearing age. Many Liberian women are still in their childbearing years. Based on these facts, we can expect an increase in Liberia's postwar population in the next decade. The irony is that there could be a dramatic population increase in Liberia at the same point in time where the social structures necessary for accommodating this growth will still be severely disrupted or destroyed: the educational sector, health care, the economy, family and village life, and the agricultural and fishing industries. Liberia will initially be unprepared to handle many of the social problems associated with rapid population growth and the return of refugees.

The prewar population distribution was very different from the postwar location of the population. Prior to the civil conflict, approximately 80 percent of the population lived in rural areas. During the war, however, hundreds of thousands of people fled the fighting and became displaced in the capital city, Monrovia, and other peri-urban areas. It is estimated that Monrovia now has a population of over 1 million people, compared to its prewar population of about 500,000. One of the challenges that the postwar government faces in Monrovia is being able to repatriate the displaced people from the rural areas back to their towns and villages. In addition to the challenge of reintegrating people into rural life, Liberia must also address the issues that will result from an exodus from urban areas.

Economy

The civil war has had a disastrous effect on the Liberian economy. For the past half century, Liberia's economy has been based on installations of and imbalanced relationships with multinational companies, such as Firestone Rubber Plantation Company and LAMCO and Bong Mining Companies. When civil war erupted, the foreigners running the multinational companies were the first to leave, creating a literal shutdown of the major employers of Liberians. Economic chaos soon followed, as the national government was crippled when the flow of hard currency generated by these multinationals ended. Out of desperation, both the rebels and the Liberian government resorted to exploiting the natural resources that were easier to extract, such as diamonds panned from the rivers and tropical hardwood cut from the rain forest. As rebel forces approached urban centers, many foreign businesspeople that owned small businesses escaped to neighboring countries.

Government

By design, the government of Liberia was set up by the political advisers to the original Americo-Liberians to resemble the United States' political system. Because indigenous people were, for the most part, shut out of the electoral process and any opposition parties were usually crushed, Liberia, for over a century, operated on a one-party system. In 1980, a coup d'état ushered in the country's first indigenous leader, Samuel Doe, who was later assassinated. During the Doe regime, indigenous Liberians who returned to Liberia after studying abroad created a number of political parties. Before the civil war, Liberia was a multiparty republic with dozens of loosely organized parties. The country still had a dual legal system based on Anglo-American common law for the modern sector and customary tribal law for the indigenous sector. In January 2006, the first postwar president was inaugurated after multiparty elections in October 2005. Ellen Johnson-Sirleaf, a Harvard-trained economist was elected president in a contest with George Weah, a soccer star and UNICEF goodwill ambassador.

The Liberian People, Ethnic Groups, and Belief Systems

Besides the controlling minority group that constitutes the Americo-Liberians, Liberia is also made up of some 16 to 23 ethnic groups. Along the coastal region are the Kru, Bassa, and Vai. The Kpelle, Lorma, Mano, and Krahn tribes are located in the interior part of the country. Most of these tribal groups retain their traditional values and orientations, tribal relationship patterns and subsistence agricultural activities as well as their customs of fishing and hunting in the forest for bush meat. Over the last several decades, some of these traditional value systems, beliefs, and customs have been loosening. As an increased number of young people from the indigenous population become educated, many adolescents and young adults choose not to continue the cultural values and beliefs of their parents or grandparents. The village chief holds tribal authority in many of the rural settings. The national and regional county governments in urban centers are aware of this power base and therefore work closely with chiefs when providing health and educational services to the populations.

While this tribal system of authority and the organization of villages based on tribes and/or chiefdoms have worked for centuries, they, too, have drawbacks. There have been reports of intertribal conflicts and raids on villages by powerful chiefs seeking to conquer another village in order to increase their power bases. Tribalism therefore became entrenched in the Liberian psyche and has continued to this day. So, while Liberia's history often involves the Americo-Liberians oppressing the indigenous population, there have also been tensions between ethnic groups (notably between the Kpelle and Mandingos), even before the civil war. The manner in which the civil war was fought, including the alignment of certain ethnic groups with specific rebel factions, made an already volatile situation even more explosive. During the civil crisis, it was common for certain ethnic groups to be targeted by a given rebel faction, especially if they were unable to speak the language in the area that they controlled.

Liberians have maintained a degree of tribalism over the years and are slow to embrace ideologies that are more nationalistic. They are proud of being part of a specific ethnic or tribal group. The latter part of the civil war disintegrated into tribal factions, intensifying tribal identity. During the heat of the civil war, one's tribal affiliation could serve as a buffer or as a magnet for discrimination and prejudice. Even in the formal government settings, tribal affiliation is influential. Many of Liberia's past leaders, including Samuel Doe, who violently overthrew the William Tolbert government, appointed members of their own tribes to high offices, even if they were incapable of performing the duties of such offices.

Appointing one's own tribesmen is justified as a means of gaining trust and creating some loyalty among a leader's administrators. The irony here is that a leader runs the risk of paying more attention to only one of the country's ethnic groups while barely carrying development projects to other sectors of the country. The issue of tribalism is pervasive among Liberians and is a key belief for many, even among educated Liberians who have lived abroad in developed countries.

Intriguing questions to ask, therefore, are: Will the tribes ever be unified for the common good of the Liberian people? Will the suffering inflicted by the civil war in Liberia and the consequences that were borne by all ethnic groups teach Liberians a lesson on how to work together and become more nationalistic? Tribalism is a major source of corruption and retardation of development. It leads to appointment of inept individuals who do not have the necessary, prerequisite skills to lead the people. In the new Liberia, high ethical standards must be developed and implemented, both in the governmental and private health care sectors. Health development programs must also be spread around the country, but implementation decisions, for example, a maternal-child health program in Bong County, must be based on sound assessment of the county's needs and not solely on whether the minister of health is a Kpelle individual from Bong County.

Political Transition and Postwar Reconstruction Development

The uneven development of Liberia's natural resources and the maldistribution of development programs to predominantly urban settings contributed to the establishment of two-tier economic structures, one consisting of a traditional, low-productivity subsistence sector and the other a so-called "modern industrial" sector. The traditional sector consists primarily of rural agricultural activities and has been the source of livelihood for the majority of the population. Agricultural activities characterized by low yields lead to problems of lack of food and malnutrition. The modern-industrial sector has, for the most part, involved the production and export of rubber, timbers, iron ore, cocoa, coffee, palm oil, diamonds, and gold. Prior to the civil war, a vibrant informal sector increasingly played an important role in the overall economy. It is important to revive this informal sector. What areas or sectors would be critical for the Liberian government to focus on or revive during this postwar era that would generate economic activities?

In terms of relative importance of individual subsectors, iron ore mining was the leading economic activity during much of the prewar era. During the decade preceding the war, iron ore production accounted for approximately 23.5 percent of the country's gross domestic product (GDP) (United Nations Development Programme, National Human Development Report on Liberia, 2000). Owing to a combination of factors, including the weakening prices of steel on the world market in the mid-1970s and early 1980s, financial problems were created that affected the Liberian government's reliance on iron ore for foreign exchange. The high-grade iron ore reserves had also begun to be depleted, and the production of high-grade ore soon declined. The onset of the civil war in Liberia led to a complete halt of the country's production of iron ore. There is speculation that this industry could be revived. However, reviving an industry that was damaged during the civil conflict in Liberia and neighboring countries will require considerable initial investment. Because the Liberian government cannot depend solely on the subsistence agricultural sector for foreign exchange, iron ore mining in Liberia may have the potential for contributing to the country's economic recovery. There are rumors that there may be high-grade iron ore deposits at the Liberian border with Guinea.

Rubber production was probably the second-ranking economic activity in the modern-industrial sector of Liberia. Apparently, Liberian farmers owned few of the country's acreage of rubber farms, while foreign companies (e.g., Firestone and Bridgestone) accounted for the largest proportion of the land usable for rubber production. In 1989, total production accounted for about 16 percent of Liberia's GDP (United Nations Development Programme, National Human Development Report on Liberia, 2000). Rubber production requires intensive labor and was affected greatly by the civil war. It too has the potential for making a substantial contribution to the postwar Liberian economy, especially since the rubber plants are still active. What this suggests, therefore, is that the postwar government of Liberia must diversify the economic activities used in generating income for government revenues. Additionally, incentives should be provided to Liberian entrepreneurs to develop local businesses and reduce over-reliance on foreign companies.

Given the devastating impact of the Liberian civil conflict on the economy, the departure of President Charles Taylor in 2003 hopefully will help create a positive environment for Liberians themselves to participate in the economic recovery process of their beloved country. The challenges in this regard are daunting, but with great planning and commitment on the part of the Liberian government and the international community, the Liberian people will start anew in rebuilding their country. In the short term, local and international efforts should focus on consolidating the peace and creating a framework for free and fair elections to be conducted, ensuring personal and national security, rehabilitating the health care and social service sectors, and resettling and reintegrating displaced people and ex-combatants while promoting sustainable programs and strengthening community-level capacity building.

Note

1.   *Hosties Noires*, 1948 - Black Hosts. In *The Collected Poetry*. Translated and with an introduction by Melvin Dixon. Charlottesville: UP of Virginia, 1991.

CHAPTER 3

HEALTH STATUS OF THE LIBERIAN POPULATION: CRITICAL ANALYSIS AND PRIORITY AREAS

The extent of the influence a nation's economy has on health can probably be seen most clearly in the extreme case in which an economy is almost absent: in a war-torn nation in which the agricultural and industrial production, the networks of trade, healthcare sectors and even the economy itself has been disrupted to the point that many of its citizens are starving and ill because they no longer have access to basic survival needs such as food, water and shelter. The existence of a sustainable economy is critical to the achievement of basic and optimal health in any country.[1]

—Brownlee, A.T

Concepts of Health and Illness: Liberian Health Belief Systems

In comparison to other countries in West Africa, Liberia and its government made some great strides in improving the health of its population before the civil war. Liberia is a multicultural society where people visit religious and traditional healers for general physical ailments and mental health-related problems. However, whenever modern health care services are made available and accessible to the population, people do utilize these services if a resolution is not found with traditional healers. In the past, one of the challenges that faced all Liberian governments was being able to provide optimal modern health care to all the people. Certain beliefs and values ingrained in the Liberian culture have been influential in laying the foundations for a dual health care delivery system: traditional and modern. Although the preference for traditional healing practices is weakening, especially as more Liberians have begun to join other organized religions, the basic belief system of most Liberian tribes includes the conviction that some kind of external or magical intervention is directly responsible for an individual's health.

Illness and death are usually attributed to the effects of witchcraft. For example, a person who has fallen ill may believe that the illness is due to witchcraft practices that had been perpetrated by a close relative that is jealous of the achievement of the person. In the Liberian setting, especially the rural areas, anyone may be suspected of "making medicine." People are therefore suspicious of one another and cautious about establishing a friendship with a stranger. Understandably, many Liberians are reluctant to reveal personal health information that might be used by potential enemies to harm them. The belief systems and dynamics involved in the dual existence of modern health delivery systems and traditional health delivery practices must be clearly understood when the Liberian health care system is being reorganized.

Population Health Trends: Major Causes of Morbidity and Mortality in Liberia

In a developing country such as Liberia, the paramount indicators of the functionality of that country's health care system are morbidity and mortality rates. The most critical indicators include maternal health and population trends; child health and infant morbidity and mortality; life expectancy; and physical and social environmental factors influencing health. These indicators are direct measures of the level of socio-economic development of a country. Figures reported for these rates are based only on estimates because collecting accurate data during the civil war, and even prior to the civil war, proved to be challenging. These estimates were, however, made by the UN and related agencies providing direct health care in Liberia. Table 3-1 sets forth recent basic background statistics for Liberia, sub-Saharan Africa, and the world.

Table 3-1: Socio-demographic information and health-related indicators for Liberia, its region, and the world

	Liberia	Sub-Saharan Africa	World
Demographic and Health Indicators			
Total population			
(in thousands of people)	3,298	683,782	6,211,082
Percentage of population			
Under age 15	43	44	29
Over age 65	3	3	7
Living in urban areas	45	34	47
Average total fertility rate per			
population			
1975-1980	6.8	6.7	3.9
2000-2005	6.8	5.6	2.7
Infant mortality rate per 1,000 live			
births	157	89	55
Child mortality rate per 1,000 children	235	175	83
Life expectancy at birth in years	43	49.8	68.1
Births attended by trained personnel			
(percent)	51	39	57
Percent of adults ages 15-49 infected			
with HIV	5.9	9.0	1.2
Proportion with Access to Safe			
Water			
Urban	NA	72	85
Rural	NA	44	40
Proportion with Access to Improve			
Sanitation			
Urban	NA	82	95
Rural	NA	47	71
Adult Literacy Rate			
Female	30	55	75
Male	60	71	86

Source: United Nations, *Human development report 2006*. Oxford University Press: New York.

Maternal Morbidity and Mortality Trends

Maternal mortality is a public health indicator that many public health experts in the West do not talk much about. Although women do die during pregnancy in developed countries, death during childbirth is a somewhat rare event because women have much better access to perinatal care and childbirth generally occurs in a hospital setting. In developing countries such as Liberia, pregnancy is riskier; many women lose their lives either before the actual birthing process or during the delivery of the baby due to lack of adequate health services and trained health care professionals.

Reports from international efforts, such as the United Nations Development Programme, suggest that Liberia has an estimated population of about 3.4 million people, with a projected annual growth rate of 3.1 percent; the associated total fertility rate is 6.8 children (United Nations Development Programme, 2006). The high fertility rate is not only characteristic of Liberia; it is a typical pattern in most other sub-Saharan African countries. Because the population increase involves a large number of women of reproductive age, this increase will also be associated with high maternal and infant morbidity and mortality associated with pregnancy.

The true picture of maternal mortality in Liberia in the near future is unknown because the full impact of this population bulge has not been realized. Another contributing factor to the unclear picture of maternal mortality in Liberia is the fact that maternal mortality rates have been systematically underreported because half the births happen outside the conventional health care system. Medical personnel in rural Liberia seldom record deaths and births. Many traditional birth attendants are illiterate and are not aware of the significance of gathering health-related statistics with regard to health system planning. Burials take place privately on family land or at the edge of the village. There are also many tribal cultural explanations and attitudes related to stillbirths and miscarriages that contribute to the underreporting of infant deaths in retrospective studies that have sought to gather data on infant mortalities. Depending on the tribe, cultural explanations for miscarriage or stillbirth could include superstitious transgressions, violating a taboo regarding pregnancy that has been handed down for generations in that family, eating the wrong bush meat, witchcraft by a jealous relative (or, in a polygamous union, another wife), or intercourse late in the pregnancy. In 2005, the lifetime risk of maternal deaths among Liberian women was 1 in 16 live births. Because skilled or trained health personnel attend only about 51 percent of all births in Liberia, it could be estimated that the actual number of women dying during pregnancy or childbirth is most certainly far higher.

There are multiple factors that spur the high rate of maternal mortality in Liberia. These risks can be broken down into (1) problems due to lack of access to and availability of modern health care as well as (2) health conditions that are endemic to Liberia being a tropical country, such as malaria and parasitic diseases. Unskilled traditional birth attendants contribute to the high maternal mortality rates because they are untrained in recognizing high-risk pregnancies that require extensive and comprehensive monitoring, they are unprepared to deal with the complications stemming from the onset of pregnancy in early adolescence, and they typically allow prolonged labor without appropriate intervention. Laws in Liberia currently allow for abortion only when it is a threat to the mother's life. A typical Liberian mother has eight to ten children; a polygamous family could have more than 20 children. Large families are valued, and children are cherished in Liberia because they contribute significantly to the family's economic and social-well being. A married woman would not consider abortion to limit the size of her family. Fulfilling the role of wife and mother is an important expectation for females in the Liberian community and confers status.

Women who have babies out of wedlock are stigmatized because they threaten the continuity of the family hierarchy. The parents of a pregnant single woman and her male partner usually negotiate the best outcome for the pregnant woman. In many instances, a marriage results in which both families unite to sponsor the marriage and set up the household. If the father abandons the pregnant woman and disowns the pregnancy, the woman's parents in many instances will care for their daughter during the pregnancy and the mother and baby become part of the household of her parents. There is no formal legal adoption process in the Liberian culture but, rather, a social contract between families to take care of children. If a pregnant single woman believes both the father and her own family will abandon her, she may consider abortion. If the pregnant woman is in school and sees a future for herself beyond her family, she may consider abortion. If the young woman was involved with a married man and is financially dependent on him, she may consider abortion in order not to threaten her relationship with him and to avoid stigmatization.

There are no free abortion clinics in Liberia, so poor women seeking abortions are faced with the choice of traditional herbal remedies that are sometimes toxic to the mother, leading to complications such as excessive bleeding, ruptured uterus, and even death. Many of these remedies are taken in secrecy to hide the pregnancy so there is no provision for skilled follow-up care, the lack of which can also endanger the woman's life. On the fringe of Liberia's modern health care sector, illegal abortions are performed by unscrupulous quacks that may have had some medical training and are now trying to make money outside the medical system by preying on the vulnerable. The quacks introduced saline solution or foreign objects into the uterus with the expectation that this will cause a miscarriage. These abortions are done under unsanitary conditions and leave the women vulnerable to serious uterine infection.

Other factors associated with maternal mortality are anemia and malaria. Anemia in pregnancy is a nutritional condition that creates risky pregnancies. Even if the mother delivers in a community clinic, if she is severely anemic, she could die during the delivery process because the community clinic often does not have resources on hand to handle any blood product needed to treat the anemia. Repeated parasitic infections, such as malaria and worm infestations, exacerbate anemia because they break down the red blood cells. There are reports that malaria accounts for almost half the complications of pregnancy for women admitted to hospitals in Liberia. For the most part, many of these complications or illnesses seen in pregnancy could be prevented with improved and available public health initiatives. These include family planning, access to prenatal care, prevention of tropical diseases, better nutrition, improved sanitation, increased education and income levels of women, and health education. Early intervention could help pregnant women with malaria manage the disease so that it doesn't put their pregnancy at risk.

Trends in Infant Health

Data on infant mortality rates vary widely, indicating the need for a better system for collecting information on vital statistics. Underreporting of death is a major research and planning problem for Liberia and many developing countries. There is a need for uniform and efficient statistical system to secure data from predominantly rural areas of Liberia, but setting up this system would be challenging. In the absence of a computerized national database that all counties could access, accurate rates of infant mortality are difficult to obtain.

In the meantime, however, there are innovative ways to carry out data collection on a smaller scale that would increase efficiency in collecting and storing data related to infant mortality. Sub-Saharan African countries are beginning to embrace information technology. Handheld computers have proven to be a useful and viable technology in the health care environments in Ghana, Uganda and Kenya (International Development Research Centre, 2006). Personal digital assistance (PDA) devices are an effective tool for collection and dissemination of health data and related information. Medical reference materials stored on PDAs can help improve the provision of health care in rural areas. The challenge here is to ensure that such technology is feasible in the African or Liberian infrastructure and appropriate to the prevalent health problems there. It is especially critical that this kind of technology be inexpensive, simple to use, and easily integrated into the daily routines of health professionals stationed in the rural areas.

Access to technology is not enough to create a purposeful national database; cultural and sociological issues need to be addressed. Health care programs have traditionally been created from a limited or "micro" perspective of health in the population. A "macro" perspective on program design, implementation, and evaluation would require health care professionals to think on a systems level and begin a paradigm shift. Funders of health information technology in Liberia need to focus on more than technology; they need to focus on the interpersonal aspects of health information: patient privacy issues, communication between providers, staff training, and respect for existing community values. In terms of infant mortality, with access to a PDA, a nurse at a remote site could easily submit data to the national database on each delivery, including outcome information on the infant and the mother.

Prior to the civil war, Liberia made some significant progress in reducing infant mortality as the result of aggressive maternal/child health programs. This progress, of course, was stalled during the protracted civil war. Recent reports suggest that the infant mortality rate in Liberia is 157 per 1,000 live births (World Health Organization, 2006). Liberia's infant mortality rate is now higher than those of many other African countries. According to the WHO, general factors associated with trends in infant and child mortality in the developing countries of Africa fall into five categories: fertility behavior; nutritional status, breast feeding, and infant feeding; the use of health services by mothers and children; environmental health conditions; and socioeconomic status (Rutstein, 2000). As the stability and prosperity of Liberia improves, these factors could be positively addressed by an integrated approach to development by different sectors of the government.

Trends in Child Health

Statistical data on population trends, age distribution, and associated infant and child mortality are derived from international sources such as UN agencies and the World Bank. In Liberia, there is a large proportion of women of reproductive age (46 percent of the total female population). Early marriage and a high fertility rate result in a population with a large proportion of children. More than 60 percent of the country's females have their first birth before age 20 according to the Human Development Report (United Nations, 2006). Demographers suggest that the age distribution seen in Liberia reflects the usual patterns seen in countries with high fertility rates and low contraceptive use. Under harsh Liberian environmental conditions, risk factors that contribute to child and infant mortality include low birth weights, malnutrition, inadequate health education, low literacy among women, and exposure to communicable and tropical diseases.

It is not clear what impact the civil war has had on the growth rate of the population. Although half a million people were killed, there are still thousands of young women of childbearing age left in the population. The war, therefore, may have had little impact in reducing the 3.1 percent growth rate. This may be especially true given how the fertility rate for women in Liberia is high and many women on average give birth to about eight children. Anecdotes and reports indicate that many women who fled to neighboring countries (e.g., Côte d'Ivoire and Guinea) are giving birth to children in refugee camps and their new places of residence. This increase in population growth is important to health planners to consider as a risk and with regard to the impact it will have on the economy for providing health services in the new Liberia. If the growth rate remained the same despite the civil war, the proportion of young adults will also increase in the current decade. Another factor to consider is that once the refugees return home to Liberia and settle anew, there will be an initial natural increase in pregnancy rates, thereby increasing the average number of children per woman.

Like the infant mortality rate, public health experts and demographers recognize the under-five mortality rate as an important indicator of the development level of a country. It is a measure that includes broader issues related to child survival: economic, social, cultural, familial, and gender issues. In Liberia, as in many other African countries, the under-five period is a vulnerable period for morbidity, neglect, violence, abuse, lack of breastfeeding, malnutrition, unsanitary conditions, and injuries, all of which lead to increase in mortality rate. Both Liberia's infant mortality and under-five mortality rates are significantly higher than those for developed countries. Before the civil war, Liberia had made progress on lowering the under-five mortality rate. Several efforts, including that of the U.S. Agency for International Development project for combating childhood communicable diseases (CCCD), had been very instrumental in developing and implementing health promotion programs. The World Bank and other international agencies are also involved in developing under-five programs. Measures suggested for mitigating infant mortality are also applicable to under-five mortality. Higher rates of childhood illnesses and deaths in Liberia offer some of the clearest signs yet of the impact of Liberia's prolonged war and political instability.

Trends in Life Expectancy

Life expectancy, the average number of years an individual is expected to live, is also a measure for comparing health status between countries and within a country over time. Survivors of 14 years of a brutal civil war may not be concerned with predictions of their life expectancies—they are concerned with survival on a daily basis. While life expectancy has been increasing for other countries, current life expectancy figures for Liberians (43 years) have not recently increased. Populations of neighboring West African countries, such as Ghana and Nigeria, fare better. Life expectancy in Liberia has been decimated by the civil war because it halted health and social programs designed to improve the country's health outcomes. To improve life expectancy, advances must now be made to reduce infant and under-five mortality rates. These will include increasing access to health care and immunizations, as well as necessities such as water and sanitation, usually taken for granted in developed countries.

Suggestions for Improvement of Maternal-Child Health (MCH) Programs

How can one put the high infant and under-five mortality rates in context for the people of Liberia? These factors point to the fact that the health care system has been inaccessible, inadequate, and inefficient and must be made to respond appropriately to the health care needs of the population. It is estimated that only 34 percent of the total population has access to basic health care services, with more people accessing health care in the urban areas in comparison to the rural areas. Public health experts, including those at the World Bank, attribute an increase in longevity in developing countries to multiple developmental factors, including education, good nutrition, economic development, employment, and rise in income levels. In a tropical region like Liberia, specific disease prevention measures (especially against communicable diseases) are also a very important factor in increasing life expectancy.

Liberia lacks information on vital statistics capable of producing valid and reliable infant and child mortality reports at the national level. The systems in Monrovia, the capital of Liberia, and other urban areas are inadequate and can in no way be regarded as representative of actual health indicators in the rural part of the country. Thus, all mortality estimates cited here from the World Bank, the UN, and other international agencies are based on census and retrospective survey data. Researchers wishing to examine the effects of infant and child mortality on the family and general society in Liberia will have to turn to community surveys. How can data be collected to strengthen program planning, design, and implementation in Liberia?

Both direct and indirect methods will need to be used in Liberia to collect birth and infant death rates. Each hospital can employ a direct method of gathering birth and death statistics, but in the absence of a national database that gathers these local statistics, determining trends and factors associated with births and infant deaths in Liberia will remain a challenge. Direct methods would include asking questions directly of mothers that elicit the birth dates of each of their children, whether any have died, and, if so, the days of their deaths. This type of data was collected from the Liberian Demographic and Health Survey (Chieh-Johnson, Cross, Way, and Sullivan, 1988).

A problem with using this methodology for collecting this kind of information is that many mothers may selectively omit children who die shortly after birth. Secondly, in a country like Liberia, where the rate of literacy is low and many mothers do not have access to hospital delivery, the misreporting of days of births and ages at death is prevalent.

Indirect community longitudinal surveys can also be done. If births and deaths are recorded as they occur, these types of data do not suffer from the cultural and statistical biases that affect gathering birth information through retrospective surveys. However, there are some limitations to the use of an indirect method in a developing country like Liberia. The number of mothers who would participate in this type of survey is often small and because of logistics, the areas covered have been purposely selected and should not be regarded as representative of all regions of the country. For example, because of the uneven distribution of health resources in Liberia and the variation in disease rates, a longitudinal mortality survey of children under-five done in Monrovia cannot be representative of rural areas. However, information derived from regionally limited longitudinal surveys does provide valuable insights into contributing factors, such as the age patterns of mortality, the causes of death, or seasonal fluctuations.

Another important aspect of a successful data collection venture will be to compile databases on geographic divisions and tribal groups. Currently, the Liberian government, through the Ministry of Health, requires hospitals to collect and report infant and child mortality data from all regions of the country. Like other African countries, Liberia has made progress in reducing the infant and under-five death rates, but this progress has been impacted by the protracted civil war. The rates of decline vary considerably among the counties of Liberia, with rural counties still experiencing higher infant and under-five deaths. In the absence of comparable data from each county, it is impossible to make meaningful comparisons of the causes of and trends in infant and child death between counties. It is important from a public health and prevention perspective to understand why mortality is so much higher in some parts of Liberia than in others or in some tribal groups more than others. No definitive answers exist to these questions, given the previous state of knowledge of the mortality pattern in Liberia. Previous information was not collected with these questions in mind. However, it is possible to extrapolate relevant factors from research in other developing African countries.

Two critical factors to consider are level of the socioeconomic development and the sociocultural environment. Level of socioeconomic development is a variable that can be presumed to be predictive of infant and child survivability in Liberia. In turn, infant and child mortality are frequently regarded as indices of poverty and deprivation of a population. Thus, the survival rate of children in their first few years of life may be expected to rise as a country's general level of development rises (World Bank, 1993). An index that has been used by the World Bank to measure the level of development in a country is the proportion of literate and educated women. To increase socioeconomic development in a country, the World Bank, the WHO, and other international agencies involved in health and development programs advocate sending more females to school. The more education young girls and women have, the better the decisions they generally make about nurturing and health care for their children. If literacy rates for females are a determinant of infant and child mortality, then female education is more than an index of socioeconomic status. While education cannot account for all factors related to reducing infant or child mortality, education leads to better jobs and increased income, which enable access to health care and better nutrition.

Environmental factors include a number of variables. The first environmental factor to consider is climate and its relationship, through temperature and humidity, with malaria. Liberia, like other West African countries, experiences endemic levels of malaria. The climate perpetuates the breeding of mosquitoes. Mosquitoes transmit the malaria parasite and lead to high rates of morbidity and mortality especially among children under five years of age because their immune systems are more vulnerable to disease. A second environmental factor is seasonal variations in weather. Liberia has two seasons: rainy and dry. While no data have been collected in Liberia that show the impact of seasonal variations on infant and child death rates, anecdotal evidence from health care workers suggests these rates peak in the rainy season. This may be due to a combination of factors: the increased prevalence of malaria coincides with the rains; food shortages occur as stocks of the staple rice from the previous year's crops are depleted; children search for food in the rain beyond their usual habitats; small ponds form where children swim and come in contact with multiple parasites; and run off from rain pollutes the water supply.

A Framework for Research on Reducing Excess Infant and Child Morbidity and Mortality

The level of infant and child mortality in a population is the result of the interaction between hazards present in the environment and the ability of the population to recognize and defend itself against those hazards. Postwar Liberian government and local communities must collaborate on efforts to address these hazards, such as health education, availability of medications for endemic conditions, mass immunizations, spraying for mosquitoes, ensuring safe water supplies, establishing latrines, and teaching people how to boil their water, wash their hands after defecation, and wash and cook food safely. Low birth weight, though not a direct cause of death, is a contributing factor to delays in development that make a child vulnerable to illness. Researchers interested in assessing the causes of infant and child mortality in Liberia should focus on the following conditions: malaria, diarrhea, respiratory infection, measles, malnutrition, and tetanus.

In developed countries, ethnicity has sometimes been identified as an important variable associated with infant and child mortality. Data of this type are collected mostly in the western world (e.g., the U.S.), where there are diverse ethnic groups and public health officials are interested in knowing the differences among groups in order to allocate scarce resources. Information collected based on ethnicity in the U.S. also enables public health officials to better target health education and prevention programs, to effectively engage community involvement in supporting and sustaining programs, to empower communities to define their own health needs based on their value systems and priorities, and to allow communities to feel ownership of health initiatives.

Although Liberians may seem ethnically homogenous, there is great diversity among tribes, especially in areas related to health belief systems and attitudes—or even perhaps the probability of being susceptible or immune to certain conditions. Health beliefs and customs, as well as genetics, might strengthen or weaken a group's defenses against certain diseases. Tribal customs that may affect pregnancy outcomes have long been recognized in Liberia. It would be informative to study, for example, differences in birth weights for Kpelle women versus Lorma or Gio women because differences might be traced back to a tribal practice, such as food taboos during pregnancy, that the tribe would be willing to change in order to improve health outcomes. Various forms of female genital mutilation (FGM) and infibulation on young girls is practiced in some tribes, but not others. It has been well documented in other African countries that FGM and infibulations can sometimes cause infection and hemorrhaging, which, if untreated, could lead to death. Communal support and respect for breast-feeding varies from tribe to tribe, because Western culture has infiltrated tribes to different extents. Abandoning breast-feeding for formula puts infants at risk for diarrhea and respiratory diseases, two major killers for children under five. There is also the risk of malnourishment and stunted growth due to a family's fluctuating capacity to buy formula. Forced marriage for girls as young as 12 years of age, to older men is also a tribal practice that needs to be addressed. The resulting health risk to young girls includes exposure to HIV/AIDS, sexually transmitted infections (STIs), and complications arising from prolonged labor caused by the pelvis being too small to deliver, including urinary fistulas for the mother and infant death.

Other sociocultural factors and customs affecting maternal/infant/child health include the following:

- Delivery methods used by traditional tribal birth attendants, especially the type of dressing put on the umbilical cord.

- Tribal traditions affecting the duration of breast feeding and determining the appropriate period before breast-feeding should cease altogether.

- Tribal customs concerning the type of weaning foods generally given to infants and the methods of their preparation, particularly those affecting their nutritional value and susceptibility to bacterial contamination.

- Traditional tribal diets and food avoidances (taboos) likely to affect the nutritional status of pregnant and breast-feeding mothers—and, hence, the birth weight of their children and their own ability to breast-feed adequately.

- Traditional tribal treatments and remedies prescribed for childhood sickness, particularly diarrhea, with particular reference to possible withdrawal of fluids and other practices likely to aggravate the condition and weaken the child.

- Traditional tribal practices relating to sanitation and the disposal of human excreta.

- Modes of living that affect crowding within a tribal community (whether, for example, the women and children in polygamous households live in the same dwelling or are housed separately).

Compared to other sectors, such as the military or the economy, the health care sector of Liberia has not really received the type of attention that it deserves from its national government. Stopping short of blaming any one regime for that neglect, now is the time to seize the opportunity to work on rebuilding the health care system. As postwar money begins to pour in, it is time to try out new ideals for health care delivery for the greater good of the people. For instance, little attention in Liberia has been paid to environmental or cultural hazards to health. Which sociocultural practices enhance health, and which ones negatively influence health? To probe into this question further, it is necessary to determine first the principal causes of morbidity and mortality in Liberia. Rates of these phenomena can then be quantified for use in program planning. With analysis of a national data base, regional and national variations in infant and child mortality in Liberia can be explained by a variety of factors, such as variations in the provision of health services, the endemic nature of diseases such as malaria, or maternal education.

The leading causes of infant death in Liberia, tetanus and diarrhea, can be attributed to complex environmental and cultural factors. For example, due to a lack of knowledge, traditional birth attendants may use rusty razor blades to cut the umbilical cord and may use cow dung to promote healing at the navel. Both practices can introduce the tetanus bacillus to the infant. The use of unsanitary water to bathe or feed the baby can introduce gastrointestinal infections in the infant, leading to diarrhea. Until the contributions that tetanus and diarrhea make to mortality in each district have been quantified, the significance of other variables that cause death cannot be properly assessed.

Data on mortality in Liberia is crude and inadequate for assessing the overall levels and trends in morbidity and mortality on a national basis. It is in this respect that small-scale, in-depth surveys and surveillance systems can make their most valuable contribution to our knowledge of morbidity and mortality in Liberia. The challenges facing current and future governments of Liberia to provide optimal health for its people are insurmountable without achieving a macro perspective and understanding of how it explains micro perspectives. Liberia will need substantial financial and research assistance as it tries to gain micro and macro perspectives on the health care needs of its people.

Description of Endemic Health Conditions and Population Health Trends

Infectious and Communicable Diseases

Because Liberia is a developing country, health planning and management in the country is dominated by concerns over control of infectious and communicable diseases rather than over chronic diseases. For several decades before the civil war, much of the funding of health programs in Liberia had been geared toward reducing diarrheal diseases in children under 5, tuberculosis, malaria, cholera, and worm infestations, which are all diseases that are endemic to developing countries. Although the government and non-governmental programs have made great efforts over the years in lessening the magnitude and severity of infectious diseases, these diseases still constitute a major public health problem and consume a significant portion of the country's Ministry of Health dollars. To aid in disease control prior to the civil war, the Liberian government, through the Ministry of Health and Social Welfare (MOH&SW), initiated a number of health programs, including the National Malaria Eradication Program, the National Diarrheal Control Program, and the National Tuberculosis Control Program. Because of security issues for patients and medical personnel, all these programs came to a virtual halt during the war and will need to be revived.

It is difficult to determine the disease rate during and after the civil war in the absence of morbidity and mortality studies. Major infectious diseases lead to serious social and economic burdens on the individual, family, and community at large. Prevalence rates for some of the major infectious diseases and other health risk conditions in Liberia are as follows:

Malaria

The annual rate for malaria cases in Liberia has never been known. However, it is estimated that approximately 70 percent to 80 percent of the Liberian population are infected with the malarial parasite at some time in their lives. The symptoms experienced from being infected with malaria can be debilitating. All segments of the population are at risk, but certain subpopulations are more vulnerable: pregnant women, infants, children, and the elderly. Even some of the UN and West African peacekeepers in Liberia developed malaria and had to be evacuated, despite taking prophylaxis.

According to the WHO, malaria is one of the most severe public health problems worldwide and is a leading cause of morbidity and mortality in many developing countries (WHO, 2006). WHO estimates that 41 percent of the world's population is exposed to malaria. According to the U.S. Centers for Disease Control and Prevention (CDC), globally, each year approximately 300 million people experience episodes of acute illness and at least 1 million people die from malaria (CDC, 2004). Malaria occurs mostly in tropical and subtropical areas of the world. It is estimated that 90 percent of the deaths due to malaria occur in sub-Saharan Africa (CDC, 2004). This is due to a combination of factors: temperate climate, rainy seasons, travel, and poor living conditions.

Temperate weather conditions allow for year-round breeding of mosquitoes, which are the carriers of the malaria parasite. Malaria transmission peaks during the rainy season when oases of water are left in gutters and small ponds, serving as ideal breeding grounds for mosquitoes. If one person contracts malaria and travels to another area, mosquitoes in that area can bite that individual, become infected, and in turn transmit the malaria parasite to another individual. Many Liberians live in poverty and are unable to afford window-screening, mosquito netting over the bed, or insect repellent. Liberians consider malaria endemic and unavoidable, as most Americans would regard the common cold. It is common for every child in a household to become ill with malaria on the same day.

Malaria is an important disease to consider because of the serious economic and social impact it has on the Liberian population. Malaria imposes substantial costs on individuals and families, as well as governments. Although no specific study on the economic burden of malaria in Liberia has been found in the published literature, studies from other countries, including Uganda, found that malaria has a great impact on the economic development of families in the country, as well as the government that must meet the health needs of its people. Social impacts are harder to measure because they are intangible and involve lost opportunities for development.

CDC summarizes major areas of economic and social impact to individuals and governments. Costs to individuals and their families include purchase of drugs for treating malaria at home; expenses for travel to, and treatment at, dispensaries and clinics; lost days of work; absence from school; expenses for preventive measures; and expenses for burial in case of deaths. Costs to governments include maintenance of health facilities; purchase of appropriate or essential drugs and supplies; public health interventions against malaria, such as insecticide spraying or distribution of insecticide-treated bed nets; lost days of work, with resulting loss of income; and lost opportunities for joint economic ventures and tourism.

These tangible and intangible costs, according to the CDC, can add substantially to the economic burden of countries where malaria is endemic, thus impeding economic growth. It has been estimated in a retrospective analysis that annual economic growth of countries with intensive malaria was 1.3 percent lower than that of countries without malaria (Chima, Goodman, and Mills, 2003). Malaria is just one disease that a country has to grapple with that impedes economic growth. For many African countries in economic decline, such as Liberia, the burden of malaria and all the other communicable diseases only adds to economic woes. Because malaria is an extremely challenging disease and has not been eradicated around the world, studies are needed to assess effective ways that households and businesses can positively respond to cases of malaria.

Since Liberia is predominantly an agricultural country, it will be important for Liberian Ministry of Health officials to commission a study in cooperation with the Ministries of Agriculture and of Planning and Economic Affairs to assess the impact of malaria on small farmers. Because malaria can cause lost days from work, it is essential to explore the economic losses farmers incur when they become ill. How much money does a subsistence farmer lose when he or she is ill with malaria and must miss more than five days of work in the rice fields during harvest? If public policy planners have an understanding of the impact that diseases such as malaria have on the economy, both at the micro and macro levels, this will assist the government in reframing their paradigms of economic development to include response to diseases that incorporates diverse factors. Studies that include epidemiological and socioeconomic geographic variation data would help the government to have a sound understanding of the health burden. Information on the economic burden of malaria in Liberia is also needed to target interventions efficiently and equitably, and to justify investment in research and control.

Lassa Fever

Lassa fever is a viral infection that is usually contracted by contact with the fecal matter of rats that carry the virus. It is also highly contagious and can be transmitted when contact is made with an infected person. The disease can be found in mostly the Central and West African regions. Symptoms start with generalized malaise, such as fever and body aches. The patient's health status quickly disintegrates into vomiting, diarrhea, and bleeding, potentially leading into disorientation, coma, and death.

Lassa fever is another disease that is endemic to Liberia. Tropical-disease researchers have been working hard at understanding its epidemiological processes. Researchers were extensively searching for treatment prior to the civil war at the Liberian Biomedical Research Institute. Like the malaria control programs, these field investigations on Lassa fever were discontinued during the civil war. It is generally estimated that 15 percent to 20 percent of cases of Lassa fever end in death, but some studies estimate the mortality rate as high as 45 percent. Like other infectious diseases found in the tropical regions, Lassa fever also causes high mortality in pregnant women and their fetuses (WHO, 2004).

Like malaria, Lassa fever is also a huge challenge for health care providers in Liberia because it is highly infectious and is mostly found in rural areas where there are poor sanitation levels and the least amount of health care. When there is civil conflict in bordering countries like Liberia and Sierra Leone, it is impossible to implement successful treatment or prevention programs because the disease is carried back and forth across the border. It becomes even more difficult for government and humanitarian agencies to deliver medical aid and provide treatment for people who are infected with Lassa fever. During civil conflict, people are usually uprooted from their normal places of residence. These types of population move- ments, which are inevitable during conflict, greatly increase the risk to individuals of contracting the disease because of extreme fatigue, weakened immune systems, and malnourishment.

Like malaria, the major impacts of Lassa fever go beyond diminishing the health of individuals. They also test the integrity of the health care system. The process of detecting and controlling Lassa fever and other communicable diseases also puts extra strain on the already overburdened health care infrastructure in Liberia. Compounding this burden, some health care workers—fearing illness themselves—may be reluctant to work in areas where such a contagious disease is endemic, leaving the nation's poor and vulnerable population uncared for.

It will be important to commission studies similar to those proposed for malaria to investigate the unique socioeconomic impact and consequences of Lassa fever on the family unit. Because the disease leads to convulsions, even if an individual survives, she or he may be stigmatized as being possessed with evil spirits or engaging in witchcraft. After recovery, he or she may become a social outcast and may be unable to contribute to generating income for the family, including through communal farming.

Cholera

Cholera is an acute bacterial diarrheal illness that is endemic to Liberia. The disease is caused by infection of the intestines with the bacterium *Vibrio cholerae*. Cholera is transmitted by drinking contaminated water. CDC information suggests that approximately one in 20 infected persons will have a severe case characterized by profuse watery diarrhea, vomiting, and leg cramps (CDC, 2006). In these persons, rapid loss of body fluids leads to dehydration and shock. Without treatment, death can occur within hours. Immediate replacement of the fluids and salts lost through diarrhea with oral rehydration solution and large amounts of fluids is critical.

Cholera outbreaks have been constant in Liberia but are on the increase because of population displacements. In July 2003, the month when fear gripped the capital of Monrovia as rebels besieged the city, an extremely high number of cases of cholera were reported to WHO. The worsening security situation in the capital then may have prevented cholera patients from going to health care facilities, thus increasing the possibility of the disease spreading to other people. Sanitation is poor and safe water is scarce for displaced populations.

As more people are now leaving the refugee camps outside Monrovia, cholera outbreaks can be certain to occur in the peripheral areas of the city and neighboring districts if proper measures are not taken to contain the disease. In order to reduce the risk of waterborne diseases and to limit cholera transmission, all water for drinking and cooking needs to be chlorinated and/or boiled. WHO and other international agencies have launched a campaign for the chlorination of water in the Monrovia area because it is the most effective method of killing cholera bacteria. Teaching people to boil their water is less effective because of the possibility of cross-contamination. The prevention of cholera is easier to accomplish compared to preventing other communicable diseases. To prevent Cholera, clean water should be provided. The Liberian Ministry of Health should develop special health promotion campaigns to better inform the population about cholera prevention measures.

Sexually Transmitted Diseases

Even before the civil war, reliable data about sexually transmitted diseases in Liberia were not available because of the poor disease surveillance system, cultural taboos about discussing sexual behaviors, and an environment where people commonly self-medicate rather than seek help from a health care facility. Sexually transmitted infections (STIs), including HIV/AIDS, are generally spread through heterosexual contact in Liberia, rather than through homosexual contact or intravenous drug use. Understanding the dynamics of HIV/AIDS and STI transmission in Liberia, as with other sub-Saharan African countries, is very complex because it involves cultural mores and traditions, economics, gender relationships, literacy, and empowerment of women. Lack of knowledge of the seriousness of HIV/AIDS and STIs contributes to unsafe sex. The widespread acceptance of polygamy, infidelity, prostitution, "sugar mamma" and "sugar daddy" roles, and multiple sexual partners puts people at risk for contracting and spreading HIV and other STIs. Figure 3-1 shows the HIV seroprevalence rate among pregnant women in Liberia.

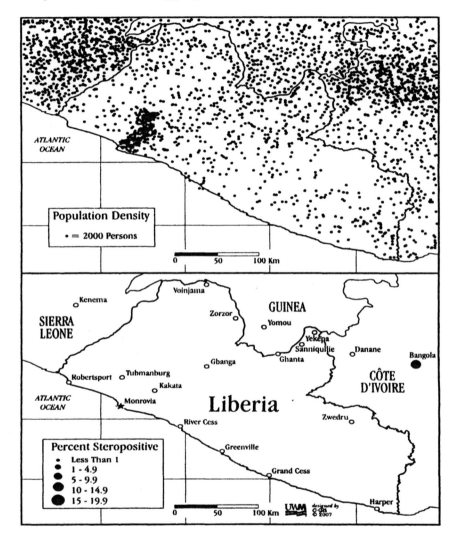

Figure 3-1. HIV sentinel surveillance in pregnant women in Liberia. Figure modified from UNAIDS data. Used with permission. For further information please view the following link: *http://www.who.int/globalatlas/predefinedRepor ts/EFS 2006/EFS_PDFs/EFS2006_LR.pdf*

There are specific and broad prevention measures for preventing sexual transmission of HIV and STIs that should be implemented. Some of these measures include understanding the sociocultural dynamics within the African setting in general and local tribal communities. These measures include increasing the knowledge level of vulnerable and at-risk populations; appreciating the influence of gatekeepers in sexual and marital relationships; acknowledging gender-based economic factors that create dependencies for women that might lead to risky decisions; job migration issues that create circumstances for men that might lead to risky behavior; empowering women to protect themselves; and empowering men to protect their wives and families. No nation on this planet is immune to the HIV pandemic. Other nations, however, have used the stability they enjoy to develop programs aimed at reducing the number of infections. Liberia, like most African countries, has in no way been spared from the impact of HIV/AIDS. The precise rate of HIV infection of individuals in Liberia is hard to determine because there is no ongoing surveillance. Estimates of HIV rates in Liberia are based on limited health care-seeking populations, such as men experiencing symptoms of STIs and pregnant women. The UN AIDS Programme estimates that at least one out of 20 adults in Liberia is HIV-infected (UNAIDS, 2005).

Early screening and treatment of people with other STIs is also an important component of effective HIV control strategy. Monitoring trends in STIs constitutes an indirect measure for assessing the progress made in reducing the spread of HIV. Ironically, the current health infrastructure in Liberia is ill equipped to carry out such STI surveillance processes adequately. Studies that help increase understanding of the conditions contributing to the spread of HIV and STIs are critical for creating appropriate behavioral interventions. These studies could look at factors such as the onset of first sexual intercourse, issues related to multiple sexual partners, attitudes and cultural perceptions regarding condom use, availability and affordability of condoms, and the prevalence of prostitution in the community. Increased understanding of these factors would contribute to better programs for delaying initial sexual activity among young people, reducing the number of sexual partners, and increasing the proportion of individuals using condoms, all of which could help reduce the spread of HIV.

Establishing viable, functioning health care centers that offer comprehensive STI services and care in all parts of the nation would be an important step in the prevention and treatment process. Identifying people with STIs allows for not only the benefit of treating the STI, but for HIV and STI prevention education, HIV testing, and notification of partners at risk. This kind of health initiative will be a huge challenge for the Liberian government during this postwar era because the health infrastructure has been destroyed. Over a decade of public health efforts to reduce the rate of HIV and other STIs in the country has been wasted as a direct consequence of the civil war. Action needs to be taken immediately to stem the spread of HIV because the impact of HIV on both the people and the economy of Liberia could be worse than that of 15 years of civil war.

Studies from sub-Saharan African countries have found the disease affects the population sector that is in its most productive years (Grassly, Desai, Pegurri, et al., 2003; Guinness, Walker, Ndubani, et al., 2003; Fox, Rosen, MacLeod, 2004). The HIV pandemic not only guts a nation's health care system, but destroys every other infrastructure that holds a nation together, including education, agriculture, business, and the family. In countries such as Zambia and Zimbabwe, the impact of HIV/AIDS on these sectors has been tragic. For example, the AIDS epidemic in Zambia has severely depleted the number of high school teachers, thus perpetuating the poverty cycle into the next generation. In Zimbabwe, the nursing shortage—in part due to the AIDS epidemic—has reduced the number of trained health care workers to care for people in the general population with other health problems (Marchal, De Brouwere, and Kegels, 2005; Habte, Dussault, and Dovlo, 2004; and Minnaar, 2005).

Lessons can be learned from successful HIV prevention programs launched in other sub-Saharan African countries and incorporated into new health care initiatives for Liberia. Because of the dire threat HIV poses to a country's economic development, postwar HIV initiatives will entail radical response. Liberia's National AIDS and STI Control Program, established prior to the civil war, needs to be run by an autonomous agency, apart from the more traditional structure of the Ministry of Health. The program should be revived with allocation of monies separate from the annual budget of the Ministry of Health. Financial autonomy and decentralization will allow the program to develop innovative ideas, encourage international donor agencies to contribute even more money to the cause, sidestep bureaucracy that could foster corruption, and allow for a specialized perspective for immediately and specifically evaluating the cost-effectiveness of HIV and STI initiatives. Innovative approaches could start with HIV/AIDS awareness campaigns as part of local community interventions. This would mean training health care professionals and community health workers, including traditional birth attendants (TBAs), about HIV/AIDS so they can be part of the HIV initiative. For a nation that is struggling to recover from a devastating, protracted civil war and is unable to provide for the most basic health needs of its people, preventing HIV/AIDS may not be a priority. It needs to be one because the civil war created the conditions for this epidemic to explode.

The long civil war had all the ingredients of a health nightmare. Most of the rebel fighters, who were "child soldiers", were manipulated into ingesting drugs in order to carry out the will of the rebel leaders. Thousands of children are currently addicted to illicit drugs. Young girls are especially vulnerable to exploitation because of the immense pressure put on girls in the Liberian culture to play a role in providing food and other necessities for their households. In some instances, sibling groups were orphaned when both parents were killed in the civil war. In such cases, the adolescent female often becomes the breadwinner for her younger siblings. She may be left with no other option than survival sex. Without access to birth control measures, it can be assumed that many of these girls became pregnant, adding considerably to their burden in caring for themselves and their siblings. Thousands of soldiers from various West African states who came as peacekeepers were well disciplined and went to Liberia to help the people, but there are reports of peacekeeping troops exploiting young people for sex. As peacekeepers returned to their native countries, many are reported to have left behind the children they had propagated with Liberian women with no consideration for how they would survive.

Other Population Wide Health and Social Problems

Gender-Based Violence Against Girls and Women in Liberia

The violence during almost two decades of civil war in Liberia caused at least half a million men, women and children to lose their lives. But even survivors of violence suffer a tremendous loss. Men, women, and children, who were victims of wartime violence, lose hope in their community, lose the presumption of safety in their environment, and lose a sense of self. Wartime violence against women and girls, in particular, creates an intangible loss for a society because women are often the gatekeepers of culture. Women are pivotal in creating stability, family unity, health, and wealth in a society. Although not an infectious disease, violence against women is a social contagion because abusive behaviors learned during the civil war will be hard to stem after the barrels of the guns are silenced. The long-range impact of the vicious process of forcing young boys to rape young girls during the civil war is not yet known. More research, of course, is needed on the profoundly damaging effect of rape on girls and women during wartime. In addition, research is needed on the future psychological impact on young boys who perpetrated these vicious acts, often out of fear for their own lives and typically while under the influence of alcohol or other drugs. How are these boys, and the women and girls they raped, going to be integrated back into their local communities? The girls and women—and the children resulting from rape—may face stigma and discrimination when they return to their communities. The boys who were perpetrators of rape and violence may also face stigma and be subject to violence by vigilantes—or victims—seeking justice.

Violence against women and girls is connected with other health conditions, such as STIs and HIV/AIDS. In one study conducted in Monrovia among 205 women in displacement camps, investigators documented women's experiences of wartime violence, including rape and sexual coercion, over a five-year period (Swiss, Jennings, Aryee, et al., 1998). Young Liberian girls and women gave chilling accounts of war-related sexual assaults, including being beaten, tied up, detained in a room under armed guard, strip-searched, or raped. Forty-nine percent of the participants in the study reported experiencing physical or sexual violence by a government soldier or rebel fighter. Although all women were at risk of sexual assault in the civil war, some women were at greater risk: women accused of belonging to a particular tribal group or fighting faction, women who were forced to cook for a soldier or fighter, and women younger than 25 years of age (Swiss, Jennings, Aryee, et al., 1998).

The impact that wartime violence against women will have on the future of Liberia should be of particular concern to the postwar government. This concern might be slow in coming, because even in peacetime the value of women in the Liberian culture was minimized. Who will be expected to open the soup kitchens? Who will be expected to organize the orphanages? Who will be expected to welcome the child-rebels back into the family? Who will be expected to be the teachers in primary and secondary education? Who will be expected to provide health care? Who will be expected to develop and sustain small market ventures? It is obviously clear that women are critical in sustaining these formal and informal sectors.

If the government expects women to pick up the pieces after the war, it should prioritize resources for meeting the needs of women who suffered violence during the war. These women need food, clean water, shelter, counseling, and health care. It is a given that these women are experiencing psychological trauma, but it is yet to be determined, in a systematic manner, what their health concerns are, including whether they contracted an STI or HIV infection. Women who have been victimized by rape during the war are a new subpopulation through which HIV/AIDS can be spread throughout the country. If the Liberian government responds comprehensively to the health and social needs of Liberian women during the postwar era, other African countries faced with similar challenges could learn important lessons.

Rebuilding Liberia's social structure after the war is exceedingly complicated due to the intertribal nature of the war. For example, because the different warring factions in Liberia's civil war were mainly tribal-bound, systematic rape became a tool for assaulting the integrity of the bloodline of another tribe. The children borne from systematic intertribal rape would be relegated to the lowest rung of the tribal hierarchy.

Chronic Health Problems Due to Lifestyle Changes

In addition to encountering endemic infectious diseases, Liberia's health care workers have begun to see patients with chronic diseases that mirror those currently seen in developed nations: diabetes, hypertension, heart disease, stroke, and various forms of cancer. This is due in part to rapid urbanization, which has changed many families' lifestyles. People still eat their traditionally high-fat and high-carbohydrate meals, but engage in less physical activity. A typical rural Liberian meal consists of rice; salt, and hydrogenated palm seed oil. Vegetables from the family's vegetable garden and fruit from trees in the village supplement the meal. Protein comes from any wild game or fish caught that day or any domesticated chickens, ducks, rabbits, or pigs recently butchered. Daily routine activity for a rural person entails getting up at dawn and walking several miles in the bush for water and firewood. Rural people often then walk several miles to the family's rice farm, where they engage themselves in rigorous farming activities for the rest of the day, such as digging, slashing, cutting down trees, planting, harvesting, and weeding—all done by hand. Then they walk miles back to the village, carrying heavy bundles of firewood on their heads and buckets of water. Women are involved in domestic chores and childcare in the evenings, and men walk into the bush to check their game and fish traps. This high level of physical activity counteracts their high-fat diet and results in optimal physical condition, as long as one does not get an infectious disease.

The massive rural-to-urban migration that occurred during the civil war has changed the eating and activity pattern of Liberians. Rural people—displaced to an urban center and living in makeshift tents for years—still want to eat their typical meal of rice and hydrogenated palm seed oil. But they now have to buy processed rice and manufactured palm seed oil rather than using homegrown. They can no longer supplement that meal with fresh fruits and vegetables because it would cost money they do not have. There is no wild game or fish to catch and no place to raise domestic animals. Meat and fish must be purchased in the marketplace, and most urban refugees are unable to do so. The result is a highly processed low-protein, high-fat, high-carbohydrate diet.

The amount of physical activity an urban refugee engages in is a tiny fraction of what she or he exerted while living in a rural setting. A typical displaced urban Liberian spends the day sitting, watching, and waiting for some change to occur. There is no employment, no family farms, no garden plots, no bush for hunting or fishing, and no domestic animals to tend. There is practically nothing to do. People don't even need to walk to and carry firewood or water. There are nearby wells, and fire coal is purchased for fuel. Because of safety issues, families stay close to their tents, protecting what few possessions they have. This change from a highly active lifestyle to a sedentary one has taken its toll on Liberians' health. The elderly are particularly vulnerable because physical activity has traditionally helped them enjoy good health and mobility into old age. Exacerbating this change in lifestyle, of course, is the extreme stress and psychological impact of the war. The enormous amount of uncertainty drains people of hope and of aspirations for the future. Depression sets in and takes its toll on physical health. Anecdotal reports suggest that some Liberians are experiencing an increase in hypertension rates and are dying from strokes and heart attacks, an unusual phenomenon in Liberia.

Injuries and Road Traffic Accidents

The level of development of countries in West Africa contributes to an increased risk of injuries for their populations: dangerous agricultural methods, uncontrolled traffic, and daily interaction with the tropical rain forest. Many Liberians suffer injury and sometimes death due to road traffic accidents; falls from trees; burns from wildfires during farming; poisonous scorpion, snake, and spider bites; lethal African bee stings; wounds from cutlasses and axes; drowning during floods; and smoke inhalation from cooking fires. The causes and extent of injuries in Liberia and other African countries are poorly known and the burden injuries place on the population is not well studied. The incidence of injury is on the increase, partly due to industrialization without adequate safety precautions and partly due to the growth of motorized transportation in a country where walking is still the standard mode of transportation in remote rural areas.

According to published reports on road traffic injury around the world, vehicle-related injuries are becoming a major cause of death and disability in the developing world, a public health problem that is expected to increase in the current century as developing countries become more motorized (Peden, Scurfield, Sleet, et al., 2004). These reports suggest that although sub-Saharan Africa has far fewer cars on the road in comparison to industrialized countries, it leads the world in deaths from traffic injuries. This shocking statistic is due to terrible road conditions, inadequate safety standards, and the inability of the health care system to respond adequately and quickly to traffic accidents. Because the transportation network in Liberia is built on public mass transit rather than individual and family cars, when there is an accident, a hundred people could die at once.

In Liberia, as in most sub-Saharan African countries, the increasing frequency of mass transit traffic accidents has become a public health issue, but is rarely regarded as such by the government. Because this is a public health issue where government and communities could work together to make both immediate and long-term positive impacts on Liberia's death and disability rates, there is an urgent need to take appropriate action.

A typical family in Liberia does not own a car because they live in poverty. People walk everywhere. In the rural areas, people walk together to the bush to get firewood and fetch water, to the market, to school, to the hospital, to neighboring villages, and to their farms. An average rural Liberian could walk 30 miles or more a day. Urban Liberians walk through highly congested unregulated traffic or, if they can afford it, they take overcrowded taxis or buses moving at breakneck speed through the city. There are daily reports of accidents involving overturned buses on the major highways in Liberia in which the majority of the passengers die. Travelers stop to look at such accidents and sometimes become the only rescuers, as there are no emergency or paramedic systems. Traffic accidents of major proportions seem to be part of the driving experience in Liberia.

Such accidents bring more than just personal tragedy for the individuals involved; they bring tragedy for a family and community. If a farmer (assuming he is head of the household for a family of 10) was killed or disabled in an automobile accident, eight children and their mother would suffer grave consequences. In a typical Liberian rural community, without a male head of household, a family struggles to survive. If the farmer lives but needs prolonged medical care due to a disability, the impact on the family could be even worse because medical bills will swallow any income. In Liberia, the government provides no social security or aid to the disabled or their families. Any assistance this farmer might receive will be from sympathetic friends and relatives in the village who are also struggling financially themselves. If the farmer does not survive the crash, his wife and children are stuck with the cost of the funeral, which could cast the family into debt for years.

There are many more pedestrian deaths in developing countries than in developed countries for a number of reasons: no sidewalks exist in rural and periurban areas, so pedestrians walk on the narrow roads, increasing their risk of being run over by speeding traffic; roads for commercial traffic are built to run right through the middle of small villages that are completely unprepared to deal with traffic; literacy levels are too low for many Liberians to understand traffic signs; there is an unresolved power struggle between pedestrians and drivers, and drivers tend to disregard any traffic regulations meant to protect pedestrians; it is a necessary part of family life to have children run errands throughout the day, putting them at risk of being run over by a careless driver; and commercial drivers are motivated by profit and deadlines rather than community safety. The drivers of "money buses," public transportation vehicles owned by transport companies, are under immense pressure to overload their buses and to make many trips to meet a quota. Money buses frequently tip over, killing 40 or 50 passengers at a time. Multinational companies, motivated by profit, create road systems that serve their short-term purposes rather than long-term community development. Transporting of harvested natural resources (e.g., lumber) by multinationals is often done during the night because the harvesting and loading of the trucks is done during the day. Only the headlights on these trucks guide the drivers because there are no lights on the narrow, dusty, rutted, and rocky roads. Oncoming drivers are blinded by their "brights" and must pull off the road to let them pass. For example, timber companies cut down enormous trees in rural areas and stack up a load so heavy that it makes it very difficult for the trucks to stop. They are transporting raw logs from the rural area to a seaport on the same roads that money buses are traveling with people packed in like sardines.

These road systems, built with gross disregard for the villagers, leave pedestrians, including children and the elderly, vulnerable to being hit by speeding buses and trucks. In the interior segments of Liberia, many of the roads literally divide villages in half, separating families from sources of water, the market, or other villagers. During the evening hours, children then must take their buckets to fetch water from across the road in order for their mothers to prepare the family dinner. Careless and irresponsible drivers fail to slow down as they drive through the towns or villages. Left without sufficient time to get out of the way of an oncoming vehicle, many young people are hit and killed or become disabled from the resulting accidents. Such vehicles also sometimes hit older people as they return to their homes from visiting other family members.

Connected to this is the fact that many of the health centers are not equipped to treat accident victims. Besides the distance and the lack of ambulances to transport accident victims, whenever auto or farming accident victim reach the hospital, doctors and nurses struggle at times to determine the extent of their injuries. Medical equipment needed to do the necessary examinations, including x-rays, is usually out of service at government hospitals. If a family member decides to seek care at a private hospital, it may be too expensive for the person or the individual may in fact die before being transferred to the private hospital.

Reducing road traffic accidents should become part of the reconstructive agenda of the new Liberia. Multinational companies need to be held accountable for their contributions to traffic hazards. The Liberian government should focus on the behavior of drivers and the police. The police should hold drivers accountable for speeding and overtaking other cars on curves or below hills. Police officers should patrol the highways, and motorists found violating driving rules should pay fines and, in cases of frequent or repeated offenses, should be made to give up their driving privileges or serve time in prison. Liberia must find ways to make police officers resist corruption, as bribery is the norm in the Liberian setting. One way is to ensure that officers are paid a living wage on a timely basis. Many drivers who violate traffic rules are likely to walk free without being prosecuted because of the ineptness of corrupt Liberian police officers. This ineptitude and corruption could be reduced if police and other law enforcement officers would be paid a reasonable amount commensurate with their qualifications and responsibilities—and paid on time.

Liberians generally blame the drivers of public transport vehicles for their lack of road sense. But they also should hold the local and national governments accountable for not maintaining the dilapidated road infrastructure. Most roads in Liberia have huge potholes that often cause accidents when motorists try to avoid them, while many of the streetlights in Monrovia and other urban settings do not work, making it difficult to see pedestrians in the dark. The protracted civil war exacerbated the already endemic problem of poor roads.

Pedestrians can also play a role in reducing traffic accidents. Even in the cities, there is a lack of road safety awareness among pedestrians. Children and the elderly are particularly vulnerable because they often do not understand road signs. Like other school-based health promotion programs, it would be a great idea to seek funding and introduce road safety awareness into all school curricula, especially in elementary and junior high schools. Also, it is safe to assume that because of lack of standards and poorly implemented policies, many of the so-called drivers in Liberia have not gone to driving school. They learned from spending time assisting bus and truck drivers in packing and transporting loads in vehicles; later, when these senior drivers become tired, they would pass the steering over to their assistants. Because many towns are far away from urban centers, driver fatigue often sets in at night. Additionally, at night, because the roads are not paved, there is poor visibility as large lorry trucks speed to transport lumber and other goods to the ports. It is common for drivers to fill a bus with more passengers than the number allowed by the government. Additionally, many of these passengers are transporting materials to and from the city, and then load areas atop pickup trucks and buses are often stacked beyond capacity. The slightest mistake a driver might make in speeding on a curve can send the bus or truck tilting over.

As Liberia is reconstructed, new roads will be built. That will be an excellent opportunity to respond to the crisis with new, better-planned highways. For example, on sharp curves, improved guardrails to lessen vehicle impacts and save lives should be incorporated. Rather than simply considering road traffic accidents as human error, those rebuilding roads in Liberia should pay attention to the design and layout of roads, the nature of the vehicles on the roads, and the development, implementation, and enforcement of traffic laws. While it is impractical to expect that the police will patrol all rural roads, periodic checkpoints could be set up in an effort to get bad drivers off the road before they injure or kill people. Road traffic deaths and serious injuries are largely preventable. Health officials will need to deal with road traffic injury along with communicable diseases and other public health issues. Government should implement low-cost technologies, such as speed bumps in urban areas and rumble strips to slow down traffic at dangerous intersections and when drivers are passing through towns.

Mental Health and Delivery of Needed
Mental Health Services

Mental health needs of the population constitute yet another concern that will need to be considered during this postwar era. Even during peacetime, previous Liberian administration has not made the mental health of Liberians a priority. As a result, there was only one poorly run and underfunded mental health hospital in the entire country, Catherine Mills Rehabilitation Center.

Many individuals do not stop to think and understand the interrelationships between physical and mental health. Research over the years, however, suggests that the mental health consequences of armed conflict can be deplorable and are interrelated with physical health. Even in peaceful countries like the United States, people are distressed and under immense stress. Reports examining the prevalence and severity of mental disorders globally suggest an estimated 26 percent of Americans suffer from a mental disorder, as measured by the *Diagnostic and Statistical Manual of Mental Disorders, Fourth Edition (DSM-IV)* (WHO Health Survey Consortium, 2004). The prevalence, severity, and unmet needs of mental health issues may be even more critical for the people of Liberia, who have lived through warfare for over a decade. A new challenge for the government of Liberia is that many Liberians, in the wake of the civil war, will experience post-traumatic stress disorder (PTSD). Although Liberians are a resilient set of people, some PTSD symptoms may manifest themselves only years later. A necessary condition for the development of PTSD is exposure to a traumatic event where the person experienced, witnessed, or was confronted with an event or events that involved actual or threatened death or serious injury. The person's response to the event or events must have involved intense feelings of fear, helplessness, or horror. This definition is obviously synonymous with what many Liberians experienced during the civil war. The long-term effects of stress experienced from the war may hinder the functioning of individuals, families, and Liberian society as a whole, long after the war. Moreover, mental health services in Liberia during the war were inadequate and inaccessible; therefore, the psychological impact of the civil war will be felt among all sectors of the population.

What then can be or should be done? The integration of essential mental health services into the provision of primary health care should be considered a priority. This process will take commitment from the health authorities and will include the purchasing of essential and adequate drugs.

Because of the immense stigma and lack of early care for most individuals with mental illness in Liberia, approximately 80 percent of such cases may require some institutional care. Many individuals, obviously, will not be able to afford private psychiatrists. As a result, the Liberian government, in rebuilding the health care system, should focus not only on reviving the Catherine Mills Rehabilitation Center, but undertake efforts to expand or create psychiatric units—a minimum of 50 beds per unit at each county general hospital. In so doing, effort should be made to recruit one trained psychiatrist or psychologist for each county hospital. Primary care physicians, physician assistants, and nurses are often the first health care professional to see patients with mental health issues, and therefore should be trained in basic areas of mental health in order to screen patients for early intervention and perhaps refer patients to mental health specialists. This would allow patients to seek help early and be put in therapy before their conditions worsen. A broader vision is needed to ensure the availability of and accessibility to minimum health care for all Liberians, but particularly the most vulnerable and underprivileged and the mentally ill.

The reconstruction of the mental health sector of Liberia should focus on improvement in training opportunities for health care professionals and community mental health services for the people. The traditional belief system of what causes illness and/or disease discussed in the chapter must clearly be understood prior to designing and implementing any mental health care program in Liberia. A system of collaboration is suggested between the modern health care system and the traditional healing systems. In the beginning, there may be some feelings of distrust; however, identification of the reasons for such distrust is a major first step in building a trusting relationship.

Access to and Utilization of Health Care Services

Accessibility and utilizations are two important variables that interact in any health care delivery system. These two concepts are critical in understanding the relationship between patients and health care providers. Access is defined as the ability of the population to utilize services, including factors such as distance, effort, cost, and awareness of services (Meade, Florin, and Gesler, 1988). In Liberia, where significant proportions of the general population are poor and lack stable income-generating sources, accessing health care and related services is sometimes difficult or even impossible. However, economic factors are not the only factors; other variables, including sociocultural factors, perceptions regarding health and other health-related belief systems, must be understood. Health care delivery may be impacted by political and environmental factors, as shown from the protracted Liberian civil war. In the following section, access to health care and challenges are discussed from both urban and rural perspectives. In reconstructing the health care delivery system of Liberia, health care planning strategies are needed that can respond to the needs of the rural population as well as people residing in the urban and periurban areas. There may be some similarities in conditions and diseases or in health needs; however, the design of health care services for people in the rural areas of Liberia should be different from those services provided in the urban areas. This does not mean that modern health care services developed for the people in the rural areas should be inferior to those in urban areas. All services, regardless of location, should be appropriate, culturally relevant and cost-effective.

Urban Health Care Needs and Challenges

Prior to the civil war in Liberia, there was an observed internal migration trend in which more individuals (especially young people) migrated to the urban centers, including Monrovia, for school and in search of potential employment. The prewar Monrovia population was about 500,000 inhabitants. Because of internal displacement due to the civil conflict, there are over 1 million people now living in the city. The overflow of people in the urban centers brings new challenges. There is a lack of basic sanitation, a lack of water, and extra strain on an already dysfunctional health care system. Recent reports suggest that many displaced individuals in the city and usual inhabitants have suffered from diarrheal-related diseases such as cholera, typhoid fever, and amoebic dysentery. Because of the overcrowding and people sleeping in the open, malaria has also increased due to an increase in the mosquito population. Additionally, in many of these settings, the presence of traditional or alternative health delivery systems may be limited. Even in the absence of sociological or anthropological research, it is known that people living in crowded urban and periurban settings in Liberia may be prone to increased morbidity and mortality rates.

Living in the urban center of Monrovia does not mean that an individual there will have complete access to health care. For instance, there are reports that the population on one side of the St. Paul River bridge (the once-famous bridge that was the division point between Charles Taylor forces and rebels), generally does not have access to many of the government health care facilities. Many of those institutions were destroyed and looted. Government has been unable to restore health care delivery in this area to its prewar level. In the absence of government health programs, many of the individuals involved turned to private pharmacies or vendors to purchase medications for their ailments. The irony here is that many of the individuals who sell pharmaceutical products to those living in the district do not have the least idea about the dosages, actions, effectiveness, and/or adverse effects of many of the medications they sell to the general population. In the absence of government control over pharmaceuticals, it is common for individuals to take the wrong medications and/or experience immense suffering and even disability from incorrect prescriptions.

In the prewar era, with the existence of contemporary care facilities, people walked significant distances to seek health care. But other factors must be understood in the Liberian context. In an effort to improve the Liberian health care system, effort should be made to collect information on accessibility and utilization of health care services based on population characteristics such as age, geographic location, tribal affiliation, income, gender, and the like. It will be important to understand these factors in Liberia. Research done in developed countries, including the United States suggests that people of lower socioeconomic status or belonging to minority groups often have less accessibility to health care (Fiscella, Franks, Gold, and Clancy, 2000). What do the Liberians believe about the causes of illness and the appropriate treatment of illness also affects when, where, and what kinds of help they will pursue. It will also be important to keep data on the type and severity of each illness. These factors are important to understand in order to institute an optimal distribution of health care resources in a new Liberia.

Rural Health Care Needs and Challenges

Rural populations in Liberia remain especially vulnerable to certain diseases and health conditions. Because they reach the health centers and hospitals late, they may suffer more from chronic conditions, including cardiac-related conditions (e.g., hypertension); rural women may have higher maternal morbidity and mortality rates. The infant mortality rate is obviously higher in the rural areas due to diverse factors. Farming of rice and other crops is a major agricultural activity in rural Liberia. Hunting and fishing are also major activities. At rural hospitals, such as Phebe Lutheran Hospital and Ganta Methodist Hospital in the central and northern parts of the country, emergency rooms are overburdened with cases of farming accidents, gunshot wounds, and snakebites. This suggests that even though rates for all causes of death in Liberia may be lower in the rural areas, the rural populations experience greater poverty, substandard living conditions, agriculture-related injuries and illness, and scarcity of basic primary health care services. These factors increase the magnitude of the health problems that they face and increase their mortality rates.

The distances a patient travels can also interact with other factors. Meade and colleagues (1998) referred to this concept as "non-spatial variables" to aid in understanding patient-provider contacts. Approximately 85 percent of the Liberian population resides in rural areas or the interior; however, in many rural areas, there is no primary health care center. Those centers that do exist in some rural communities are usually barely staffed with trained and experienced health care workers and, in many instances are poorly equipped. The lack of supplies and the availability of trained health care providers (nurses and midwives), groups that are regarded as the front line of health care delivery in Liberia, is endemic. This does not encourage people to seek health care in a contemporary health care center.

The notion of what constitutes a rural community is debatable, and interpretation varies. Politics may also come into play when defining communities as rural or urban. Villages and towns in Liberia are sparse, and in some counties, there may be concentrated villages or towns surrounded by forested or jungle areas. There may also be great distances between few people. Even with the availability of funds, the challenge for the Liberian government here is how to provide optimal health care to the people in these rural communities. Forested terrain, poor-quality roads, and/or lack of public transportation may greatly lengthen travel time across relatively few miles.

Specific to the rural populations in Liberia are the intangible costs of seeking health care. Many women and men in the rural areas of Liberia are subsistence farmers. Besides having to travel long distances to seek health care, they may also be faced with lost time from work in their rice fields. While many health care providers may focus more on the capability of the patients to pay, rural families must weigh the cost of being able to pay for health care service against that of leaving their rice fields for a day or two to travel afar in an effort to seek health care. For example, assume that the Liberian government came up with an excellent policy to provide free or low cost prenatal care to all pregnant women in an effort to improve infant and maternal mortality in the country. A superintending nurse or midwife assigned to a primary health care center may be more focused on the costs of such care and assume, wrongly, that because the care is free, or less expensive, more women in the rural area will now take advantage of the new program. A factor to consider in many rural areas is that a pregnant woman may have other obligations, such as taking care of other young children, and may not want to take time off from protecting her rice fields from destructive birds and other animals. In rural areas of Liberia, because of the travel distances involved, a prenatal care visit to a health center may take all day. Indeed, in some cases, women may even have to travel a day or two, both before and after a day set aside for a prenatal care clinic visit. Health services such as these carry costs that too often are not included in assessing rural health care services and their feasibility. Such costs and the perceptions of these costs by women and men and families in rural communities are critical factors in service utilization.

Opportunities and Implications for New Directions for Health Care Delivery in Both Rural and Urban Settings

Prior to the civil war, Liberia embraced the primary health care (PHC) approach described in chapter 1. In this postwar era, it will be critical to revive most PHC programs. It may be important to create a bureau of primary health care services or a bureau of rural health care to address health care needs of rural populations. Because the nurses in Liberia are the first line for the provision of modern health care for the majority of the Liberian population, innovative nursing strategies need to be tested in community-based settings aimed at improving and enhancing the availability, accessibility, acceptability, adequacy and appropriateness of health care services in the rural areas of Liberia. Instead of focusing on training nurse managers, educational institutions such as Cuttington University College should direct their efforts in training postbaccalaureate nurses skilled in assessing, implementing and evaluating patient care. These individuals should be trained in the areas of community health, epidemiology, and research, in addition to at least basic managerial and economics principles. Besides being able to provide care, a nurse, even in a rural setting, should know how to collect and keep disease surveillance data and how to keep stocks of supplies and pharmaceuticals.

Primary and secondary prevention will be important in both rural and urban areas. Worldwide, the discipline of nursing has been instrumental in providing health promotion and health education activities. In the rural areas of Liberia, nurses are mostly likely to be assigned to a village or town instead of a physician. They will therefore have the advantage of working with rural farmers, women and children. Nurses in the rural areas can use their communication skills to effectively reach rural populations on matters related to infant mortality, women's health, agricultural injuries and illnesses, and immunizations. The involvement of the family in many health care-related activities, including involvement of males in family planning programs, will be essential in rural areas.

The tertiary care settings and linkages between acute care and chronic care facilities require critical examination. Nurses and midwives in rural settings usually refer a chronic or difficult-to-solve problem to a larger healthcare facility. However, there are no tertiary prevention strategies currently in place in the Liberian care delivery system. What happens when a congestive heart failure patient or a diabetic patient is discharged from the hospital and sent back to her or his rural community? Who should he or she talk with if a problem arises? Is the nurse assigned to the nearest clinic aware of her or his treatment regimen? Is there any collaboration between the formal medical system and the patient's family or informal support systems? In an effort to rebuild the health care delivery system in Liberia, appropriate and cost-effective strategies for implementing postdischarge care for chronic illness in the rural areas are also needed. In these cases, extensive nursing case management may be important. Although difficult to sustain in the absence of electricity, modern technological methods, including handheld radio messages to nurses twice daily in the rural setting, could help provide some of the needed information about patients.

In the urban areas of Liberia, some segments of the population strive while others live in despair, searching for opportunities. Liberia, like most developing countries, has had people migrating to not only the main city, but also to surrounding areas of the city known as periurban areas. These individuals live in shacks and dilapidated areas where they become highly vulnerable to contracting various diseases. In order to survive, many engage in risky activities including use of illicit drugs, alcohol misuse, violence, and other detrimental habits. They also face other contemporary health and social problems including HIV/AIDS and unplanned pregnancies. Comprehensive programs will need to be developed that address physical, psychosocial, and structural barriers to obtaining help for these problems.

Healthcare issues will have to be viewed from a broader, holistic perspective to include the factors of meeting housing and other needs.

Just like their rural counterparts, such programs in urban areas should be based on a continuum of services encompassing primary, secondary and tertiary care. Nurses are also paramount in providing services to urban areas. They can help in focusing interventions while establishing centers where people could obtain all their services. It is assumed that many vulnerable urban residents will not be insured and will probably be small-market vendors; they therefore cannot afford to get sick. Others may be partially employed on an hourly basis and cannot afford to miss a day or even several hours of work.

Although costly for small companies in the Monrovia area, businesses, especially larger companies, may want to start thinking about having at least one nurse on site. The nurse would then act as an in-house expert on health-related issues and develop a referral system for employees who may need tertiary care when a chronic problem needs resolution. If a company can afford it, it may attempt to provide basic primary care services to all its employees. Smaller companies may combine their resources and hire a nurse who would provide basic services to employees of three or five businesses. The goal here is to develop a nurse-managed primary care delivery strategy at or near where people work to help meet the health care needs of urban employees. In this case, employees may be asked to pay a reasonable price for such services, something that is not currently done in many Liberian companies.

Note

1.   Brownlee, A.T. (1978). *Community, culture, and care: A cross-cultural guide for health workers (pp33)*. Saint Louis, MO: The Mosby Company.

CHAPTER 4

HEALTH CARE IN LIBERIA:
UNDERSTANDING ITS ORGANIZATION
AND DELIVERY

But in a turbulent environment the change is so widespread that
it just routes around any kind of central authority. So it is best to
manage the bottom-up change rather than try to institute it from
the top down.[1]

—Kelvin Kelly

The way to build a complex system that works is to build it from
very simple systems that work.[2]

—Kelvin Kelly

The Concept of a Health Care System: Liberia

Every country faces challenges as to how to distribute health care to its
entire citizen. The challenges for developing countries are compounded by an underdeveloped health care delivery system and the scarcity
of financial resources. The provision of modern health care is even more
problematic in many sub-Saharan African countries because civil war has
disrupted the socioeconomic development process. As in most countries of

the world, the health care system of Liberia consists of a combination of many subsystems. For instance, while the Liberian government primarily provides health care in Liberia, it is also provided by the private sector, including companies and nongovernmental organizations (NGOs). Additionally, there are private clinics, pharmacies, and "medicine stores" run by individuals with no medical training.

The modern health care delivery system in Liberia operates parallel to the traditional health care delivery system. "Modern health care system" is defined here as those formal institutions that are built and staffed with health care workers trained in the area of the biomedical treatment processes: nurses, doctors, pharmacists, and other allied health care professionals. "Traditional health care delivery systems" employ non-scientific or other alternative treatment modalities. The health care system in Liberia could also be grouped into health promotion, curative, or disease prevention services. The modern health care system could also be viewed according to the type of services provided: outpatient care, community-based services, hospital or institutional care, pharmaceuticals, and diagnostic services. The health care system in Liberia could be divided geographically into urban and rural subsystems. Politically, Liberia is divided into 13 counties, with the majority of the population residing in the rural areas during the prewar era. Within the counties are tribal clans and townships that carry certain local governmental responsibilities. The chief of the tribal clan has power over the chiefs of the townships in his or her area. The smallest social units are the villages. Some villages are more populated or more remotely situated than others. Accommodating these intricate socio-political-cultural structures, and at the same time providing health care to all people in Liberia, presents logistical, human resource, financial, and management challenges.

Organizational Structure of the Liberian Ministry of Health and Social Welfare (MOH&SW)

The principal governmental agency responsible for health services in Liberia is the Ministry of Health and Social Welfare (MOH&SW). The MOH&SW utilizes a quasi-centralized administrative approach to organizing and delivering health care. The Minister of Health, a cabinet-appointed official, is the chief health officer of the country. Through the years, the MOH&SW has undergone several reorganizations and at the time of conducting the research for this book, its responsibility was divided among six bureaus: the Bureau of Central Administration; the Bureau of Planning, Research and Development; the Bureau of Vital and Health Statistics; the Bureau of Curative Services; Bureau of Preventive Services; and the Bureau of Social Welfare. There are also semiautonomous governmental health institutions that have responsibility for health care delivery and are under the auspices of the MOH&SW, such as the National Drug Service, the John F. Kennedy Medical Center, and the Tubman National Institute of Medical Arts. All these bureaus and agencies are based in Monrovia, the capital of Liberia. In the other large cities, there are government-run hospitals and clinics that fall under the administrative structure of the MOH&SW. For rural health administration, there is a network of 13 county medical directors. These county health officers are the decision makers for health care delivery in their respective counties.

Figure 4-1. Prewar organizational structure of the Liberian Ministry of Health and Social Welfare. (Adapted from the MOH& SW annual report, 1991). Note. MOH&SW postwar organizational structure is purported to be similar.

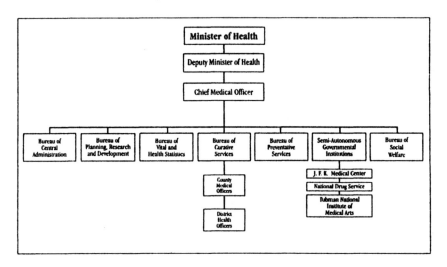

During the prewar era, the six bureaus of the central MOH&SW were each further organized into divisions with a wide variety of functions. For example, the Bureau of Preventive Services of the MOH&SW included the following divisions: Environmental Health; Family Health; Communicable Disease Control; Health Information, Education and Communication; and Primary Health Care Coordination. Figure 4-1 presents a flow chart that illustrates the administrative structure of the Liberian MOH&SW. The administrative structure of the MOH&SW in the postwar era is purported to be similar to the prewar structure.

Bureaus and Autonomous Health-Related Agencies of the MOH&SW

Bureau of Central Administration

The Bureau of Central Administration is responsible for ensuring the availability of health care, the proper management of infrastructure, the financing and provision of materials, and other logistical matters necessary to provide health care to the general citizenry. This centralized structure sometimes creates a bureaucratic nightmare in providing medical supplies and materials and labor for repairing and maintaining hospitals and related buildings. In the past, the Bureau of Central Administration has been plagued with accounting inefficiencies. Poor record keeping and insufficient accountability for expenditures are two of the many problems that cripple the system. Strategies need to be developed to ensure that the limited resources are efficiently, cost-effectively and fairly distributed. Also, although many health conditions affecting the general population in Liberia are preventable, the MOH&SW spends more money on curative services than it does on preventive health services.

There are also inefficiencies in how health care professionals are employed and compensated. When MOH&SW employs health care professionals, such as nurses or physicians, there is usually a lengthy process of approvals. As a result, a nurse who is assigned to a rural part of the country must remain in the capital city until the Ministry of Finance approves his or her payment. Leaving early for one's assignment in the rural area means one will be unable to get one's salary. Also, the Ministry of Finance pays health care providers in the form of checks, which makes it difficult to cash. A nurse or physician is employed by the MOH&SW but is actually not paid by the ministry itself. Except in urban areas such as

Monrovia or Kakata, it is very difficult to cash checks. Banks and other financial institutions are few or nonexistent in the rural areas, making it difficult at least for employees to cash their checks. As a result, employees are often absent from their posts in the rural areas when they travel to urban locations to have their checks cashed. This means often that patients in need of services, are unable to see the only nurse or physician assistant assigned at a given health center because she or he has traveled to the nearest city to cash her or his paycheck. As the economic sector of the country improves, more banks will be established in the rural areas. Decentralization could mean that the Ministry of Finance distributes salary payments to the county medical officers to distribute to the District Health Officers, who could then distribute individual salaries to health care professionals. Each County Medical Officer could set up the most efficient payment system for his or her area.

This existing pattern of the personnel system is not unique to the health care sector. It is common to all Liberian governmental or public sectors, including the Ministry of Education. An extreme centralized decision-making process precludes responsibility for assessment and appropriate assignment, things that lie more in the direct experience of the county health officials. When rural health care workers are not paid on time, it creates economic hardships for them. Many of these rural workers are tempted to seek employment in the urban areas, where it is often possible to supplement income by working in the private health care sector. To retain these workers, their salaries must be provided on time and opportunities should be created for in-service training and career enhancement.

Bureau of Planning, Research and Development

The Bureau of Planning, Research and Development is responsible for conducting health assessments, identifying health problems, and developing health programs and projects that would improve or enhance the health of the people of Liberia. This arm of the MOH&SW works collaboratively with other ministries to strengthen and provide health care services. At the same time, this bureau tries to understand the dynamics of the provision of health care, including access to health care. International agencies, such as UNICEF, estimate that only approximately 35 percent of the Liberian population has access to basic health care. In this postwar era, the goals of the Bureau of Planning, Research and Development could be achieved by decentralizing some of its activities, increasing the training of more Liberians in the areas of health and planning. External resources may have to be obtained to finance such human resource development projects.

Bureau of Vital and Health Statistics

The Bureau of Vital and Health Statistics, collects data on morbidity and mortality rates from health facilities throughout the country. As in other African countries, vital statistics about Liberia are insufficient and in some cases unreliable. The civil war also exacerbated and constrained the already poorly functioning statistics gathering system. Annual reports from the Ministry of Health admit to poor data collection, incorrect reporting, underreporting, and late reporting.

Collecting relevant health, morbidity, and mortality information is essential because health policy should be based on sound evaluation of health problems impacting the population. Policy should be based on need rather than on political ideologies, tribal affiliation, economic gain, and regional favoritism. Policy should be linked to the morbidity and mortality data, so diseases and injuries have to be defined and ascertained and their frequencies noted. This calls for an organized approach to the collection, analysis, and use of the information contained in health statistics.

The manner in which previous governments collected information on morbidity and mortality is a reason for concern. The collection of health statistics from various clinics and health centers is not automated and requires patience, effort on the part of health care professionals to complete long and sometimes confusing government forms accurately. Erroneous reporting leads to deficiencies in existing data bases, but that is only part of the problem. Analyzing data requires the use of sophisticated data management skills with training in statistical analysis programs of a type that is optimal for medical, public health, and social science research. Interpretation of these statistical analyses requires advanced skills in biostatistics, demography, and epidemiology. This information then needs to be put into language that planners can comprehend and use to make intelligent policy. Research results need to be disseminated to the various levels of health care professionals so it can inform their health care practice.

To establish adequate health data bases and health information systems on a national basis will require some serious short- and long-term research planning. Some reforms in the Liberian economic and political structure will also be required. For instance, the government of Liberia will have to view the health and well being of its people as a priority that is critical for the development of the country. Importing hundreds of computers with spreadsheet software, by itself, will not be adequate without extensive human resource planning. In addition to acquiring the necessary hardware and software packages, the perspective of health care workers must evolve to embrace research-driven allocation of funds. Doctors and nurses, for instance, must see the link between contributing data on patients to the national database and a more effective and fair distribution of national funds. Finally, prevention and treatment programs must also be evidenced-based.

Bureau of Curative Services

The Bureau of Curative Services is responsible for providing clinical medical treatment through its network of health facilities: hospitals, health centers, and clinics. This bureau is made up of four central divisions, dealing with, respectively, medical and dental services, nursing services, pharmaceuticals, and laboratory services. In predicting and ameliorating clinical health needs, the bureau sometimes collaborates with some other government agencies as well as NGOs. The bureau sets standards for the provision of clinical care by hospitals and clinics, as well as doctors, nurses, and other health care professionals.

Currently, 13 County Medical Officers report to the Deputy Chief Medical Officer who heads the Bureau of Curative Services. While the responsibilities for county activities are largely delegated to the County Medical Officers, the Deputy Chief Medical Officer is still responsible for implementation of health programs and policy adherence. Within the MOH&SW is also a Director of the Division of Nursing. This individual recruits and assigns nurses for all government hospitals, health centers, clinics, and health posts.

Postwar budgets are lower for every government ministry and bureau. The Bureau of Curative Services faces shortages of key personnel, especially nurses, in rural areas; insufficient funds to maintain and build new facilities; shortages of equipment and essential medications; and inadequate transportation for fieldwork. Many health care professionals should be lauded for their tireless efforts in working to improve the health status of the population with scarce resources.

Because the current pattern of health conditions in Liberia pivots on preventable communicable diseases, these conditions cannot be reduced only through the expansion of the curative or acute health care system. Yet, the curative health sector consumes more of the funds and efforts than preventive services. Creating a better balance between curative and preventive services will be a more prudent approach.

Bureau of Preventive Services

The Bureau of Preventive Services is crucial to improving the overall health status of the Liberian people. This bureau includes central divisions for environmental health, family health, communicable disease, and information and communication, as well as a primary health care coordination office. Bureau objectives, according to MOH&SW, include (1) minimizing the prevalence and incidence of diseases attributable to environmental factors; (2) establishing and operating maternal, child, and family planning services in all political subdivisions; (3) motivating and educating the public on the importance of personal hygiene to good health; and (4) controlling and preventing the spread of communicable diseases.

Like other bureaus, the Bureau of Preventive Services also faces budgetary constraints, and as a result, many of the bureau's programs have progressed slowly. Before the civil war erupted in Liberia, programs with international funding, such as the Expanded Program for Immunization (EPI) and the South Eastern Region Primary Health Care Program (SERPHC) progressed faster than the programs funded only by the Liberian government because international funding was more dependable. Like the curative bureau, the preventive bureau also is faced with constraints in transportation, staffing, and lack of incentives for rural services, equipment shortages, and poor national policies regarding preventive health programs. The imbalance of MOH&SW expenditures on sickness rather than prevention is indicative of a strategy that ultimately results in poorer outcomes than would be experienced if more money were spent on preventative programs. This disparity prevailed even before the civil war; the faulty allocation of health expenditures probably relates to the overall poor management and direction by the MOH&SW. The very centralized nature of strategy formation means that there is limited opportunity for counties to distribute funds as they see fit, which would correct a strategic error made at the highest level.

Based on the advice of the World Health Organization (WHO) in the 1980s, the government of Liberia agreed to follow the primary health care (PHC) framework, which balances both prevention and treatment approaches. However, in practice, the PHC framework is not fully supported organizationally, financially, or strategically. For example, the training of health care workers at the middle and lower levels of the health care delivery system has been inadequate to support the PHC framework. And even when training occurs, financial support is not sufficient to sustain the programs that these health care professionals have been trained to establish.

An Understanding of Structural Factors, Including Inputs and Outputs of the Health Care System

Along with understanding the health care delivery processes in Liberia, it is also essential to understand factors related to the inputs and outputs of the system. Inputs include how the system is financed; the number and distribution of facilities and personnel; and the inpatients, outpatients and population covered by the modern health care system. Outputs include data on morbidity and mortality rates; life expectancies; patient satisfaction with the system; and improvement of overall health status of the population. According to reports from international agencies, the distribution of health care facilities in Liberia is inadequate. Before the civil war, UNICEF reported that Liberia had 33 hospitals, 32 health centers and 343 health posts (UNICEF, State of the World's Children, 1990). It is not clear how many of those hospitals exist after the civil war. Table 4-1 presents the distribution and availability of health care resources in Liberia—many of which, if they still exist, are currently inoperable.

Table 4-1. Distribution and Availability of Health Services and Resources in Liberia.

Indicator	Value/percent
HEALTH RESOURCES/DISTRIBUTION	
• Percent of national budget spent on health care	5.0%
• Health care expenditures per capita (U.S. Dollars)	$10.0million
• Health care expenditure as a percent of GDP	9.0%
• Population per doctor	10,000
• Population per nurse	5,000
• Total number of hospitals	30
• Total number of health centers & clinics	301
AVAILABILITY OF HEALTH SERVICES	
• Percent with access to safe water	93 (%Urban)
	22 (%Rural)
	50 (%Total)
• Percent with access to sanitary facilities	24 (%Urban)
	8 (%Rural)
	15 (%Total)
• Percent with access to health care services	50 (%Urban)
	30 (%Rural)
	34 (%Total)
• Percent of women with prenatal care coverage	85
• % Births attended by trained health personnel	50
• % Mothers breast-feeding at 6 months	75
• % of pregnant women immunized against tetanus	35
• % of 1 year fully immunized	TB= 84
	DPT= 43
	Polio= 45
	Measles= 44
• Prevalence of anemia in pregnant women (% below the norm)	78

Source: UNICEF (2005). *State of the World's Children*. New York: Oxford University Press.

The structural organization of the MOH&SW is, for the most part, not very different from the health care systems of many other sub-Saharan African countries. Before the wave of independence for African countries of the 1970s and 1980s, colonial powers instituted health care delivery systems that mirrored their own. Because the colonizers were immediately susceptible to endemic tropical diseases, they made the decision to develop health care systems and facilities that supported their own health needs. Large tertiary health care facilities (specializing in treating local tropical diseases and chronic diseases seen mostly in Western countries) were initially built to provide treatment for colonizers and upper class Liberians.

The colonizers and the Liberian government made this decision in spite of the fact that the major causes of morbidity and mortality among impoverished Liberians—who made up the majority of the population—were conditions that could be remedied through primary health care initiatives at the community level. As WHO and other international agencies began to define health more comprehensively, many African governments, including Liberia's, began to embrace primary health care and prevention-oriented services when they decided to offer universal access to health care. This new direction has been evolving gradually. This is partly due to budgetary constraints and lack of commitment to develop sound strategies and policies that would emphasize using primary care to prevent and treat conditions that would otherwise lead to complications that would require more costly tertiary care.

Ironically, in a country where there are so many people without access to health care, many hospitals and clinics operated by the MOH&SW are not cost-effective because they are underutilized. Some tertiary hospitals in the country have a low occupancy rate due to cultural, economic, and geographic reasons. Hospitals need excess capacity to accommodate disease outbreaks and other health crises, but an occupancy rate of less than 50 percent signals the need for hospital mergers or closings. Due to current population dynamics in Liberia, hospitals are mostly serving children with serious illness and women with complications of pregnancy. Risk factors for many of the problems seen in children and pregnant women occur in the communities where they live, work, and play. In essence, modern health care services (e.g., childhood immunizations, prenatal care, etc.) need to be provided in the villages where people will live, especially as the post war population shifts back to rural areas. Now that the war is over, a group of internally displaced people will choose not to return to their villages and instead will continue to live in periurban and urban settings. These people, too, will need community-based primary care. Although a rural health care framework and emphasis is suggested, individuals remaining in the urban slums should not be neglected. If modern health care is not offered to Liberians in a way they can access and accept, they will continue to seek help from traditional healers, including traditional birth attendants (TBAs).

As table 4-1 shows, only 34 percent of the total population of Liberia has access to modern health care services. A significant rural-urban disparity is the legacy of the small but influential segment of the Liberian population that influenced the earlier decisions about the organization of a modern health care delivery system in the country. A lesson to be learned from mistakes made during the prewar era is that critical policy decisions made during the postwar era could have a lasting positive impact over time if they are based on improving health for the entire population, not just a privileged few.

The breakdown of the health infrastructures in Liberia because of the civil war will make it difficult to see immediate improvement in health outcomes for the people. An increase in the MOH&SW budget alone will not solve the entire health problem in Liberia. Other important actions must be taken, including retraining health personnel and offering low-cost, effective, and appropriate services at the community level. These actions must be tailored to the appropriate stage of social and economic development in Liberia. For example, the John F. Kennedy Medical Center could be used to provide tertiary services for indigent urban Liberians in the Monrovia area and as a training facility for primary care health professionals who will serve the population in community-based settings in urban and rural areas.

Liberia laid the groundwork toward building its national health system before the civil war erupted. The Liberian civil war led to acute financial crisis and chaos in a system that had barely been established, exacerbating the problems in providing essential health care to the population. In this postwar era, the manner of investing in the medical system of Liberia should be based on prudent financial policies and management of scarce resources. Everyone at the MOH&SW will have to be held accountable to higher standards in providing health care to the people who really need it.

The principles of public health and primary health care that were endorsed, but not fully implemented, by the Liberian government in the 1980s should be revisited. Liberia needs to move beyond the point where it was allocating funding disproportionately to treatment-oriented programs and facilities while neglecting primary prevention and public health programs. A new system will call for a balance between the tertiary care treatment facilities and community-based health care delivery. Securing this balance involves a strategic shift toward prevention-oriented programs like the PHC programs that were already being implemented in many areas of Liberia during the prewar era. This strategic shift will require not just a shift in funding allocation, but also a shift in purpose from the treatment of chronic conditions in urban settings to the prevention of communicable diseases in local Liberian communities.

Major Stakeholders in the Organization and Delivery of Health Care

The Role of Religious and Philanthropic Organizations and Institutions

Religious groups and philanthropic organizations influence politics, education, economics, and health care delivery in Liberia. In addition to the Liberian government, religious groups have been instrumental in the provision of medical care to the Liberian people. During the civil war, religious and philanthropic groups—at great risk to their staff—provided acute health care to thousands of internally displaced Liberians. For example, before the war, the Lutheran and Methodist Churches provided modern health care to the northern and central provinces of Liberia. The Lutheran Church has two major hospitals and health training facilities in the country—one located in Lofa County and the other in Bong County. The Methodist Church also has a major hospital and training facility for registered nurses in Nimba County. These institutions are, for the most part, the only comprehensive health care facilities located in these areas. Although government clinics and health posts may be present, they lack pharmaceuticals and sufficient staff to provide extensive care to the people.

None of these facilities was spared damage during the civil war. They were looted, some nurses and other staff members were killed, and physical facilities were grossly damaged. The Liberian government will need to negotiate with religious and philanthropic organizations to continue to provide health care for their clienteles, especially in the rural areas where their institutions are based. When these facilities were initially established, they provided free health care services to needy people; in the future, individuals may need to make a small contribution toward payment for their health care.

Countries throughout much of Africa are suffering from sociopolitical and health-related crises and are vying for help from church-related institutions. Philanthropic budgets are strained. The Liberian government may have to subsidize the rebuilding of health care facilities and supply some staff in order to restore health care services to prewar levels. The return of Liberian refugees and internally displaced people poses an enormous health care burden for the country, and the Liberian government needs to take responsibility for carrying this burden and to support other organizations that are willing to carry part of it.

The Role of Multinational Companies in Health Care Delivery

When the Liberian outposts of multinational companies were functional, prior to the civil war, many helped develop medical facilities, primarily used by their employees and their families. Some of these companies include the Firestone Rubber Plantation Company, Bong Mining Company, and the Liberian-American Mining Company. These companies, especially the Bong Mining Company, conducted valuable research on some of the endemic and fatal tropical diseases found in Liberia, such as Lassa fever, yellow fever, and schistosomiasis. These companies supported the establishment of the Liberian Institute of Biomedical Research and the Tropical Medicine Institute of Hamburg, located near the German headquarters of the Bong Mining Company. These institutes conducted research on malaria and other vector-borne diseases that helped the health care field better understand the prevention and treatment of these diseases. These programs all ended during the civil war because the multinational companies pulled out of Liberia for the safety of their expatriate employees. After the civil war broke out in Liberia, they moved on to profit-making ventures in other African countries, taking their biomedical resources with them.

During the postwar redevelopment process, multinational companies will again be interested in Liberia's natural resources: diamonds, gold, iron ore, and timber. This will be an opportune time for the Liberian government to press upon these profit-making companies to participate in an equitable and just development of the country, including health care research, health care delivery, and prevention of diseases. Previously, the distribution of health care services was confined primarily to the areas where the companies were located. Since the natural resources these extract are actually a national resource, they owe the people of Liberia compensation. A commensurate compensation would be a contribution to health care on the national level. The leaders of these companies need to contribute their resources in the reinvention of Liberia's health care system. If companies that did business in Liberia before the war decide to come back, they need to be challenged by the government to move beyond the exploitative approach of compensating only the top echelon of Liberians in return for draining Liberia of its natural resources. If new multinational companies come to Liberia to participate in the reconstruction process, the leaders of Liberia, including MOH&SW officials, will need to negotiate terms up front, including devising important and productive opportunities for philanthropy on the national level.

The Role of Private For-Profit Health Services

Liberia is one of the sub-Saharan African countries that managed to develop facilities for training its own health care professionals. The sole medical school is located at the University of Liberia, in Monrovia. Cuttington University College, which trains the country's advanced nurses, is located in the central rural area of the country. They both barely survived the civil war. The damage incurred by these institutions of higher learning in the areas of material losses and displaced human resources are staggering. Rebuilding these institutions of higher learning will be pivotal in re-staffing the health care system with qualified health care professionals. During the civil war, there was an exodus of trained health care professionals from the country. Even those professionals who remained fell behind in their practices because continuing education was nonexistent.

Almost all physicians, physician assistants, and nurses are employed in a Liberian government hospital, a church-related health institution, or a company hospital. Prior to the civil war, few health care professionals embarked on the business venture of establishing their own private practices. As for those who did establish a private practice, there are inadequate data to provide a clear picture of the variety and extent of their private practice in Liberia. Enterprising nurses and doctors—suffering from low morale in the government sector—began capitalizing on the dissatisfaction that patients with the ability to pay for health care had with government-run health care. As an alternative to establishing their own clinics or medicine shops, some physicians and nurses held salaried positions with the MOH&SW while working in a private clinic to augment their salaries.

The economic crisis in Liberia has spawned a private sector that has the potential to become a significant area for health services in the future of Liberia. The private health sector could help the overall health care system in a number of ways. For example, they could raise the standard of medical practice. There could be contractual links and alliances between government hospitals and private health institutions. The networking contacts of health enterprises in Liberia with other businesses in sub-Saharan Africa and the rest of the world could serve as a medium for new partnerships with the MOH&SW. When information from private practice is collected and entered into the national health database, it will contribute to a more accurate picture of the health status of the Liberian people. Alliances with the private sector will also help to raise standards of practice and will, hopefully, help improve the overall image of government's efforts in providing health services for the general citizenry.

In order to understand the coverage areas and avoid duplicating services, the government will need to identify the number and location of registered practitioners, so better registration of private practice is necessary. In Liberia, as in other sub-Saharan countries, both bureaucratic public health care systems and scattered small private practices exist, and, as an unintended result, provide greater accessibility to essential health services. With the majority of the Liberian people living in poverty, privatizing the health care system would preclude most Liberians from obtaining health care. Under the "market justice" approach, health care is not viewed as a basic right but rather, as a commodity. In the "social justice" approach that Liberia aspires to, health care is viewed as a collective responsibility. Liberia is experiencing the limitations of the social justice approach, through a lack of sufficient financial backing and political commitment. One can argue that although the Liberian healthcare system is primarily based on the social approach to healthcare distribution, market- driven approaches also exist alongside the social approach and thus the Liberian healthcare system could be described as a "quasi-social approach."In the future, it may be helpful to explore the potential of increasing the role of the private sector in the provision of health care to the Liberian people.

The Role of Local Pharmacies and Medicine Stores

The exact number of pharmacies and medicine stores in Liberia is not known. A medicine store is a quasi pharmacy that sells over-the-counter and some prescription drugs as well as toiletries. While pharmacies are registered with the MOH&SW, medicine stores are not. There are few pharmaceutical regulations in Liberia. Hospitals and some clinics typically dispense drugs from their own supplies. Instead of going to a hospital to be diagnosed, a person who is ill could go to a medicine store and describe her or his symptoms. The salesperson, who is seldom a trained pharmacist, will select a package of medicine or dispense a quantity of some herbal remedy that he or she advises the patient to take in a certain way. Only rarely does the patient present a doctor's prescription to be filled. Often, the client simply requests the compound he or she wants, based on his or her own past experience or the advice of others. Self-care recommendation by the medicine store salesperson is the most common initial response to sickness in the country. This approach is especially widespread among Liberia's rural population, where the lack of modern health care and the unavailability of medications at clinics and health posts is a chronic problem.

Despite their shortcomings, pharmacies and medicine stores are a potentially valuable adjunct to the health system of Liberia. Private pharmacies, and even medicine stores, are more efficient at building inventory than government-run facilities. By their very nature—small-scale and community-based—they expedite the distribution of valuable items such as oral rehydration salts (ORS), family planning supplies, pain medications, and supplies for minor injuries. Despite the risk of potential problems in the misuse of ORS, contraceptives, or antibiotics, there is a place for private pharmacies and medicine stores in the Liberian health care system that nothing else fills yet. Currently, the government has a shortage of foreign currency for the purchase of medical supplies, so the privately operated pharmacies and medicine stores offer an alternative, although the cost may be higher. The government can negotiate for large quantities of drugs at a reduced cost, relying on international agencies to do the bulk purchasing. However, the costs of the most basic, essential drugs for a developing country are already set low, so the increase in cost in the private sector may be relatively insignificant to the consumer. The MOH&SW should study the problem of increased cost and the actual effects on the consumer.

The Role of Traditional Health Healers

For centuries before modern "Western medicine" was introduced to Liberia, in the early 19th century, traditional healers rendered healing services. Throughout Liberia, traditional healers are respected and continue to provide services, for better and for worse. They employ a variety of treatment methods, including both invocations of supernatural forces through magic and empirical physical procedures such as massages, bone setting, and giving patients various ingested herbal remedies.

Thousands of traditional healers still render services to the sick in rural villages and even, to some extent, in large towns and urban areas. It is in fact safe to assume that the traditional healer is the first line of health care worker available to most Liberians, especially in rural settings. As more effective, scientific services became available, the relative importance of traditional healing started to decline before the civil war. During the civil war, traditional healing practices in Liberia lost their social context. The reverence for traditional healing was threatened by the insurmountable chaos and brutality of the war. Anecdotal reports suggest that some traditional healers were murdered or displaced along with the common people and consequently lost their status. The lineages of certain traditional healers and healing practices were cut off. The extended family structure that supported seeking health care from traditional healers was decimated.

Despite the adversity of the war in Liberia, some traditional healers continue to practice, and belief in traditional healing endures. In a country with strong roots in traditional practices, cultural attitudes are an obstacle to the accomplishment of improved health results within the modern health care system on a national scale. The prevailing cultural theories about the causes of disease make turning to the respected traditional healer for treatment, both in its magical and physical modalities, a logical response to the treatment and prevention of diseases for many Liberians.

Traditional healers include Traditional Birth Attendants (TBAs) who perform an array of services for women of childbearing age. The TBA is a traditional health worker category has been endorsed by the MOH&SW. It is estimated that over half of all deliveries in Liberia are performed by TBAs. Some sources estimate there were approximately 20,000 TBAs in Liberia before the civil war (Liberian Health care Assessment, 1988). Increasing numbers of TBAs are receiving orientation to Western concepts about pregnancy and delivery from the MOH&SW

and international agencies. TBAs are invariably experienced older women in the villages who have apprenticed with other TBAs during the delivery process and who have given birth to many children of their own. Through these activities, they have experientially and intellectually acquired skills for performing deliveries for women in their villages. Many TBAs have also been given training by MOH&SW authorities and play roles within organized modern health systems.

Traditional healers are usually not engaged full-time in the activity of healing. They could also be farmers, blacksmiths, or homemakers. If they render service only occasionally, they may not expect payment, either in money or in kind, for what they do. However, the majority of traditional healers in Liberia charge fees for their services. In this way, one would consider them to be in "private practice," even though their charges may be very low in comparison to those of the formal modern health care sector. For example, a TBA may charge only a few dollars for delivering a baby or even barter for rice, plantains, chickens, ducks, or a goat. A traditional healer who has won a reputation for her or his gift for healing may charge higher fees than inexperienced and less effective healers.

Traditional healers employ certain practices that reflect long tradition but may actually be useless and even harmful to their patients. Some of these practices may have no medical value, and the time spent on using these traditional remedies delays individuals from entering the modern health care system. Other practices may mask or exacerbate symptoms. For example, a toddler could experience 90 percent dehydration while the mother faithfully uses the herbs recommended by a traditional healer to stop an acute episode of diarrhea. Traditional healers have not established dosage, toxicity, and efficacy levels of herbs for the age of the child. Traditional healers do not conduct clinical trials on the remedies they use. Blind faith in both the traditional healer and the herbal remedy, combined with ignorance about how the body functions, could lead to overuse of the remedy. This medical error by the traditional healer could result in the child suffering from paralysis of the gastrointestinal tract and subsequent intestinal obstruction.

Traditional healing practices, however, undeniably hold an important place in the Liberian culture. To maximize the delivery of effective health care and minimize complications from ineffective practices, Liberia needs to explore ways to increase cooperation between the traditional healers and modern health care professionals to achieve MOH&SW health objectives in postwar Liberia.

Opportunities and Implications for New Directions
for Health Care in Liberia

As in other sub-Saharan African countries, health in Liberia is fundamentally related to the availability and distribution of resources. The viability of a health care system depends on more than just health resources such as doctors, nurses, health care centers, and pharmaceutical products; it also depends on socioeconomic resources such as education, the supply of safe water, and the availability of adequate food. A priority concern for the Liberian government, therefore, is to ensure that available economic and social resources are distributed equitably. Vulnerable populations, including internally displaced Liberians and returning refugees, will have the greatest need. As Liberia emerges from the civil war and economic development projects begin to take hold, policy makers must view health as an integral part of the overall development process of the country. Thus, factors that influence the health of the Liberian population—social, cultural, economic, biological and environmental—must be understood when developing health programs.

Achievement of better health in Liberia will also require active participation on the part of the general citizenry. It will require individuals, families, and communities to adopt healthy behaviors and to ensure a healthy environment. A reorganization of the health care system should embrace individual self-reliance, as well as collective responsibility, for health. With this in mind, the following strategies are suggested for reforming or reorganizing the health care system in Liberia: (1) voluntarism in health care; (2) stimulating citizen participation and community involvement; and (3) increased support for health programs from the Liberian government.

Volunteerism and Altruism in Healthcare
in Postwar Liberia

In developed countries, such as the United States, health care volunteerism is making a comeback in the form of community mobilization and local health and education initiatives. More recently, the U.S. government launched the AmeriCorps citizen participation program, which recruits young individuals from their local communities and trains them to provide an array of civic services to their local communities ranging from health education to work on environmental health issues.

In postwar Liberia, health care volunteerism could play a critical role in rebuilding the health care system as well as rebuilding a Liberian identity on an individual, community and national level. For individuals, volunteering would be a unique way of fostering self-worth and reestablishing a work ethic and sense of social responsibility. Currently, thousands of Liberians are internally as well as externally displaced. The life of a displaced citizen consists of hopeless inactivity and passive acceptance of food rations. Volunteering is a way to play an active role in the redevelopment of society, which will help reduce overdependence on foreign aid. Creating volunteer opportunities that will encourage Liberians to work toward the common good of all is a way to foster peaceful solutions to the many crises facing Liberia, including complex health problems. National leadership in the volunteer sector will be a critical component for Liberian policy makers to embrace because government endorsement and financial backing will help sustain long-term volunteer initiatives.

Tribal tradition in West Africa places high value on successful communal living where people share resources and take care of each other, especially in matters concerning health and sickness. Health care volunteerism in the modern sense builds on existing Liberian cultural traditions and values and expands them from the tribal group to the national level. The strategy of health care volunteerism in the formal health care delivery sector could be the backbone for local community health initiatives. During the protracted civil war in Liberia, many local health coalitions and traditional alliances ceased to function. Many of these organizations and relationships need to be revitalized; new initiatives must be undertaken to address new health and social issues that were spawned by the civil war.

There is a Liberian proverb, which states: "It is easier to break a single stick than to break several sticks in a bundle." Liberians already know the power of working in unison for a common good; for centuries, the tribal groups have been the most powerful units of identification and action. The positive aspects of tribal affiliations were exploited in intertribal conflicts that led to the civil war. All citizens can become activists on issues that influence their communities. According to Miller (1992), "in turbulent times, government by itself is unable to be solely responsible for society as a whole." Liberia is going through tempestuous times as the country emerges from a civil war. Community decision makers and respected civic leaders were killed or forced to flee into exile. As new communities emerge from the ashes of the old ones, it is the responsibility of the national government to encourage new civil leaders to take on the critical issues of their communities. In the aftermath of tragedy, Liberians must remember the positive power of a community working together, but they also need to expand their sense of community beyond their tribe to the national level.

Women, working together, have always been the source of altruism in building community in Liberia and have laid the social and cultural bedrock for community health and development initiatives. During the civil war, women created community wherever they were-in the jungles, the refugee camps, the shantytowns. The strategy forming women as community-builders, to share resources and protection increased the chance of survival for many, especially the most vulnerable: children, the elderly, and those who were ill or injured. Women traditionally instill in the young a spirit of altruism, and that cultural transmission process could empower the youth of Liberia to get involved in volunteerism. The current population of young people in Liberia is projected to increase in the future. Because of the conditions of the civil war, young people in Liberia are experiencing an unusually high level of health problems related to infectious diseases, violence, and pregnancies. Whether young people took part in the fighting or tried to escape, they all were profoundly traumatized. The meager mental health services in Liberia will barely make a dent in alleviating the suffering of Liberia's youth. Being a vital part of a community can be a healing experience, and volunteerism opens that door. Career direction can stem from volunteer work, and meaningful work can continue young people's healing process.

As young people return to schools around the country, students could pitch in to rebuild their educational institutions and tutor younger students to catch up on the education they lost during the civil war. Once a system of volunteerism has been established in educational settings, health professionals can tap students to play a greater role in providing health education to local communities. For some of the communities in Liberia, the critical question is whether young Liberians—whose socialization process has been disrupted by civil war—will have the motivation and patience to understand the political and cultural context for the revival of the health care system. To play an integral role in the redevelopment of the health care system requires careful consideration of the priorities, needs, and perspectives of others. Youth in the new Liberia must be proactive on issues paramount to communities' survival, as well as their own. They must help the Liberian authorities identify and define the many problems influencing their communities, not sit passively and react to policies once they are developed.

Liberian health care workers already have great understanding and appreciation of how to prevent many of the conditions that adversely affect the health of the general population. The piece that is missing is how to convey persuasively health related messages to the younger generation. During the civil war, older siblings raised many young people and they did not develop the traditional respect for older gatekeepers in the community. Health care professionals need to develop models of peer mentoring in order to reach young people. An autocratic hierarchical approach will not work for current younger generations whose members under terrible circumstances, became disillusioned with authority, and were disconnected from tribal and cultural socialization.

Stimulating Community Involvement in Health Care Delivery

In Liberia, the role of the public in steering health development policies has not been fully realized. Reasons for this are varied and include the fact that health is not considered a high priority by either the government or the people themselves. Poverty pushes people to the bottom of their hierarchy of needs: food and water. Health comes later. Liberians have also not held their elected officials accountable to the electorate. Because people don't demand health services from their leaders, the government has shortchanged the general population in terms of health care. The priority for previous governments has been to sustain their power base in a volatile political climate. These governments underestimated that assuring health and economic development for the people might have been another strategy for retaining power.

Health is a universal human right, and the process of attaining optimal health is empowering. Because of the history of unjust distribution of education and economic development, many Liberians were accustomed to become passive recipients of health care. Help or treatment must be received from someone else—be it a modern trained health practitioner or a traditional healer who has some special healing gifts. Health is seen solely as the absence of a disease or sickness. With this sickness approach, the prevention of diseases and health conditions in local communities becomes more challenging. If health care is viewed as the process in which only sick people in the village are treated, then what possibilities exist for the local community to become involved, other than to pay out money for medications or to contribute toward the building of the health center?

The prevention of diseases by taking particular proactive actions has gained public recognition in sub-Saharan Africa, especially as researchers are able to discover the causative agents of particular diseases (e.g., tuberculosis, measles, malaria, schistosomiasis, and other infections). Even when the causative agents are discovered and the means of prevention are understood, the effective implementation of mass preventive measures is not guaranteed. Individuals outside the community who are professionally trained, such as doctors, nurses, or environmental health specialists are involve in implementing many of these preventive efforts. They are experts in the medical—rather than the sociological and anthropological—aspects of how these health problems exist in a community. Because primary health care emphasizes community involvement and intersectoral cooperation, it is a better approach.

Primary health care (PHC) is a way to help a community achieve better health status through a combination of prevention of disease, promotion of good health practices, and treatment of those who are sick. Conceptualized in the late 1970s, PHC was and still is a revolutionary approach to health care delivery. The key to embracing this approach of community involvement is to have an understanding that public demand for participation in health delivery programs will not occur without a thorough process of information and education at all levels.

It is conceivable that as many internally and externally displaced persons return to their local communities, health care will be one of the priorities addressed by the Liberian government. In refugee camps, health care was limited or nonexistent. For many of the returning families, there is a pent-up need for health care services. Officials from MOH&SW should make contact with the communities in the early stages of redevelopment, when new patterns of behavior and new relationships are being established. The time of first contact between the residents and the public health or outreach workers in villages and towns will be crucial, since that is when important first impressions are made. A village chief may question the underlying purpose of a visit from a government representative wishing to discuss community involvement in a health and development project in the village. Before the civil war, many such programs in

Liberia were structured using a top-down approach in which government officials felt they knew what was best for the people in a certain village. Some of these health projects were poorly planned and irrelevant to the true needs of the people. Memories of failed projects and wasted resources persist in the postwar era. From the community's point of view, there are grounds for the village chief and his or her people to be suspicious about government health projects.

The best person to make the initial presentation of the program on behalf of government agencies is a local person whose familiarity with the community where the program is to be established will help reduce suspicion. For example, a respected member of the local health center who has treated many of the villagers and their children may be ideal for the task. In the absence of a health care institution in the village, a local school teacher or a member of a local women's organization are possible alternatives. Even a person with national connections to the village would be suitable.

Starting a dialogue with the community about the project will also be important in the process of involving the community. The community involvement model constitutes a partnership approach that advocates an equal partnership with the villagers and the government personnel from health and other related governmental sectors. Informing and educating the villagers about the project and their roles in planning and implementing a project is the first step. It is also necessary to use a participatory evaluative approach whereby community members are actively involved in the exchange of information, views, and perspectives. Community members need to learn about the health care project, but equally so, health officials and project staff need to learn about the people and their community. Such an exchange can take place only by means of an open and honest dialogue, which may not be easy to achieve. Health care professionals have a particular difficulty in establishing a true dialogue, since their training often leads them to believe that they possess certain special skills and knowledge that should entitle them to special status in society. This elitist attitude is an important reason for health care professionals to be trained regarding the value of listening to people at all levels of the socioeconomic strata within a community. To make an impact on the health outcomes for a community, health care professionals need input from people who will give them a clear, comprehensive picture of the overall health care needs of the community.

Government Support for Health Programs
at the National Level

The nature and extent of support from the national government of Liberia will determine the opportunities available at the county and local levels to rebuild the health care system. Support may take the following forms: (1) political support; (2) administrative support; (3) planning support; (4) research support; and (5) decentralization of decision-making.

Political Support

Restructuring the health care system in Liberia should be seen as a political issue, since the health of the population is an integral part of the country's socioeconomic development process. When the Liberian government embraced the PHC approach in the 1980s, it accepted the challenge to ensure that essential health care is accessible to all, with emphasis on those population groups that are most vulnerable. The PHC approach is also concerned with the rights of people to acquire a fair share of the health care that is available. Thus, PHC is concerned with justice and an equitable distribution of resources.

Political activity is an essential ingredient in the furtherance of health for all the people of Liberia. An example of reconstruction would be to devise health policies that are compatible with the PHC approach. Political policies should be integrative; what is good for health should be considered and treated as good for education, agriculture, and commercial sectors. If politicians view health as separate from other sectors of socioeconomic development, interests incompatible with health promotion compromise health outcomes for the people. Paramount to reconstruction would be the policy governing the ways in which financial resources are distributed to counties. The health care and social needs of the people vary widely from county to county. If the Liberian government is not committed to just policies based on need rather than political power, some segments of the population will be deprived of health.

National commitment to health development is sometimes measured by the percentage of the annual government budget allocated to the health care sector and specific health initiatives. However, that percentage does not reveal the way in which resources are distributed within the health sector. The amount spent on preventive and health promotion initiatives may be miniscule in relation to the amount spent on treatment-oriented programs. The Liberian government, like the governments of most sub-Saharan African countries, has the tendency to focus more on curative care through the establishment of tertiary centers that are highly technological. For many of these African governments, establishing high-tech hospitals satisfies their superficial desire to look as though they are providing state-of-the-art health care to their people. This misguided and shortsighted policy has inherent weakness because only a small percentage of the national health budget reaches the rural hospitals and health centers.

A PHC-oriented policy would be more appropriate for resolving Liberia's health crises and requires strategic financial allocations within and between sectors. It may be important, for example, to create a national advisory board to the MOH&SW where factors related to health and national development can be freely discussed and coordinated. Such an advisory board must be intersectoral and interdisciplinary to be effective and should have a direct link to the MOH&SW in order to ensure appropriate action on proposals. Another possibility is to create a wider body health policy body (example, a Liberian National Health Council) that would be made up of representatives from every county. This council would keep the Minister of Health up to date on regional concerns about health care.

Administrative Support

As seen in Liberia, the fact that governmental policies are developed does not necessarily mean that such policies will be implemented. Successful implementation and evaluation of any health initiative in the new Liberia will require committed administrative support from the MOH&SW at the national level. Administration can be manifested most strongly through the allocation of needed resources, distributed swiftly and regularly, for use in the rural counties of the health care system. These resources would include monies for training of health care workers; maintenance and repair of vehicles; purchase and maintenance of equipment and buildings; and staff salaries. Other resources would include pharmaceuticals and supplies, refrigerators, motorcycles and bicycles, and even stationery and computers to maintain the health information system.

Unfortunately, the MOH&SW in Liberia has had a dismal record at the national level in providing effective administrative support. In the prewar era, while a majority of the people lived in the rural areas, most of the financing of health care in the country was focused on urban setting—specifically the John F. Kennedy Medical Center, a tertiary health care facility located in the capital city. Additionally, the highly centralized structure of the Liberian MOH&SW makes it difficult for staff in many of the rural health centers to function well. In many instances, the national focus is on reducing the risk that local staffs will mishandle funds or misappropriate resources rather than on how to expedite funds and resources so that staff at local clinics can function well. As a result, the system in place for releasing funds and accounting for their proper use can be very cumbersome, resulting in funds being delayed in reaching the rural areas. This problem is often compounded by some Liberian MOH&SW officials working in urban settings who have limited understanding of priorities for needs in the rural areas. This lack of understanding can create prejudice about the capability of health care workers in rural areas to managing resources, especially money earmarked for programs.

In this postwar era, these administrative problems may be difficult to resolve. One way to resolve them is involve community representatives in the political process of controlling health institutions at the local levels. A village or town chief in a rural area could appoint individuals (e.g., a local school principal) to sit on the health committee. This proactive approach enables central administrators to anticipate problems early and take action before implementing a health project and during the implementation and evaluation stage.

Planning Support

In many sub-Saharan African countries, the process of making long-term plans is not totally valued or appreciated. Rural indigenous people negotiate their lives on a day- to- day basis by being flexible in dealing with the natural forces out of their control. They respond to crises one at a time, using community networks and bonds as their strategy for resolving crises. Indigenous people hope and plan for health and prosperity just like everyone else. But traditionally, in many sub-Saharan African countries, the resources necessary to implement plans are limited or unpredictable. Add the sporadic and unpredictable catastrophic events that are part of the nature of the way of life in a developing country, and the efficacy of health planning are significantly diminished. Civil war all but demolished the desire to plan on the part of the people. Cultures like Liberia's have been able to perpetuate a laissez-faire way of life for centuries.

But today, countries in sub-Saharan Africa emerging from civil conflicts are faced not only with war and famine, but a plague of endemic and emerging diseases. Addressing these health and social crises will be insurmountable challenges without carefully planned and comprehensive health care initiatives that can be implemented on a macro scale. The traditional approaches to community health are not enough to handle these new kinds of epidemic health problems. The health care system in Liberia will need to overlay the Western idea of planning on the indigenous ideology of community sharing in order to resolve these problems. The resources needed to combat diseases and health care problems on a grand scale will require a skillful approach to seeking funding and creating partnerships with international organizations that value a proactive style of planning as done in many developed countries. The need for comprehensive planning at the grassroots level cannot be overemphasized. The reluctance of many Africans to embrace long-term planning—based on tradition, tribal myth, and the disappointments of experience—must be overcome. Liberians lost their homes, their farms, their livelihoods, and their villages during the civil war. Especially after the loss of so many lives and the deterioration of the health of the survivors, it will take some effort to persuade Liberians that participating in planning will lead to positive health outcomes.

Within the formal modern health care sector, the concept of health planning was paid lip service. Prior to the civil war, much of the health care planning in Liberia was based on a top-down approach that minimized the importance of the opinions of the people who would benefit from the programs the most. A bottom-up approach would be more effective because the voice of the people would be heard, not only in terms of their health needs but the overall economic and development needs of their communities. Currently, health care planning in Liberia takes place in the centralized bureaucratic structure of the Liberian MOH&SW. Rural counties and other sectors of the country are usually left out of the planning process because the value of representation is underestimated. Even if administrators are recruited from rural areas, they are usually medically trained individuals focusing on specific service programming and have few links with overall development planning. Since the mid-1980s, however, there has been increasing interest on the part of several sub-Saharan African countries in embracing a decentralized approach to planning health activities. Liberia could learn from the experiences of these countries and embrace the positive aspects of decentralization.

Research Support

Many of the difficulties encountered in the implementation of health care in Liberia will require careful study in order to identify appropriate remedies. For this reason, the research branch of the MOH&SW and other research institutions, including universities, all have very important roles to play. Important areas that need to be studied include how communities are organized to resolve health problems; the role of community health workers; intersectoral action on health care delivery; and management information systems. These areas require skilled attention on the part of health institutions and social scientists.

Decentralization of Decision-Making

Over the past decade, decentralized decision-making has gained widespread appeal in many sub-Saharan African countries. In postwar Liberia, there will be the need to balance local and national opinions about health and development, especially as the country faces the grave economic difficulties involved in rebuilding a war-shattered nation. A primary problem is the centralized control over the national distribution of resources. Since Liberia has 13 mainly rural counties with dire public health needs that are best solved with PHC approach, a decentralized approach may need to be explored for more optimum health care delivery in Liberia.

As far as 1987, the WHO was advocating the decentralization of health care delivery in developing countries. According to WHO, decentralization has the following advantages: (1) it facilitates community involvement, making it easier for communities to convey their needs and problems to the level of the decision makers; (2) it speeds up the process of communication and thus facilitates the swift distribution of resources; (3) it facilitates the development of plans in keeping with local needs and local variations in needs; and (4) it facilitates good intersectoral co-operation (World Health Organization, 1987). In the same report, WHO describes the considerable difficulties to be overcome in creating an effective decentralized system of decision-making framework. There is a risk that local communities may demand services that are greater in extent and diversity than those that the national government is able to deliver. However, if leaders in the rural areas are aware of the central government's overall agenda, they will be better prepared to submit proposals that fall under the umbrella of overall national health goals and therefore will be more likely to be funded. Staying informed about national health plans and agendas will help empower local communities as they develop their primary health care systems. In some instances, however, local agendas may conflict with national health goals. For example, the national government may be inclined to infuse financial capital into building new tertiary hospitals, as opposed to small rural clinics.

There is also the need for individuals with appropriate training and skill to undertake necessary financial management and accounting functions at the local levels. Before the civil war, the launching of many rural health initiatives in Liberia was impeded by a shortage of trained personnel (including doctors and nurses) who were willing to work outside the urban areas. In the prewar era, the MOH&SW provided few incentives for working in the more challenging rural settings. Additionally, if decentralization is accomplished, there will be a need for qualified planners and managers willing to work in rural settings. The protracted civil conflict damaged health-training programs; those individuals studying abroad could not return to their country for fear of being persecuted; many health care personnel who chose to remain were either tortured or killed. The shortage of trained health personnel will require the revitalization of health training facilities, which will be costly and time-consuming.

It may be necessary to phase decentralization incrementally over a number of years. Creating a hybrid organizational structure of health care delivery that balances the best of centralized and decentralized approaches is important for revitalizing the health care system in Liberia. Before transformation can happen fully, reformers will have to work within the existing centralized structure for some time. The government of Liberia may have to rely heavily on external collaboration—without which it has no hope of putting new health policies into action.

On the other hand, there are unscrupulous individuals who try to take advantage of the difficulty many Liberians experience in accessing modern health care. These individuals are the itinerant "black baggers" or quacks who offer nonprofessional services. The number and distribution of quacks are not well documented by the MOH&SW officials. The quacks do not abide by any theoretical concepts, but simply give injections for any ailments. Importantly, these quacks should be distinguished from the classical traditional healers and it is understandable why MOH&SW officials refer to them as "black baggers." They are sometimes former students who have failed out of a training program (e.g., a medical school, physician assistant school, or nursing training program) or simply unscrupulous persons who take advantage of a widespread belief by uneducated people that taking injections is suitable treatments for all illness.

The balance between the public and private sectors is a common problem in health care systems in most sub-Saharan African countries because they are too economically strained. Where the economy is strong, private investors often support government policies that, in turn, are supported by well-organized infrastructure; a stronger role for the government is possible. But the reality for Liberia (after a protracted civil war), and now in history, is that the government will be constrained in performing a strong public sector role. In very practical terms, the ability to provide access for the majority of the population to essential health care—and the provision of adequate medicines, supplies, and services, including oral rehydration solution and family planning services—will depend on the cooperation of a strong private sector. In view of the private-sector orientation to clinical medicine, there is a greater reason for the government to concentrate its limited resources on those services that cannot be provided by the private sector, namely, the prevention of diseases, improvement of nutrition, maternal and child care, and advocacy in family planning. Government must be willing to fill the gap in the provision of healthcare where the private sector or market fails.

The proper aim of health policy is to improve health, not just to provide health services. Priority should be given to health improvement for those with the lowest health status as part of a unified plan to improve the quality of life. Health policies and strategies should not be seen as permanent decisions. As suggested above distinct roles for the private sector and the public governmental sector in providing health care appear to fit Liberia at this moment in its health care development history. Health care reform in postwar Liberia should be centered on incremental approaches and pragmatism that such proposals will succeed. Modification of the health care delivery system should be made depending on current and future political, economic, social, and health-related conditions of the future.

Notes

1. Kelvin Kelly. *Out of control: The new biology of machines, social systems and the economic world.* 1995, Perseus Books Group: New York, N.Y.

2. Kelvin Kelly. *Out of control: The new biology of machines, social systems and the economic world.* 1995, Perseus Books Group: New York, N.Y.

CHAPTER 5

FINANCING HEALTH CARE
SERVICES IN LIBERIA

As a nation we shall measure our progress by the improvement
in the health of our people, by the number of children in
school, and by the quality of their education, by the availability
of water and electricity in our towns and villages, and by the
happiness which our people take in being able to manage their
own lives and affairs.[1]

—Kwame Nkrumah, President of Ghana,
December 24, 1977

Postwar Economic Strife in Liberia

The civil war in Liberia resulted in the destruction of critical infrastructure in the country, the very infrastructure that is necessary for
maintaining health care delivery services: hospitals and clinics, roads and
transportation networks, communication systems, educational institutions, electricity, sanitation, and garbage disposal. The war also interrupted the revenue stream needed to carry on meaningful health programs in the country. A broad measure of how a country is functioning
economically can be taken by examining that country's output of goods
and services. The most widely used indicator of economic output is gross

domestic product (GDP). The GDP is an indicator of the market value of all the goods and services produced by a country. It is a critical indicator for comparing development levels and economic progress among nations. During the civil war, Liberia performed dismally with regards to the amount of goods and services produced in the country for local consumption and exports.

One major reason for this poor economic performance is that, to date, the production and export of iron ore in Liberia has not resumed. Iron ore production accounted for about 10 percent of Liberia's GDP and 50 percent of its exports before the war. Mining facilities were looted and destroyed during the war; no major reconstruction activities have yet been undertaken to rebuild the infrastructure of iron ore mining. Other commercial activities in rural areas, such as logging, rubber processing, and farming, were also disrupted due to fighting. In urban areas, where people are dependent on manufacturing and service industries for employment, the economy was also destroyed. Foreign investments in Liberia were almost nonexistent during the civil war. Even with UN peacekeepers on the ground, foreign investors are hesitant to invest in a war-ravaged nation. International companies fled during the peak of the civil war and have since been leery about returning to and investing in the country because of lack of confidence in both the economic reform process and the political leadership.

The Liberian capital is overcrowded with internally displaced people, and unemployment in Monrovia is at an all-time high of approximately 90 percent. Of those who have jobs, most are drastically underemployed. For example, salaries in the government, which is the main employer in the country, are below sustenance level. Reports suggest that a person with a bachelor's degree teaching in a public school earns a monthly salary of less than $100 in U.S. dollars. Besides being low, salaries are not disbursed on time. Dedicated teachers struggle to survive while they wait for paychecks that can be delayed for months while the Liberian Ministry of Finance searches for money. This situation is demoralizing for thousands of teachers and decreases the number of Liberians who would have considered entering the profession of teaching.

The protracted period of the civil war also increased the number of dependents for those individuals who are employed. Liberian families (parents and children) are very large and could range from 10 to 15 per household. If only one person in a family of 10 is employed, there will still not be enough money to provide food, clothing and health care to the whole family. Compounding this stress is the expectation that an employed person will also take care of members of his or her extended family (aunts, uncles, cousins, grandparents, nieces, nephews, or even just people from one's village who may consider one to be family).

Coupled with all this is the uncontrolled depreciation of the Liberian dollar. In Liberia, the U.S. dollar is legal tender alongside the Liberian dollar. Many small business owners are now demanding that customers pay for their goods and services in U.S. dollars, so people need jobs that pay U.S. dollars. Some employers paying in U.S. dollars take advantage of this crisis and offer workers even lower wages.

Other factors exist that exacerbate the current economic plight in Liberia. Public transportation is limited or nonexistent in some areas. Public transportation is paramount to finding and keeping a job in sub-Saharan Africa because owning one's own car is a luxury only for the rich. Liberians who lived in exile in Western countries during the war and who have since returned to Liberia report the challenges they encounter while trying to navigate their way in the city. To get a ride on one of the minibuses and taxis in the capital city, one must be strong enough to fight off others in order to board the vehicle. In a recent visit to Monrovia, a colleague described the public transportation experience as "survival of the fittest," a process one expects only to see when visiting a safari hunt in an African game park. He remarked: "I woke up one morning and sat in front of my sister's house near one of the busy boulevards in the capital. I was used to transportation problems in Monrovia before the civil war. But what I saw now was unbelievable. Hundreds of commuters try to push their way to the bus so they can virtually throw themselves on it during the morning and evening rush hours." It is a life-and-death struggle because if one does not get to work on time, one could lose one's job. This would mean losing income that may be providing dozens of people with minimum sustenance. After 14 years of lawlessness and dire circumstances, many Liberians must operate with a survival mentality. One who does not get on the bus will have to walk miles to get to work. People also have to take the bus to health care facilities. Pregnant women, children, and sick people are too weak to compete for transportation, and in the absence of an ambulance system, so their health suffers.

Travelers to the capital have remarked that Monrovia is the "darkest city in the world." The one hydroelectric plant that provided electricity to the entire city and its environs prior to the civil war was totally destroyed during the peak of the fighting. In July 2006, after years with no electricity in Monrovia, President Sirleaf made good on one of her promises and restored electricity to some parts of the city. The most wealthy and powerful citizens have personal generators that they run a few hours a day. The majority of the people live their lives from sunup to sundown. After work, people must rush to get home before nightfall; otherwise they will become stranded in the dark. Venturing out at night puts one at risk of being robbed or killed, harassed by corrupt police officers, or, in the case of females, being raped. Although there is an elected government in place, the city is still without other basic necessities, including safe water, reliable communication systems, and a working sewage and garbage disposal system.

While the UN and the African Union must be commended for the successful disarmament process that ended the civil war, the millions of dollars pledged by international donors for the reconstruction of Liberia have not been forthcoming. One reason could be because of donor fatigue in developed countries and because sub-Saharan Africa continues to be plagued with new problems. Economic conditions in Liberia continue to deteriorate while government revenue fails to increase. With unemployment so high, there are no citizens to tax; with no new investment coming into the country, there are no corporations to tax, either. Previous tax enforcement and collection policies were weak because of political corruption and ineptitude. It will be difficult to generate funds for reconstruction programs if existing tax laws are not enforced. The government should not rely only on the infusion of international dollars; there needs to be a mechanism for generating internal funds to finance critical health programs.

Several questions therefore arise related to the planning and financing of health care services in postwar Liberia. Prior to the civil war, there were funding inequities and mal-distribution of health resources based on geographic location; how will these funding disparities be addressed in the postwar era? What are some major obstacles to health care financing in Liberia? What are some ways to share best practices for reforming the financing processes of health care services in Liberia? Are there any lessons to learn from other sub-Saharan African countries that would be applicable to Liberia? Lastly, how should any health financing reform scheme or programs be implemented, evaluated and sustained?

Factors Influencing Health Care Organization, Financing and Delivery in Liberia

Both developing and developed countries face problems with health care financing. Developed nations face problems with scarcity but they are mostly due to inefficiencies rather than an overall lack of funding. In developing countries, due to severely limited economic resources, there is a true scarcity, of medical resources to provide health care to the people. In comparison to developed countries, many developing countries experience a greater illness burden and higher mortality rate. There is not one nation in sub-Saharan Africa that is not faced with the challenge of how to fund and distribute scarce health resources to its population in the face of endemic diseases and competing social problems. A country's health care financing warrants political solutions because it requires a complex web of cooperation within multiple social systems. In developed countries, such as the United States, Canada or the United Kingdom, focus is on those aspects of the health care delivery system that relates to the containment of the skyrocketing costs in such countries. On the other hand, in the developing countries of sub-Saharan Africa, health care reform centers on securing and maintaining the ability to provide basic health care to all people.

Because of a number of complicated economic, social, and epidemiological factors, many African governments including Liberia, can no longer live up to the social dream of providing basic health care "free of charge" to everyone. Just as in developed countries, as life expectancy increases in developing countries and an expectation for optimum health becomes the norm in those countries, the cost of providing health care there imposes an ever-increasing national burden. The nature of basic health care has evolved into a more expensive endeavor due to the prevalence of chronic diseases overlapping endemic diseases. In addition, the emergence of new diseases, such as HIV/AIDS—which requires an expensive, complicated, and prolonged treatment regimen—is also draining the funding for other programs.

In order to reform a health care delivery system, policy makers must pay attention to individual and systems factors that influence the manner in which health care is organized and delivered. These interrelated factors include the general political climate of the country, the socio-cultural values and beliefs systems of the people, general economic conditions, development of low but relevant technology for economic development, physical environment as a determinant of health, and the general population characteristics of the country (see Figure 5-1). Even in nonfragile sub-Saharan African states, these factors are important to consider because they determine whether health care delivery will be a priority among all the competing needs. In fragile states like Liberia, it becomes even more critical to understand these interrelated factors, because a change in even one of these factors can lead to poorer health outcomes.

Figure 5-1. Factors Influencing Health care Organization, Financing and Delivery in Liberia. (Adapted from Shi, L. and D. A. Singh. *Delivering health care in America: A systems approach.*) Third Edition, Boston, MA: Jones and Bartlett Publishers, 2004.

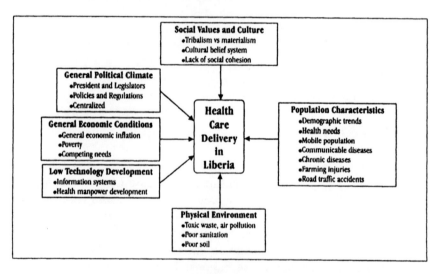

The Liberian health care system shows many scars from the protracted civil war. Inadequate health care is provided to the people by a severely underfunded, highly stressed and fragmented health care delivery system. International agencies such as the World Bank, the World Health Organization (WHO), and the International Monetary Fund (IMF) have addressed health care financing reform in developing countries. The World Bank proposes three financing strategies that would be useful when considering the postwar financing of health care in Liberia and other sub-Saharan African countries emerging from a civil conflict. These strategies include: (1) establishing or increasing revenue recovery through user fees and by establishing insurance plans; (2) enhancing the allocation and management of existing scarce health resources; and (3) outsourcing and expanding some health care delivery activities to the private sector. It is critical to examine the interrelationships between socioeconomic and cultural factors and health in Liberia when analyzing the choices available for allocating the country's current meager resources. A unified, comprehensive approach is advocated in order to meet the basic health care needs of the people of Liberia and other sub-Saharan African countries emerging from civil conflicts.

A Legacy of Disparities in Urban/Rural Health Development and Financing

Although temporarily displaced in urban settings during the civil war, the majority of the Liberian population came from rural areas. In the past, due to inequities in the allocation of resources, these rural areas were slow to benefit from government development programs. Life in some areas of Liberia continues much as it did centuries ago—apart from the "progress" of dusty and rutted dirt roads, poorly operated radio stations, and understaffed primary government schools or health centers. Unemployment, underemployment, malnutrition, infectious diseases, poor housing, and unhealthy environmental conditions have persisted through generations. Because schools are not available in every village, it was common for young children to walk over 10 or more miles to another village or town to attend primary school. Many of the clinics and schools in the rural areas were poorly staffed and lacked textbooks or chairs for students to sit on during school hours. Children in Liberia, like children in other developing countries, often attended school hungry and did not have access to food during school hours, thereby diminishing their growth and development as well as their academic performance.

During earlier Liberian administrations (the Tubman and Tolbert administrations), past development policies emphasized economic growth for its own sake, without careful planning and examination of who would benefit from the growth. Most development programs were focused on the urban areas of Liberia with the assumption that the rural areas would eventually benefit indirectly from urban growth. Even though Liberia depended on rural areas for food, the government failed to provide those areas with essential amenities and services such as safe drinking water, sanitation, public transportation, primary health care services, and educational and cultural facilities. The lack of these amenities and services substantially diminished the health of the rural population.

What is the purpose of national health care policies when such policies do not help the majority of the people, especially the most vulnerable rural inhabitants: the poor, women, and children? The objective of public policy related to health care delivery should be to improve the health of the people, not just to deliver the services to improve delivery statistics. In Liberia's postwar era, priority must therefore be given to improvement of the health status of those most in need while enhancing the quality of life for all people.

Health care, unlike other economic goods and services (e.g., personal vehicles), is not a luxury. Basic health care should be regarded as a universal human right, regardless of people's ability to pay for such services. The ideal of universal access to health care will be a challenge to sub-Saharan African countries, including Liberia, where financial resources are meager and equity is a difficult concept to embrace. Also, the failure to provide health care to certain groups of individuals based on their tribal affiliation, gender, or geographic location will uncover the hidden hatreds between groups that in fact helped spark and fuel the civil war. If more health care is provided to a favored ethnic group, other tribal groups may feel disenfranchised and regard the central government as unfair. Provision of health care services by the national government is certainly a means to create unity and peace among all people in Liberia regardless of their socioeconomic status, tribal affiliation, or geographic location.

The primary health care (PHC) model, rather than the curative biomedical model, is a better approach for resolving the many health problems facing the Liberian population today. Equity is an important component of the PHC approach. In the review of the literature on primary health care, several authors have defined equity. Whitehead (1992) suggests "equity in health implies that ideally everyone should have a fair opportunity to attain their full health potential and, more pragmatically, that no one should be disadvantaged from achieving this potential, if it can be avoided." Musgrove (1986) also defined equity as "equal treatment for all of the population" and an equitable health care system is one that assures the same probability of access and "will be equal across population groups for a given set of health problems."

Given these definitions, it is clear that the concept of equity in health care, delivery is a complex process to evaluate. However, to achieve equity in health care factors related to the distribution of health care should be considered. Health distribution factors include resources such as the ratio of doctors to population; the ratio of nurses to population; the probability that all individuals will receive treatment based on need; and an individual's ability to pay for the services.

How does one go about assessing equity in health care? There are two pragmatic ways of assessing if health care is equitable. One way is to determine if the same amount of money is spent on health services per person in every part of the country. A second way is to determine if the same standard and quality of care or services is being provided everywhere and for everyone (i.e., both rural and urban areas), even if there might be cost differentials. What is considered a fair distribution of health care resources? There must be the realization that health services will cost more to provide to the dispersed rural populations in Liberia than to urban populations. This is in part due to the increased transportation, refrigeration, training, communication, and reporting costs that are incurred in providing health care across great distances. It also costs a rural patient more to access health care than it does in an urban patient due to increased transportation costs and lost agricultural work time at critical times in the harvest cycle due to days of travel. For example, absence from the rice fields at a critical point means that a crop that has been growing for months could be destroyed in a few days by birds or groundhogs.

Health officials in Liberia will have to devise a clear definition of what equity is, and such a definition could serve as the basis for providing health care to all people, especially disadvantaged populations such as refugees and internally displaced individuals returning to their villages. The poor residing in periurban slums are also disadvantaged and shut out of health care because of transportation costs, and their desperate attempts to sustain precarious employment that supersedes seeking health care services. The same techniques used to bring health care to rural people, such as use of medical vans that are set up in marketplaces, could be used for the periurban poor.

A definition of equitable health care that sets the same standards and quality of care for all people, regardless of socioeconomic status, culture, or ability to pay for such services, will have a profound effect on the rural and urban poor of Liberia. There will also be future implications for health personnel training to distribute health care fairly across the country, not just in the more desirable places to deliver health care. Regardless of which definition of health equity—cost or quality—is used, the commitment to equity in health care in the postwar reconstruction era of Liberia should be a political decision at the highest central governmental levels.

The Contribution of Health Services Development in Liberia

Health services development can be viewed as the implementation of programs that enable the achievement of optimal health for the Liberian people. In Liberia, as is the case in many sub-Saharan African countries, in order to achieve optimal health, various aspects of society must improve, including problems of poverty and equality among people. Poor people in Liberia and other sub-Saharan African countries that have experienced civil war should not be viewed as a liability to society but, rather, as a casualty of civil war. Poor people are an undervalued asset in rebuilding war-ravaged countries in Africa because the quality of their lives could change dramatically from even the most minimal development project.

The wealthy Liberians who made up a small segment of the Liberian population enjoyed many advantages before the war and are better equipped to reclaim their lives because of those advantages: education, property, investments, national and international contacts, and political power. Health services development projects will not have as big an impact on these advantaged individuals as it will on the majority of the Liberian population, which includes some of the poorest people in the world. Many of these individuals were self-sufficient small farmers with a strong work ethic and numerous skills. The revitalization process needs to create more and more opportunities to empower poor people to sustain themselves and their families again, including providing for the health needs of themselves and their families.

Ill-conceived and poorly implemented international health development projects do not make a positive impact on people's lives. Only health development projects that are based on helpful input from the local communities have a chance of succeeding. Initiating health development projects is more complex than simply handing out food rations. Although they are interrelated, disease is more complicated than hunger. People from all walks of life can be instrumental in a food distribution program, but it takes trained health care professionals to address the complex web of endemic diseases prevalent in sub-Saharan African countries. Local communities must be part of the projects that donors are developing. The creation of local grassroots initiatives will help promote sustainable development. Health and illness in any society are influenced by multiple factors: political, economic, moral, and cultural phenomena, as well as the disease patterns observed in that society. Development is also linked to these same factors in society.

Before the civil war, policy planners in Liberia were preoccupied with staying in power and placed little importance on establishing an efficient health care system that would provide health care services to the general population in a cost-effective manner. International agencies and donors involved in funding health programs were more interested in enumerating the dollar figures they spent on health care in their annual reports than in reporting outcomes. While the infusion of health dollars into the system is a critical factor in providing health care, it does not explain all the difference in outcomes across populations. For example, increasing funding can increase the ratio of doctors or nurses to population density, which will help improve health outcomes for infants, children under age 5, and pregnant women. On the other hand, increasing funding for sophisticated tertiary care hospitals may not help improve the health outcomes for people in these categories, who are better served at the primary level.

Developing countries of sub-Saharan Africa could learn from the weaknesses of health care systems in developed countries. For instance, the United States spends more on health care delivery than other developed countries, yet experiences higher infant death rates. Inability to develop culturally appropriate prenatal care programs keeps the U.S. from improving health outcomes, despite its advanced financial investment in the health care system. The U.S. puts its financial investment in health technology and sophisticated curative approaches, neither of which directly addresses the factors contributing to infant mortality: poverty, culture, education, and belief systems.

In prewar Liberia, following the US model, most of the health expenditures by Liberia's Ministry of Health and Social Welfare (MOH&SW) were centered on the provision of curative services, mainly to the population living in urban areas, even though a majority of Liberians resided in rural areas. In addition, only a third of the rural population had access to even basic primary health care services. It is not surprising, therefore, that the health care system in Liberia made little progress in comparison to those in neighboring countries, such as Côte d'Ivoire, in improving health indicators such as infant mortality, mortality for children under 5 years of age, maternal mortality, and life expectancy. A legacy of the policies of the past is that the John F. Kennedy Medical Center, a large tertiary health facility located in Monrovia, consumes the largest segment of the MOH&SW budget, money that could be more effectively spent on public health programs in the peri-urban and rural areas. Although a tertiary care setting is important in the health care system continuum, the current dismal epidemiologic and disease patterns of the population of Liberia warrant substantial public health and preventive measures. Therefore, even a well-financed, highly technological hospital like the John F. Kennedy Medical Center may make only a temporary impact on long-term health outcomes for the population if the basic causes of morbidity and mortality in Liberia are not addressed at the source.

Western nations or developed countries in the latter half of the 20th century experienced a decrease in infectious diseases that led to an increase in life expectancy. Some of the measures used to reduce infectious diseases were low-cost preventive measures: health education programs, immunizations, and literacy programs. It was these simple measures—rather than high-tech, high-cost endeavors—that were paramount in reducing infectious and communicable diseases, thereby leading to an increase in life expectancy. Developing countries should take note that the Western world, including the U.S., is moving from an acute care model to a more prevention-oriented model.

Simple measures could make a big difference in developing countries of sub-Saharan Africa. When women are provided the options of family planning, they are able to direct scarce family resources to more comprehensive health care for their children. When their children are provided the necessary immunizations and nutrition, they are less susceptible to diseases that afflict children under 5 years of age. Access to immunizations and nutrition are bound by socio-cultural-economic factors. Therefore, it is important to understand how health care services must be linked with other sectors of society. For instance, improving the health status of women and children in Liberia involves understanding their role in the context of their society. For example, one who wants to provide family-planning programs to women in a village needs to understand how male and female sexuality plays into family dynamics. Childbearing gives women status in their villages because it proves their fertility, fulfills their role in society, demonstrates the potency of their men and, in terms of frequent pregnancies, ensures that they will have at least some children to survive into adulthood. Introducing family planning measures in this climate warrants connecting the diminished health outcomes for their children and themselves with the practice of having unlimited pregnancies. Women who have confidence that their young ones will survive are more apt to use contraceptives and plan the number of children they intend to have. When women are empowered to participate as full members of society, they are more likely to be proactive in advocating for their own health care as well as their family's.

Lack of National Health Planning Leading to Incongruent Health Policies

Economics and health are interconnected. Poverty is a major contributing factor to many health conditions in Liberia and sub-Saharan Africa. Some health conditions linked to poverty include malaria, diarrhea, cholera, and worm infestations. Many of these conditions have dire consequences on the individuals who suffer from them. Indirect consequences, such as financial instability for the family, a breakdown in childcare, and an interruption in farming activities, must also be considered. One reason for reforming the structure of the Liberian health care system and its financing is that the existing tertiary-based framework does not adequately address the complex socio-economic and environmental problems Liberians are faced with today. The protracted civil conflict plunged everyone into economic strife and exacerbated the conditions of those who lived in poverty conditions during the prewar era.

As countries in sub-Saharan Africa emerge from civil conflict, they should seize the opportunity to develop national health plans in a form similar to that used by Western countries: baseline health indicators, goals and objectives, implementation and evaluation plans. Careful planning at this level has not been done in Liberia before. The United States Department of Health and Human Services developed a health plan known as "Healthy People 2010." This document provides a framework for understanding and improving health for the nation. It is a statement of national health objectives designed to identify the most significant preventable threats to health and to establish national goals to reduce these threats. Many different people, government bodies, communities, professional organizations, and others engaged in developing programs to improve health, can use this information. Many states in the U.S. have also developed their own health plans based on their local population needs, but which mirror the federal government objectives.

Developing a health plan for the postwar era in Liberia will be critical for giving direction to all parties involved in the rebuilding of the country's health care system. However, such a health plan will probably not fully meet the health care needs of the people unless the plan specifies how programs will be paid for, where they will be implemented, and how much in terms of human resources will be required to implement and evaluate them. Nutritional programs for families are particularly important because they are now relying on food rations from international aid instead of Liberia's formerly self-sustaining farms. Those people who return to their villages can eventually cease their dependence on food rations if the government assists them as they resume their agricultural activities. The foods produced by small farmers in the rural areas are labor-intensive but can have a life-sustaining impact on the nutritional and health status of children and adults in local communities.

If emphasis in the postwar era focuses on encouraging farmers to grow cash crops for export (coffee, cocoa, rubber), it may compromise the nutritional status of families. The staple in the Liberian diet is rice; if it is not grown in Liberia on a massive scale to feed the people, it would need to be imported. Importing a staple food is risky and undesirable because the country would then be at the mercy of the world market and would lose autonomy. The local population may not initially accept a different variety of rice, but may eventually change to a preference for imported rice, which would affect established agricultural foundations. Liberia is a country that prides itself on a communal life, which includes the bartering and charitable exchange of agricultural produce. Imposing a market-driven approach that requires cash for food will unravel Liberia's rural safety net—a net that has been woven over generations—and the poorest of the poor will suffer. Without rice farming, a traditional way of life faces extinction; the growing and processing of rice is embedded with ritual and socialization in the Liberian culture.

The PHC framework encourages skillfully weaving health care delivery into the cultural web of a community. All private and public sectors of Liberian society should be engaged in reviving the development process of Liberia. In the public sector, for example, the Ministry of Education could develop curricula that include components of health education and health promotion, as well as information on how to use new technologies that are relevant to the local communities, and concepts of training for sustainable development and health. The protracted civil war denied many young people and adults the opportunity to learn. This profound gap in the collective knowledge of Liberian society will be hard to overcome. Institutions of higher learning must create affordable and accessible opportunities for all people to learn the skills they will need to survive in the postwar Liberia. Adults who already achieved an education before the civil war will need continuing education programs to update their skills.

In Liberia, as in many sub-Saharan African countries, poverty is a vicious cycle; many of the adults who live in poverty today had parents or grandparents who also lived in poverty before the war. It has always been difficult to escape poverty in Liberia because the country was founded on a system of inequality. Now it is even harder to rise above poverty. Formerly displaced Liberians returning to rural areas are faced with even greater challenges than their ancestors faced. Despite the resiliency of the Liberian population, civil war has severely compromised the physical, spiritual, and emotional health of Liberians. Liberians have few opportunities for lifting themselves or their children out of poverty. They will have to cultivate the same harsh land that their ancestors cultivated and are faced with the same risk of variable rainfall and locusts, but they also have to contend with the trauma of past violence and the fear of future conflicts.

The postwar era is a great opportunity for the government to develop programs that will restore the hopeful spirit of Liberians. One objective that will help empower people is to establish health education programs. There is nothing more important in the prevention of diseases than to get people involved and proactive in their own health care. Health curricula for physicians, nurses, physician assistants, and other allied health professionals should be expanded to include educational practicums in villages and in rural secondary and elementary schools. During a practicum, health profession students could teach children and adults about the causes of major health problems in their communities; why clean water is important; proper disposal of human refuse; and the importance of personal hygiene. During these forums, women can also be taught which local foods would provide their children the greatest possible nutritional values, what foods to grow around their houses to supplement their diets, and how to prepare food to maximize nutritional value. During the civil war, many women and children starved or died of malnutrition. Food is of paramount concern to Liberians now more than ever. Making the most of the food they have is important to achieving optimal health.

As the remaining fragments of families return to their villages and settle in, many young people will begin to think about establishing the next generation. Because the natural passing on of skills to nurture families has been disrupted by war, the health care sector will need to provide young people with the skills and education on how to maintain a healthy family. Some of the critical areas of health instruction will be breast feeding, weaning foods, immunization issues, the care of infants, how to recognize common diseases, and the use of simple home remedies, such as oral rehydration salts in the treatment of dehydration related to diarrhea. In many Liberian settings where child spacing is rarely practiced, health education can drive home the advantages of spacing infants with the use of contraceptives where such methods may be culturally acceptable.

The discussion of health is a useful starting point for involving local communities in identifying their own development agendas because health is vital, personal and integral to life in the family. Although many of the parents in rural areas are not educated, every parent in these settings wants her or his child to survive. Thus, a local discussion of why some children die of measles could be a great starting point for discussing community needs and talking about solutions, such as immunization programs, in which members of the community can participate.

These community-based initiatives rely on the centralized structure of MOH&SW for funding. The Minister of Health is the Chief Health Officer of the country, and one of his or her roles is to advocate for strategic funding for health care services for the people. The irony, however, is that increased spending alone may not necessarily lead to an improved health outcome for the people. In postwar Liberia, the MOH&SW must play a substantial role in designing a health care plan for Liberians. The building of a new clinic or a health care center should not be viewed as competition for another development project in a village (e.g., the development of new roads connecting three villages). Development projects often complement health care initiatives. For example, the construction of new roads may be important to the health of the people in the villages as well as important to economic development. With the new roads, pregnant women may be able to travel easily for prenatal care to the next major town that has a functional health center and trained health care professionals to monitor pregnancy. With good roads, transportation is enhanced and women will be able to bring their children for immunizations to the nearest functional health center. The MOH&SW, in this instance, has the obligation to explain to the citizens of the village why such development initiatives are critical and how they are interrelated with health care.

In the rural areas of Liberia, small farmers are still using antiquated, labor-intensive methods of rice farming, and will need to be taught new ways of improving their crop yields. One such proposal is to teach the farmers how to use fertilizers on their land. The Ministry of Agriculture may also help them establish irrigation projects for their farms. Again, the establishment of irrigation networks for small farmers should not be viewed as a competitor against health care delivery. Rather, this type of project should be embraced by the MOH&SW because of its potential for increased food production for good nutrition and for improved water supplies. If these programs are not planned well, there could be negative implications for such agricultural projects with regard to the health of the people, a good reason for the MOH&SW to be involved in the development of such programs from the onset. Research suggests that irrigation sites, if not designed and managed properly, can put people at risk for conditions such as malaria, schistosomiasis, and other water-borne tropical diseases. These irrigation sites serve as breeding grounds for the intermediate hosts for causative agents of water borne diseases. Some villages may choose to establish communal poultry or cattle farms. If the expansion of poultry or cattle farming is the project of choice for a village, the MOH&SW would want to be alert in preventing the spread of diseases from animals to people or from animals to the human food chain.

It will take patience and time, but deciding on a project to improve the health outcomes of the community should not be imposed on the people. As beneficiaries of the project, they must be involved in all its phases, including its conceptualization. Identifying what the community really needs is a critical first step. In the end, if a primary health care project is identified, the MOH&SW authorities must understand that money must be included in the budget for recruiting health care workers to help the community develop, implement, and evaluate any such project. It is best to draw upon health care workers already part of the community. But during this postwar era, there is a dearth of health care workers so expertise may have to be drawn from outside the community. In that case, the health care workers will have to find ways to become part of the communities they serve. The challenge for the government of Liberia in the postwar era is the lack of planning health policies that are congruent with other development initiatives and governmental sectors.

Major Challenges to Financing Health Care in Liberia

The problems of funding health care services in Liberia are similar to those of many sub-Saharan African countries and can be summarized into three major categories: (1) health care not being a priority in the allocation of funds by the national government; (2) government programs being bureaucratic and inefficient in distributing funds; and (3) the unequal distribution of the benefits of scarce resources. These three factors are applicable to other sub-Saharan African countries and are especially relevant to Liberia and other war-torn African countries.

Health Care Not a Priority in Allocation of Funds

Prior to the civil war in Liberia, health care was not a priority in the allocation of funds by the national government. It is still not a priority. Liberia, like most sub-Saharan African countries, embraced WHO's Alma Ata Declaration, promulgated in 1978 to declare a commitment to providing health care to the entire citizenry by the year 2000. Unfortunately, the funding commitment by the national government has been inadequate to implement and sustain many of the proposals from the conference where the declaration was promulgated. Many sub-Saharan African countries accepted the social obligation of declaring that their governments will provide health care services to all citizens, regardless of their ability to pay for such services. The irony is that countries like Liberia encountered insurmountable challenges in their efforts to provide basic health care to their people. Since the Alma Ata Declaration, funding of health care from both the public and private sectors has been insufficient to meet this goal of socializing health care delivery for all citizens. The protracted civil war has exacerbated the problem of socializing the health care system, and now there are competing needs for the limited dollars generated by the national government.

Although funding from charitable, nongovernmental organizations (NGOs) and other international agencies has been forthcoming, many of these dollars do not go to programs that are essential in improving health outcomes for the general population: immunization, HIV/AIDS prevention, maternal and child health, health education programs, and simple curative care referral networks. According to comparative information published about countries in sub-Saharan Africa, Liberia—before the civil war—spent less than 5 percent of its GDP on health care services. In light of the catastrophic health care needs facing Liberia and in comparison with other sectors of the government, such as the military, this is a paltry amount. In this postwar era, the national government is spending even less. Even if the government could achieve prewar spending levels for health care, it would barely be able to implement and sustain critical programs because the needs of the people in the postwar era are even more pronounced due to the return of internally and externally displaced populations.

In developed and developing countries alike, health care expenditures vary with the state of the economy. For instance, when a country's economy is good, the national government is able to take in more funds through taxes and other revenue-generating programs. A good economy means that government can decide to increase funding for social and health programs it would otherwise not fund during stagnation or a downturn of the economy. In most developing countries of sub-Saharan Africa, government is a major source of health care funding. Increasingly, however, many sub-Saharan African governments, including Liberia's, have been incapable of providing enough money to deliver basic health care to the general population. Sub-Saharan African countries are beginning to turn to private sources (corporations and individual fees) for payment of health care services. Reports from the World Bank and other international agencies, point to the fact that over the last two decades, the proportion of central government dollars devoted to health care in many sub-Saharan countries has declined, while in developed countries, government funding has steadily increased. The decline in government funding for health programs in countries like Liberia jeopardizes the implementation of many crucial health programs, such as those for maternal and child health.

With limited resources, the nagging question is: How do nations in sub-Saharan Africa that are emerging from a civil crisis balance the funding of programs for returning refugees with the funding of critical primary health care services? Before the civil war and currently, both government and nongovernmental spending in Liberia were geared to hospital-based acute care and curative services. This type of allocation does not adequately address the basic health problems facing many Liberians. On the other hand, funds cannot just be totally redirected to preventive programs because tertiary care is still important. Hospitals treat the most difficult and chronic cases, so it is important to sustain them in the postwar era. However, efforts should be directed to preventing many of the chronic conditions experienced by the people of Liberia at the primary prevention level.

Why has this mismatched funding situation in Liberia persisted for so long? First, it must be pointed out that the Liberian health care system is a centralized structure, which makes it difficult for a flexible and responsive process to be put in place to assist in the allocation of resources. In the prewar era, about half of the MOH&SW budget was spent on hospital services in urban settings. An estimated 40 percent was spent on county hospitals and other health facilities located in large towns, and approximately 10 percent was spent in rural areas, where the majority of the people lived. Based on these prewar estimates, it is clear that restructuring of the postwar health system in Liberia will call for the redistribution of the financing of health care for the people of Liberia.

Funding must also be based on morbidity and mortality indicators. In Liberia, most of the common causes of hospitalization are gastrointestinal diseases, complications of pregnancy, respiratory illness, malaria, tuberculosis, malnutrition, measles, and vaccine-preventable diseases affecting children under 5 years of age. Many of these conditions are preventable. If some of the disproportionate resources spent on hospitals were redirected to the primary levels of the health care delivery system, many of the health conditions seen in Liberia could be treated earlier, at a less severe stage, or prevented altogether. In essence, if the goal is to reduce the burden of morbidity and mortality on the country, monies spent on expanding large tertiary centers in the capital and other large cities would be better spent on prevention.

The beckoning question, then, is whether all tertiary hospitals in Liberia should be closed. The answer to this question is "No." Shutting down existing facilities cannot solve problems influencing optimal health care delivery in Liberia. Even if all large hospitals in Liberia (like the John F. Kennedy Medical Center, which consumes a large proportion of the MOH&SW budget) were closed down and the money used for operating them was diverted to rural health programs, there would still not be enough to fund adequate health care in rural areas. Liberia has always had serious problems with developing a cadre of trained health care providers to meet the demand for health care delivery to all people. The problem is even more acute now that the war is over. The civil war has exacerbated the lack of health care professionals. Out of fear of being killed or harm being perpetrated against their families, many nurses, doctors, and allied health care professionals fled the country and are now residing in other sub-Saharan African countries or in Western nations. Unlike in some other African countries, English is the national language in Liberia. Training of health care workers is conducted in English and based on Western models of practicing medicine and nursing. Liberian health care workers escaping the civil war were able to establish themselves in the U.S., Canada, the United Kingdom, and other European countries because they knew English and they knew Western medicine. In the short term, it will be difficult to attract some of these individuals back to their homeland, as they have settled in their new countries and are progressing in their careers. More doctors, nurses, and other health care professionals will have to be trained to replace these workers. These Liberians living abroad, however, have gained advanced and better skills in health care delivery and may be a valuable resource to tap into in the long term.

Reallocating resources away from hospitals and tertiary care facilities is not an easy proposal. If one focuses only on the largest government hospital in Monrovia, it may be possible to turn this institution (the John F. Kennedy Medical Center) into several small primary health care units, but it is difficult to transform such facilities, and the health care providers working there have been trained in treating the "sick" rather than the "well." It may make a smoother transition to build new primary health care facilities and train new health care providers in a primary health care framework. In any event, tertiary care facilities and health personnel must be linked to the rest of the primary health care system, because primary care facilities will still need to refer patients with advanced health care needs to tertiary care settings. At the current stage of Liberia's level of development, health professionals will still see gunshot wounds, severe burns due to agricultural activities, road traffic accidents, and increasingly, some chronic diseases seen only in Western countries. It is the financing of health care, rather than existence, of expensive, highly technological hospitals that needs to be changed.

Bureaucratic, Inefficient Government Programs
for Distributing Funds

In the prewar era and even now, evidence points to the inefficiency of the Liberian health care system and how the scarce funds that are allocated for health care are poorly used. Some of these problems involve charging people very low or no fees, poor-quality health centers, and highly centralized management structures. One shortcoming in this area is the inappropriate utilization of tertiary health care facilities by individuals whose conditions could be resolved in less sophisticated settings. In the urban areas, for instance, it is very common to see long lines at large hospitals with outpatient care services, while smaller health centers are underused. There are several reasons why people choose to seek health care from modern urban health centers: health care personnel may be better trained; more sophisticated equipment and laboratories are available and functional; and many of these hospitals are located in settings where, if a case is diagnosed and the hospital lacks medications for it, the patient may be able to purchase that medication from a local drugstore. Additionally, because these tertiary care modern facilities are free of charge, there is little deterrent for people not to travel to them to use the facilities. The result is that many simple services are provided unnecessarily through costly facilities, which overburdens the understaffed health care personnel at these centers. If people had a reliable option for health care in their local environment, they would be less apt to seek health care from a facility more advanced than their conditions require.

There are tangible and intangible costs for the patients and their families when they travel long distances and wait long periods to be seen for amoebic dysentery. If everyone who is sick decides to use the tertiary care setting, hospitals will remain overcrowded. At some county health centers, people wait all day to be seen by the nurse or physician assistant, only to be told that supplies or medications—or even the health care provider—is not available on the premises. For poor rural people who have traveled miles, using their last pennies to pay for transportation, this is a travesty. For rural Liberian women with heavy demands on them to care for their children, fetch water and firewood, prepare meals, and assist with farming activities, the intangible costs of waiting all day at a health care center can be very high.

There are unintended consequences to inefficiencies in the health care systems besides just the time lost by patients encountering long waiting lines at government hospitals and clinics. One unintended consequence is that instead of everyone having equal access to health care, only those who can afford to wait for a long time will receive care. Another consequence is that the system becomes corrupt when patients bribe health care workers to be seen early. Instead of seeing patients on a first-come, first-serve basis according to triage, the system is abused and those most in need may not be treated in time, if at all. The two major tenets of the PHC approach— accommodation and acceptability—are overlooked when the emphasis is on a centralized, bureaucratic structure. It is difficult to encourage Liberians to seek health care within modern health care facility because the effort is so strenuous, especially for sick people. The long lines at free government clinics mean the limited staff can spend less than five minutes with each patient. It takes more than five minutes to adequately conduct an assessment, evaluate laboratory reports, and prescribe a treatment regimen for the kinds of serious illnesses and injuries presented in these health care settings

There are also logistical problems with the distribution of health care services, equipment, and medications. Logistical problems in the supply of needed drugs, equipment, and fuel are not only the result of resource constraints, but also because of highly centralized distribution systems. Liberia, before the civil war, had a National Drug Depot under the MOH&SW through which all government clinics obtained health supplies, including medications. Compared to that in private health care facilities, the quality of health care provided at government health care facilities is low. Staffers are stretched to their limits and suffer from low morale, medications are in short supply, and buildings and equipment are deteriorating. Patients are the ones who suffer from these problems. For instance, an individual from rural area who has just experienced a severe farming injury with fractured bones may not be able to have an x-ray taken at the health center because the x-ray machine has broken down or the technician is not on duty. Some of these apparent shortcomings occur because the government accepts foreign funds and then passively allows Western-style architecture to take precedence, even if it results in a building that is not appropriate for the climate and the culture. As the health care system is being rebuilt in Liberia, the government should be more active in decision making as gifts are received so that unsolicited donations do not shape long-range planning, but, rather, long-range planning elicits donations. For example, the donation of a new magnetic resonance imaging machine may not be prudent to accept if there is no budget for personnel, operating costs, and maintenance.

Bureaucracy is built into the government health care system in Liberia because it is highly centralized in financing and management. Resources are used inefficiently and communication among the different parts of the organization is fragmented. Besides the duplication of duties or activities, a health structure highly centralized in funding and management may be subject to disruption in case of civil crisis. During the mid-1990s, when Liberia was divided with various warring factions fighting to gain territory, the northern and eastern sectors of the country, controlled by such factions, were deprived of health care. As a result, many government health care centers in these areas ceased to function. The national government in the capital city could not send supplies and found it impossible to control health clinics in these areas. With the exception of two church-related hospitals in this area of the country, civilians living in these areas over the period of the war did not have access to health care.

Inequity in Distributing Benefits of Scarce Resources

Liberia, like other sub-Saharan African countries, is faced with limited resources for the provision of health care. Because health care competes with other social needs of the people, the government cannot afford to provide free, publicly funded curative services for everyone. Liberia, like other sub-Saharan African countries, has a history of inequitably distributing health care benefits. Two major factors that drive this inequity are urban-rural disparities and income differentials among the people.

In many sub-Saharan African countries, governments spend most of their funding for health care on urban-based health care facilities. Maintenance of hospitals is expensive including the staffing of health care workers. There are urban-rural inequities because the seats of governments are based in urban settings and therefore favor constructing hospitals in large cities where government officials can receive benefits. Politicians want to display large tertiary care centers in their cities as evidence of economic development. While rural patients could conceivably be referred to tertiary hospitals in urban settings, many of these hospitals are still utilized primarily by the urban populations where they are located.

Besides the inequitable location of physical facilities, there is an inequity in the distribution of supplies and health care workers between urban and rural settings. The pattern of urban-rural disparities was seen in Liberia before the civil war and continues. For example, the per-capita numbers of physicians, nurses, dentists, and other allied health care workers were and are lower still in the rural areas compared to urban areas.

Some NGOs and religious-related organizations have long provided health care to rural residents in Liberia because they recognized and had compassion for the needs of rural people. Previous Liberian administrations had some prejudice against rural citizens benefiting from economic development programs of the country, health and education being two of the critical programs. In the yearning to evolve beyond Liberia's status as an under-developed country, previous governments equated urban development with progress. Its officials failed to value the rural nature of the country and did not see the rural inhabitants as valuable assets to the country's development. The Americo-Liberians who were in power at the time that many policies were being crafted had little association with rural life in Liberia. Additionally, those rural Liberians who migrated to cities to study became acculturated, and many decided to leave their rural roots behind. The converging factors meant that the rural health care delivery system in the country did not receive the same priority or attention given to the urban health care sector.

It may be impossible to change the attitudes of Americo-Liberians and other elitist indigenous groups in power that are far removed from the everyday lives and experiences of the rural population of Liberia. It is hard to develop compassion for what one does not understand. It would be far easier and more effective to infuse the power structure with grassroots input, specifically from rural areas. In other words, instead of waiting for the elite power structure to develop a heartfelt commitment to rural health care and development, it would be easier to tap into the commitment that rural people already have for their community and its needs. What good is it to construct a new clinic in a village when funding dries up because concern has waned? What good is such a clinic if the government fails to staff it with trained health care workers and provide it with adequate supplies for diagnosis and treatment of common ailments? What good is such a clinic when it lacks basic amenities such as water, latrines, and electricity?

In Liberia, any health care reform proposal must also take into account the income inequities that exist between urban and rural families.

In the cities, family incomes may be higher than those in the rural areas because most rural families rely heavily on subsistence farming and bartering, with little access to hard currency. If the government allocates most of its meager funds for health care to urban hospitals, it may be financing health care for families with means to pay. This is not to suggest that all individuals who live in urban areas will be able to afford health care services on their own. For certain groups and individuals, the cost of health care will have to be subsidized. Hospitals and tertiary care settings will still be an essential part of the health care delivery system in the postwar era, even as the MOH&SW embraces the PHC framework that emphasizes more prevention and treatment of illnesses at the entry level of the system.

Sources of Health Care Financing and Delivery in Liberia

Financing is a critical component of the health care delivery system in any country. Financing is the process through which funds are raised to pay for the health care before and/or after such care is delivered. In the traditional health care system in Liberia, compensation for traditional healers could be in the form of cash or in-kind contributions such as livestock, produce, or other commodities. In the modern Liberian health care system, health care is financed by many different sources, including government and private. Examples of public funding sources include revenues generated from taxes, social insurance programs for specific groups, and lotteries to fund designated health programs. Private financing sources include employment-based insurance, self-insurance, charitable organizations, foreign aid programs, and direct household expenditures by family members.

In postwar Liberia, understanding and prioritizing these methods of financing is critical to developing relevant health policies. First, it may be important for MOH&SW officials to get a clear picture of how much different segments of the population are capable of paying for their own health care. With this information, a determination can then be made on how much and what kinds of care need to be offered and subsidized.

One of the social promises that had been made by a succession of Liberian administrations has been to provide free health care to everyone, financed through tax dollars. This promise has been kept more for the rich than for the poor. The flaw in this policy is that by funneling money into urban tertiary care facilities, the provision of health care is still tied to disparities in household's income among the population. If services are free but concentrated only in urban areas, it does no good for the masses, since many people in the rural areas would be unable to travel to get to the free services. Transportation is a prohibitive cost in sub-Saharan African countries and creates an insurmountable barrier to accessing health care.

Urban-based health care policies pander to the wealthy by providing sophisticated technology in a tertiary care setting, a system that the wealthy, rather than the poor, are more able to navigate. An unintended consequence is when the wealthy use the high-tech services offered by the government; it raises the bar on what is perceived as desirable health care. Health care professionals are tempted to use technology even if a lower-tech approach would be equally appropriate. And, eventually, the poorer segments of the population will want high-tech services because they mistakenly equate them with improved health outcomes. The available resources for health care could be available for more people if everyone, rich and poor, had their condition resolved with the lowest level of health care technology that is still effective and appropriate. Anything more than that is a waste of scarce resources that could save lives among other parts of the population. If the rich want advanced technological health services, they could pay for it out of pocket rather than using up scarce resources. The public policy problem for the MOH&SW in the postwar era is to come up with creative ways to provide cost-effective care to all Liberians. This egalitarian approach would improve the overall health status of the nation.

Reforms Suggested by the World Bank for Financing Health Care in Developing Countries

As far back as the late 1980s, health policy experts at the World Bank suggested certain policy reforms to help address the complex problems faced by many developing countries in financing their health care systems (World Bank, 1987). The World Bank in one of its financial studies suggests that some of the financial burden should be shifted from national governments and transferred to the users of services themselves. Four policy areas that the World Bank recommend for financial reform of the health sector include: (1) charging fees for users of government facilities; (2) establishing insurance plans where enrollees pay a fixed amount and in turn receive full care; (3) working effectively with non-governmental health care agencies; and (4) decentralizing government health services (World Bank, 1987).

Before any of these proposals are embraced for implementation, economic and organizational challenges need to be considered. First, the Liberian national currency has a very weak exchange or equivalence value on the world market. Most sub-Saharan African countries are not manufacturing medical technology, pharmaceuticals, and supplies, so they have to be purchased on the world market at a disadvantageous rate. Many Liberians are subsistence farmers and deal in simple exchanges of goods and services rather than in cash. It will be disaffecting to tell the people seeking health care at local facilities to pay in hard currency when many of them have none. On the other hand, if the Liberian people are made to pay for their services in Liberian dollars, the health care sector will not be able to generate enough hard currency to order more pharmaceuticals or laboratory supplies in the international market. Funding health care programs in the postwar era will take the combined efforts of the MOH&SW, the Ministry of Finance, and the international monetary agencies that give loans and grants to the Liberian government.

The four recommendations suggested by the World Bank have inherent limitations and, if introduced, should be introduced incrementally and with caution. If high user's fees are charged, it may deter people (especially those most in need) from seeking health care. As seen in health maintenance organizations (HMOs) in Western countries, embracing the concept of risk sharing may lead to rationing care, and many people will be underserved. Lessons should be learned from the current system in the U.S., where reforms have gone too far in terms of implementing cost savings measures without much regard for how satisfied the users of the systems are. Privatization may be important in making health care delivery more cost-effective, but that direction could skew the health care delivery system with the most profitable areas or patients having better-quality care than to others. Abdicating government responsibility to the private sector in the most challenging areas to serve in Liberia may strain those private resources to the breaking point. Decentralization is important to enabling the people to become more proactive in health care policy, but the national government will still be responsible for making difficult decisions about training health care workers or investing in new health care facilities.

War-impacted sub-Saharan African countries may find it difficult to embrace the recommendations as suggested by the World Bank because it takes concerted effort just to emerge from chaos. It will require political will and boldness from elected officials and all others involved accepting innovative health reforms during the postwar era. Elected officials will have to pay keen attention to making the health of the nation a top priority. A healthy population will translate into increased productivity leading to economic development.

Proposal for Change: Health Care Financing in Postwar Liberia

Providing Cost-effective Health Care Services

In sub-Saharan African countries that are reeling from civil war, it is paramount to devise cost-effective ways of providing primary and secondary health care services, saving tertiary care settings for only the most critical conditions that require that level of care. To make health care even more cost-effective, it is important to encourage communities to take a proactive approach to achieving optimum health for their localities. Collective responsibility for health will be more effective in the long run than each family trying to navigate a confusing and unfair system on its own. In order to reduce the cost of health care services, the government must find a way to encourage communities to fund some of these services for themselves. Every community no matter how poor has resources and assets that could be mobilized from within. These include the ability to work together in groups to resolve common health issues. In a developing country, it is easy to succumb to the prevalent belief that there are no resources to solve health system problems. But, creative solutions to human and financial resource problems may emerge if the community believes in a project. The world over, public health experts have come to understand that it is a formidable task to collaborate with a community to change counterproductive customs, beliefs, and behavior handed down for generations. Efforts by health care professionals working in postwar Liberia should be geared toward understanding why certain beliefs and attitudes persist and how they affect on the health of the people. In essence, if certain beliefs have no harmful effects on the health of the people, they should be left intact; efforts at change should be directed toward beliefs that lead to harmful health outcomes.

Health care advocates need to work within the cultural framework of the populations they serve. Individuals from the local villages can be chosen and trained as health educators to help resolve common ailments while teaching people basic preventive health skills. Many of these local community health workers may not ask to be paid; they may be volunteering in order to contribute to the collective web of altruism that holds their community together. These community health care workers need to be provided with some training so they can be more effective and gain credibility in the eyes their fellow villagers and be linked to the modern health care delivery system. Involving the communities in finding ways to improve the health of their people may be relatively inexpensive in terms of staffing and equipment; however, it will take the political will of government officials and the commitment of any community that will benefit from such program.

In postwar Liberia, the community-based programs and outreach efforts that were previously successful should be revived and expanded. For example, rural towns and villages could recruit community health care workers to provide practical information on how to give simple preventive health messages. These health workers would then be given the necessary supplies to ensure that young children are immunized and/or, be trained to alert government health workers about infectious disease outbreaks. Community health care workers should be trained to realize when a case is far beyond their ability to mitigate and they should seek assistance from a more advanced health care worker. Community health workers are being used in both developed and developing countries as a way to increase the effective utilization of the health care system and improve health outcomes (Rodriguez, Conway, Woodruff and Edwards, 2003; McElmurry, Park, & Buseh, 2003; Nemcek, and Sabatier, 2003).

Two groups from which these community health workers are most likely to be drawn from in the postwar era will be (1) women and (2) traditional healers. As in other sub-Saharan African countries, women in Liberia have for centuries had their babies delivered with the assistance of traditional birth attendants (TBAs). TBAs receive small payments in cash or goods for the services they provide. At this point in Liberia's development, it would be impossible to supply trained midwives for every woman giving birth in the country. But birth outcomes could be improved significantly if TBAs received additional training in the labor and delivery process. Given additional instruction, TBAs could also serve at the periphery of the health care system in providing service and remedies such as oral rehydration salts to children under 5 years of age, or some forms of family planning, such as condoms.

Traditional healers are still widely consulted for a wide variety of conditions—both acute and chronic—in Liberia. This group of indigenous health care practitioners is uniquely qualified to make important contributions in improving health outcomes for the population. First, however, they will need some training and persuasion to drop or abandon practices that do not promote health, as well as encouragement to incorporate more effective practices based on science rather than on cultural traditions. Traditional healers who have been trained could use some modern remedies that do not require complex administration and monitoring. Some traditional healers may want to retain traditional healing practices because they might perceive change in their practice as a threat to cultural continuity. Traditional healers, along with other community leaders, hold the role of protector of cultural beliefs and values in their communities. In some cases, the status conferred by this role gives a traditional healer an inflated sense of importance and a feeling of infallibility. For instance, some traditional healers have claimed to have remedies for almost any ailment, including fatal diseases such as HIV infection. It will be prudent to link the modern health care system and traditional healers in a way that balances cultural respect with scientific knowledge. For example, a patient hospitalized in a tertiary health care facility dying from HIV/AIDS may request a visit from a traditional healer and should be allowed such an option because it will provide emotional and spiritual support, which is part of health care in its broadest sense. Indigenous traditional healers deserve legitimacy in the new health care system because they have long been committed to the egalitarian provision of health care to all people. For centuries, they have understood that all people deserve health care, regardless of status in society or ability to pay, an idea that the modern health care system is still grappling with.

In resource-deprived African countries such as Liberia, there are few modern health care workers in proportion to the general population. Many health care needs of the people will be unmet unless some of the responsibilities of these professionals are delegated to other staffers at lower levels of the system. Doctors must be willing to delegate some of their responsibilities to nurses and physician assistants. Registered nurses (RNs) and trained midwives must be willing to delegate some of their professional activities to licensed practical nurses (LPNs). LPNs could engage families in simple preventive health practices. Health care professionals on every level could connect to the traditional healers who are part of a community's health care system.

Economics drives the effort to resolve health conditions using the lowest appropriate level of health care professionals. Individuals at the lower level of the health care system can be trained at a lower cost than those at a higher level. Since there is a shortage of doctors and medical training comes at an exorbitant cost, it makes economic sense to train more nurses and physician assistants with advanced skills. The ideal skills mix for developing countries would involve a large number of community health workers supported by highly trained nurses and physician assistants who are, in turn, supported by doctors. Nurses with advanced training can carry out physical assessment, correctly diagnose cases, and prescribe the appropriate treatment for the patients in their health care settings. In the rural areas, all health care professionals will have to be trained as multipurpose, well-rounded, multi-tasking individuals. It would be best if health care workers were recruited from the local communities or villages where they work. Because they know the local culture and language, they can be a catalyst for change.

Community Financing as a Way of Expanding Health Care

Increasing community involvement in determining how to meet health care needs is the way for Liberia to move forward in this postwar era. If they are invested in long-term range planning, communities might assume accountability for provision of some services. For instance, villagers could build the local health clinic and residence for the nurse or midwife assigned to the clinic in a way that better integrates them into the community. It is important to understand that health care planning and financing happens within the context of a community. In Liberia, a community could be viewed as a village, town, or an urban neighborhood. Tribal groups in Liberia, even if geographically dispersed, should also be viewed as a community because they share a common heritage and are expected to maintain their identity by working together as a group. During the war, affiliations to tribal groups superseded every other community; affiliation to a tribal group meant the difference between life and death.

The acceptance of health initiatives can be accelerated if promoted among groups that regard themselves as a community. For instance, if the villagers in a rural area of Liberia recognize malaria or tuberculosis to be a common problem that affects their health status as a community, they may be highly motivated to participate in the organization of health care services for everyone in the village. If a community decides to organize around the provision of health care services, the question then becomes how the community work will finance the program so everyone in that community benefits.

As early as 1979, an economist with the WHO, Romer Milton, suggested the use of "community financing of primary health care." Community financing of primary health care is defined as "the mobilization of resources by a community to support, in part or in full, basic preventive and curative health services for its members" (Russell and Reynolds, 1987, p. 7). In most African societies, households and communities have played a central role in providing resources for health initiatives. They have provided gifts, food, lodging and other material compensation to health care professionals in lieu of monetary compensation. Because many villages are small and cohesive, it would be easy to establish a community funding mechanism (a "sickness fund") to which every family/household has contributed. Such funds can then be used to help subsidize some of the health care services offered by the central government. Individuals will also contribute a minimal fee at the point of service. The community fund reinforces the value of collective effort in meeting community health needs; the fee for service reinforces the individual's responsibility for his or her own health.

Community financing could not only be a way of providing health care for everyone, but could also be a way of creating economic and social development for local communities. A highly functioning and well-run health center would be an asset to a village. People from neighboring villages would travel there to obtain health care and spend dollars in the village in the process. It would stall the health development of the country immeasurably if it is assumed by everyone that only the central Liberian government should be responsible for health care delivery.

The PHC framework, which endorses community involvement and financing, is the most viable strategy to follow in reforming the health care system in postwar Liberia. The role of the national government will still be critical in the PHC framework, because they has the expertise, infrastructure, and access to international funding sources that are beyond the reach of local communities. This advantage should not preclude the government from engaging local communities in determining their own destinies.

The central government alone, importantly, will not be able to finance health care for the entire population; hence, the consideration of community financing. Community financing, although used in the past with some success, also has its inherent limitations. Even with community financing, the provision of health care will still be inequitable because some communities will be less able to finance health care than others. A mixed approach, with some community financing and some government financing of health care services, would be a viable postwar strategy.

Benefits and Limitations of Community Financing

Obviously, countries in sub-Saharan Africa will differ in their strategies for building community financing into the health care system. Some of these differences will involve the participating populations, methods of raising funds, procedures for setting fees and collecting revenues, and managing and supervising the financing system. To customize the approach that would be most appropriate for a country, research will be needed to inform the policy makers about factors that will influence resource allocation and, the structure of health programs. The cluster of factors related to community health financing includes the role of the community; objectives of the community financing approach; what fees will be levied for the services provided; and management and evaluation of the community financing process.

Role of the Local Community in Community Financing

The role of the community in the financing process is an important variable to consider, according to the PHC literature. Some communities will play increase roles in financing primary health care; others will be involved only minimally. The nature and degree of community involvement needs to be explored before community financing is implemented in a community. A critical question is: What is the minimal level of contribution needed from a community in order to ensure that the community financing strategy works to provide adequate health care?

Decisions must also be made concerning how the local community should be involved in overseeing financial decisions and transactions. Should it be involved in the planning processes, setting prices, collecting revenues, and supervising the collection of fees from those who use the program? For example, it may work well in some local Liberian communities for the community representatives to be responsible for collecting fees, accounting, and paying the health care workers, but in other communities where corruption and illiteracy are more prevalent, this structure may not be appropriate. Before launching the community financing approach in each community, it will be important to identify both the most appropriate activities for community participation and the level of participation in each activity.

The structure for organizing community participation must also be considered. On the village level, who should be involved (What, if any; special roles should be given to women, village chiefs, and/or others)? Should everyone be involved? How will concerned individuals participate (periodic meetings, committees, voting)? Research about community organization as it pertains to community health financing is somewhat limited. During the prewar era in Liberia, communities that participated in community financing relied on committees of village members to represent them. For example, the village chief and his or her council members may have appointed a village health committee to represent their community in financing decisions. This committee will often be responsible for raising and allocating funds for building an airstrip where a bush pilot may land a small plane to transport critically ill individuals to a secondary or tertiary health care facility in a larger city.

Decisions about how a community can continue a community-financing plan, once launched, is also an important consideration. It will be necessary to educate the members of the community on the importance and benefits of community financing. In some instances, members of the community may need incentives to serve as motivation to participate in the community-financing program. Some of these incentives would include civic pride and community recognition. Other factors that may influence the role that the community can play may be beyond the control of the national government or MOH&SW officials. For example, what is the degree of cohesion in the community? Are there several tribal groups residing in the village, and are there some groups that are marginalized because of their tribal affiliation, social unit or socioeconomic status? If community financing relies on close cooperation among kinship groups, it may be more successful. A relevant aspect of Liberian culture is that relatives from anyone's family are usually found in other neighboring villages and may make it more likely for villages to pool resources and work together. Geographic isolation may lessen the opportunities and inclination for villages to collaborate. In rural Liberia, where people live in scattered small villages, distance may limit their interests and ability to participate in the decision-making process of inter village community financing of joint projects.

Other sociological and anthropological variables can act as constraints to community financing. The leadership structures of Liberian villages and towns have evolved independently and come in different forms: democratic, autocratic, or hierarchical, depending on tribal history and outside influences on a community. Based on how the chiefs are identified for leadership and how they rule their people, they may be considered autocratic or non democratic. Educational levels of individuals in the community may determine those most likely to participate in the process. Balancing scientific understanding of epidemiological patterns of diseases in the community with sociological understandings of a community's perceptions of its health needs is also a factor critical with regards to community financing.

Objectives for Establishing a Community-financing Program

Objectives need to be established for developing a community-financing program; is the financing going to pay for preventive, curative, and/or rehabilitative services? What specific health problems will improve as a direct result of the new financing system? For example, a rural village in Liberia may decide that too many children are contracting and dying from schistosomiasis or diarrheal diseases. If interdisciplinary scientific research identifies the contributing factors to schistosomiasis or diarrheal diseases and these factors are explained to the community, then the community may decide to participate in community financing. The community could pay for the recommended medications used in treating schistosomiasis, to dig new, safer wells in the village, or to purchase more oral rehydration salts and antibiotics.

The establishment of community-financed programs implies the Liberian MOH&SW will expect individuals to contribute financially to the whole, but such contribution is dependent on the personal financial capability of the villagers. It will be counterproductive to collect money from families that are poor and may be struggling to meet their basic needs, including providing food for their children. In Liberia, many people live in subsistence farming communities; their income is seasonal, and some families may not have the funds to pay for health care services at certain times of the year. Community financing is a desirable option for financing health care even if there are some in the community who will not be able to pay cash. The poorest of the poor should still be able to use the services; however, they could also make non-cash of such contributions of such things as labor and goods.

After a village accepts the community financing option, it needs to determine which services or amenities it will finance, such as safe water, maternal and child health progress, immunization programs, or medication supplies. If a preventive health care service option (e.g., immunization) is selected, the community's ability and willingness to pay for the vaccines, supplies for storage, and human resources will have to be determined. It is important to first see health care needs from the people's perspective, even if it is an unscientific perspective. For example, many people may not see the immediate benefits of immunization against a disease. They may be more willing to pay for curative services than preventive health care services. This perspective is the point from which communication can unfold between the community and MOH&SW officials.

Fees to Be Charged for the Services Provided

Fees at the point of service are very critical to the success of community-based financing because paying for a service—even minimally—reinforces its value. Fees can enable a clinic and some health programs to become self-sustaining. Determining fee structure is a delicate matter to be considered by both MOH&SW officials and the village involved. Should everyone be charged the same fees for services provided, or should there be a sliding scale? Are there vulnerable populations that should be totally exempted from payment? For instance, what should be the fee for prenatal care and delivery? Special provisions must be made for segments of the population that will be unable to pay for services (e.g., subsistence farmers, elderly people, or women and children who may have little access to funds).

Management and Administration of the
Community-Financing Program

A major decision affecting success of the program will be the one as to who will manage the funds from the community-financing program. If funds collected are poorly managed, embezzled, or misused because of corrupt management, the project is likely to fail. As PHC literature notes, many management options have been used. Health care workers, members of a health committee, project staff, local businesspeople, and, in some instances, a paid individual with prior management skill may be hired. The best option for management will depend on local circumstances. In Liberia, a setting plagued with corruption, it may mean using checks and balances to reduce the likelihood of embezzlement. Other questions to consider are: should one person or a group of individuals manage community financing? Should the managers be compensated for work? And if so, how much compensation? Where should the administrative or management team be located—at the health center or at the MOH&SW? To whom will the managers be accountable?

The management of community financing for health programs will require business skills: bookkeeping, inventory planning, budgeting, and reporting and analyzing past activities. Good management of community financing will be critical for the achievement of the program's objectives and lead to sustainability. In prewar Liberia, some communities in rural areas established community funds called "revolving drug funds" (RDFs). An RDF serves as a communal fund for purchasing essential supplies for a local health center. RDFs enable continuous replenishment of critical medications and medical supplies. However, like any other small enterprise, if good inventory is not maintained or payments are not documented, an RDF program would soon become ineffective. Some of the RDF programs in Liberia were terminated because of poor management—inventory was not maintained; stock was lost because of poor storage; and because of inflation, costs increased faster than fees. In some instances, then, a solution may be to rely on a village health committee to manage the RDF.

If this option is chosen, relevant social and cultural factors need to be considered. For example, if literacy skills of community members are low, a village health committee may not be able to administer the program. Because most Liberians live in a community with extended families, the potential for social pressure on health committee members to give family members special treatment may strain the system and eventually cause it to crash. In other cases, committee members may be the politically acceptable choices the government officials and/or even the local committee itself, but they may lack the skills and experience necessary to manage. For any of these reasons, it may be more advantageous to hire a paid manager who possesses the required skills than to use a community volunteer manager. Health committee members from the community could then serve as advisers to the manager and act as a liaison to the community.

Monitoring and Evaluation of the Community-Financing Program

Monitoring and evaluation is an important component of community financing, although often overlooked. An accurate and reliable monitoring and evaluation system is important for current and future decision-making. A clear and simple monitoring and evaluation system should be designed so that all stakeholders involved are aware of the outcomes of the program. Good decision-making will depend on accurate information about users of the services; awareness of the greatest obstacles to community financing; and understanding of the opinions community members have about the program. Evaluation assessment should gather data on both processes and outcomes. Data collection should occur in all phases because the community financing process is developmental, each phase building on the next. If the community-financing program is extensive and receives international funding, it may be prudent to use an outside evaluator to assess the strengths and weaknesses of the health project. In either case, either an internal or an external evaluator will need to work closely with the community financing committee (if one is established) or government officials in prioritizing health programs for evaluation. Evaluation will help more securely link community health programs to national goals and objectives for reducing morbidity and mortality among the Liberian people.

Sustaining Health and Development Programs in Postwar Liberia

All governments in sub-Saharan Africa, and certainly that of Liberia in the postwar era are faced with the tremendous challenge of providing health care services to their people. With a near-total collapse of the health care delivery system in Liberia during the war, it will take considerable political savvy and courage on the part of Liberian government health officials to inform the Liberian people that they cannot fulfill the prewar promise of providing free health care to the people. The prioritization of health services provided by the government is an important decision to convey to the people. To drive this message home, MOH&SW officials must be able to inform and engage the public about health care initiatives.

Strategies to sustain health programs were outlined in WHO's 2000 World Health Report. In that report, the health status of a population is assessed based on the proportion of the general population that has access to health care services. Equity and efficiency in financing health programs were also discussed in the report. In the same WHO report, 191 member countries were each graded on their performance in relation to that expected from the financial resources and educational levels of the country. Among the 191 countries, Liberia is ranked 187th in health attainment and 186th in overall performance. The only countries in the world with worse health status for their populations were the Democratic Republic of Congo, the Central African Republic, and Sierra Leone—all sub-Saharan African countries currently either engulfed in civil wars or just emerging from them.

With these dismal odds, how can health programs be sustained and health status improved in postwar Liberia? Attainment of national health goals and provision of health care services will have to be viewed as a central focus for all governmental sectors in the new Liberia. In a war-torn country, decisions made in all sectors of the government can be a determinant of health. Any government coming to power in postwar Liberia must put health at the forefront of a strategy for sustainable economic development. As the UN has proclaimed: "Human beings are at the center of concern for sustainable development. They are entitled to healthy and productive life in harmony with nature. The primary health needs of the world's population are integral to the achievement of the goals of sustainable development" (UNCED, 1992, Principle 1, p. 1). Integrating sustainable development into the political decision-making of postwar Liberia will require more than just financial resources. It will also require the recognition on the part of health policy planners that local communities must be involved in their own well being, including through recognizing their own health needs.

Because the PHC approach is best suited for providing health care to the people of Liberia at this current stage of the country's development, many primary care health projects (e.g., maternal-child health initiatives) will need to be sustained, even when funding for such programs comes to an end. In the last two decades, much attention has been paid to understanding the concept of sustainability in health care delivery in both developed and developing countries. However, conceptualizing what sustainability means in its true sense has been difficult. Sustainability is more than funding; its ownership by a community, vital links with other health care programs and integration with comprehensive development initiatives. While some international projects on health care claim they have achieved sustainability, there is limited empirical research to provide a clear understanding of the indicators that are used in evaluating the sustainability processes and outcomes of a health program.

Some researchers who have done work in this area list three important indicators in assessing the extent of sustainability of community-based health programs: (1) continuation of the health benefits accomplished through the initial program, (2) understanding the level of the institution of the program within the organization, and (3) assessment of the level of empowerment—the building of capacity—in the local community where the program was implemented (Shediac-Rizkallah and Bone, 1998).

The level of sustainability should be clearly delineated from the outset in any health program. For instance, an RDF program in a Liberian village will have a better chance at sustainability if the program is well designed and effectively implemented; if it reflects the organizational structure of the MOH&SW; if it is congruent with applicable sociocultural beliefs about health; and if it echoes the predominant value system in the local community. A major weakness of many well-intended health programs in sub-Saharan Africa is that their developers and implementers have no plan for creating sustainability. Because of this shortsightedness, many health-related programs implemented in sub-Saharan Africa are discontinued when the initial funding runs out. During the conceptualization phase of a project, the following questions need to be addressed: What would be the individual benefits of the project? Will the benefits be substantial enough to change the attitudes of the people using the project? What's the role of the funders and managers of the program? Will the community perceive the intended project as theirs or as just another irrelevant health program that is dreamed up by some health care bureaucrat?

Swerissen and Crisp (2004) have also discussed and presented an excellent framework for the sustainability of health programs at different levels of an organization. It is critical to the sustainability process for program designers to determine whether sustainability is feasible and to delineate exactly what they seek to sustain. Swerissen and Crisp (2004) posit that health programs are sustainable if they make significant changes at both the individual level and organizational level, if they lead to community action, and if they result in institutional change.

Individual Level of Sustainability

At this level, examining the impact on individuals assesses change. This involves evaluating the impact the program has on the participants' knowledge, attitudes, beliefs, and practices (KABP) in relation to a specific health intervention. For instance, if in the postwar era, the MOH&SW discovers that there is decreased breast-feeding among rural women, one strategy would be to develop a health education and social marketing approach in which women would receive messages on the benefits of breast-feeding for their newborns and themselves. To assess the impact of the program, the usual KABP surveys would be carried out in the communities that benefited from such programs. For example, if rural women modify their breast-feeding habits, what is the probability they will continue breast-feeding until the child is ready to be weaned? Are the skills learned by the women in the breastfeeding program transferable to other health issues in their communities? Swerissen and Crisp (2004) suggest health programs that are targeted to individuals require a continuation of funding and necessary resources to sustain a comprehensive impact on the general population. Targeting individuals without altering their environment, results in limited impact because people live in communities that inversely influence healthy behaviors.

Organizational Level of Sustainability

As at the individual level, sustainability at the organizational level also has its advantages and pitfalls. Over the years, we have learned that improving the physical environment in organizational settings, such as schools and work places, can lead to positive health outcomes (Leeder,

1997; Nutbeam, 1997). For example, the physical settings in many sub-Saharan African countries could be altered to reduce the spread of certain endemic diseases, such as malaria or diarrheal ailments. Establishing policies to reduce risks found within the physical environment will affect individual behaviors. In developed countries, we have seen health policies that reduce risks in certain environments, such as bans against smoking in buildings. The literature on sustainability suggests that once a health policy is established organizationally, there may not be the need for repeated doses of intervention because the policy is reinforced with sanctions (Jackson, 1985; Rappaport, 1995). The sustainability of programs at the organizational level is linked to the existing rules and policies governing the organization. For example, once a new "no smoking" policy in a building is established, individuals will have to conform to the new rules if they want to remain in the building. While some of these institutional changes have been successful in protecting the health of employees of an organization, those most directly affected by the rules could experience some social stigma, i.e. the smokers relegated to standing by the back door to smoke. A balance between individual rights and organizational policies will help reduce the stigmatization.

Action Taken by the Community

This aspect of sustainability is the most critical for long-term maintenance of health programs in local communities. In order for community sustainability to occur, according to Crisp, Swerissen, and Duckett (2000), there must be recognition of the relationships among organizations and among organizations and individuals. It will, however, require infusion of intensive resources over much longer periods, than those allocated for sustaining change at the individual or institutional levels. In some instances, individuals in the community may be resistant to change and may feel that diversion of resources from one program to the next is inappropriate. Due to this resistance, new community-based health care programs may require longer-term maintenance support. If funding or other support for a program is withdrawn too quickly, the intended effects may abruptly disappear.

As Liberia emerges from the protracted civil conflict, what may be more critical is for MOH&SW officials to assist communities with capacity building by developing, reviving, and maintaining the infrastructures required for achieving optimal health for the general population.

The notion that sustainability of health programs is only based on financial support should be dispelled. Health care projects that are implemented at the wrong level of the local Liberian social system will likely be less effective and will probably not be able to be sustained over time. In most Liberian and other sub-Saharan African communities, there are great social cohesion and supportive networks. These good social relations and strong supportive networks will help improve the health of individuals and families as well as the community at large, but many of the social bonds that held Liberians so tightly together have been destroyed because of protracted civil war. There continues to be evidence of high levels of inequity of income and social status, which tends to lead to less social cohesion, more violent crimes, and increased morbidity and mortality rates among the general population.

Hopelessness and depression are pervasive in Liberian communities in comparison to their levels in the prewar era. A feeling of well-being is rare among internally and externally displaced people. It will take the integration of the actions of individual Liberians with the changes made at institutional levels to produce sustainable health gains in Liberian communities. International organizations working with the Liberian MOH&SW will also have to review their expectations for program outcomes as they supply funds to implement health initiatives in Liberia. All parties involved, including the Liberian government, must take shared responsibilities in these efforts. In some instances, this may mean that programs with no immediate visible outcomes may have to be funded for a long period before any impact is realized. The goal is for local communities to be able to build capacity and become self-sufficient.

Notes

1. Nkrumah, Kwame (1977). *Africa must unite*, p. 55, quoted in Axioms of Kwame Nkrumah (Freedom Fighters' Edition), Panaf Books Ltd. Stafford, Staffordshire, England

CHAPTER 6

HUMAN RESOURCE DEVELOPMENT: A CRISIS IN THE PREWAR AND POSTWAR LIBERIAN HEALTH SECTOR

Furthermore the people, through their own hard work and a little help and leadership, have finished many development projects in the villages, have built schools, dispensaries, community centers, and roads; they have dug wells, water channels, animal dips, small dams, and completed various other development projects. Had they waited for money, they would not now have the use of these things.[1]

—Julius Nyerere, Former President of Tanzania,
The Arusha Declaration, February 5, 1967

Background Issues: Human Resources Development in Sub-saharan Africa

According to Becker (1993), it is the people of a country that possesses the energy and ability to create true prosperity for their country, the kind of comprehensive prosperity that will make their country competitive with other countries. Human capital, Becker posits, can be increased or decreased, depending on the situation in which people exist. Human beings are competitive and creative creatures. We invest our time and energy in acquiring new knowledge, which leads to improvement in our health and quality of life. In any country, the development of human resources can be summed up as the core foundation of prosperity in that country. Acquiring new knowledge and skills leads to enhance self-actualization and good health outcomes. People must be able to provide for themselves certain amenities: shelter, food, clothes, education, and transportation—all of which are interrelated with good health outcomes. Because of a complex web of factors, it is impossible for some individuals in society to achieve self-actualization. Government has a social obligation to step in and provide certain services for the general population, one of which is basic health care. Governments must provide the infrastructural and financial resources needed to achieve a healthy population, which will, in turn, produce a productive workforce.

While countries in both the developed and developing regions of the world experience different challenges related to human resources development, the region of sub-Saharan Africa faces the daunting task of developing and maintaining its human capital. In sub-Saharan African countries, the development of human capital is critical to delivering adequate health care to the people. Many sub-Saharan African countries lack the means to develop their own human capital in needed health care disciplines. Inadequate development of human resources is also helping to fuel the high level of poverty that exists in many of these countries. Human resource development has been recognized by international organizations such as the World Bank and the International Monetary Fund (IMF) as an effective strategy to reduce poverty in sub-Saharan African countries. Over the years, these agencies have invested in education, health, and agricultural sectors. Investment in a population's education, health, nutrition, and family planning is widely thought to broaden its skills, improve population health, and lead to increased economic growth for the country. In essence, beyond individual gains, such investments by African governments do have ripple effects for the broader society. An increase in literacy levels, for instance, has been shown to strengthen the participatory process of the general population in politics, health, and the economy.

For adults in sub-Saharan Africa, good health is critical, not only for themselves, but also for their children and families. The sickness or death of an adult family member may mean a child's withdrawal from school to assist in the fields and care for siblings. The loss of household income due to sickness or disability, especially if this adult family member is the main breadwinner for the family, would precipitate difficulty in the family being able to pay tuition and other school expenses. This lost opportunity experienced by children is now reported in many sub-Saharan African countries where HIV/AIDS is ravaging the productive adult segments of the population.

Even before the discovery of HIV infection in many of these countries, the record of human resource development in Africa was dismal and limited in its ability to reverse poverty. Some sub-Saharan African countries made some economic progress in the 1990s; others are still struggling to help pull their people up to minimally acceptable levels of basic social and health care services. United Nations Development Program (UNDP) reports suggest that some of the sub-Saharan African countries experienced a decline in the number of young people enrolling in primary school. Compounding this fact is that sub-Saharan African countries have the fastest-growing population in the world. With this trend, an increase in the population will inevitably lead to an increase in the number of poor people. Large households will also lead to an increase in dependency on the few who work, which makes family systems more vulnerable.

The delivery of quality and efficient health care in any country is heavily dependent on the effective development, deployment, and utilization of well-trained health care professionals (Green, 1994). The training of health and allied health professionals calls for crucial planning and management of health care and related structures. In Liberia, like other sub-Saharan African countries, personnel salaries and the monies it takes to maintain them requires a significant proportion of most countries' health care budgets (Walt and Gildon, 1994). Given the fact that there are finite public resources in Liberia to be spent on health care and other competing needs, it will be important to address the efficient use of human resources during the postwar era. An integrated planning and management strategy will enable Liberia to meet the health needs of the population with the limited dollars generated by the government and international donors.

The protracted civil war in Liberia had devastating effects on the country's economic and social fabric, including the health care system. The war left nearly 90 percent of all health care facilities damaged or destroyed. But even before the civil war, minimal progress was being made by prewar governments to improve the already poor health outcomes of the people. From the perspective of the health planning and organization framework, the modern health care system in Liberia, when functioning well, could be regarded as a pyramid with three basic levels: primary, secondary, and tertiary. The primary level is the first level of entry for the patient into the system. This level is supported by lower-level trained health care professionals and includes the community health workers (CHWs) and traditional birth attendants (TBAs). Qualified health practitioners train these individuals. The secondary level includes a local clinic or health center staffed usually by a professional nurse, a physician assistant, or a trained nurse-midwife. This level includes basic services, routine checkups, and treatment of common illness. Cases not handled by the staff at the secondary level are then referred to the tertiary level (large health centers and hospitals, including teaching hospitals). At the tertiary level, patients receive care from doctors and specialists. In order for this system to work, a trained and dedicated workforce needs to be in place at each level. If one level is staffed inadequately, the continuum of care is interrupted and compromises the health outcome for the population.

The primary health care (PHC) framework is suggested as the appropriate approach to help revise the health care delivery system in postwar Liberia. With this in mind, policy makers and health care providers in Liberia and other sub-Saharan African countries emerging from civil conflicts will need a clearer understanding of the PHC framework if it is used as the basis for health reform. This PHC approach must also be used to develop a plan to meet the critical human resource needs that face the national health care system. The current organization of the Liberian health care delivery system and the infrastructure of the Liberian Ministry of Health and Social Welfare (MOH&SW) are inadequate to meet the needs of providing health care to all Liberians. The most important resources in any health care system are trained personnel with various health care functions. For many sub-Saharan African countries, these personnel include doctors, nurses, physician assistants, trained midwives, lab technicians, environmental sanitation workers, and CHWs. To perform effectively, the Liberian health care system needs professionally trained and strongly motivated personnel who are paid fairly for what they do. Unless harmonious conditions prevail, the quantity and quality of health services will be severely compromised. Inequity can make or break otherwise cost-effective approaches to health care.

The Impact of Liberian Civil War on Development of Health Human Resources

Scarcity of Trained Health Professionals and Need for Advanced Training

Liberia, like most sub-Saharan African countries, is committed in principle to the Alma-Alta declaration of 1978 to provide "health for all" by 2000. This goal, which would have been an elusive one even if the civil conflict had not broken out in Liberia, required the training of the health care workers who would staff the system at all three levels: primary, secondary, and tertiary. In a sub-Saharan African country such as Liberia, an optimal level of health care services is just a dream for most of the population; there are too few health professionals being trained in modern health care delivery to adequately provide health care services for the people. To understand the gravity of the situation, the United Nations Children's Fund (UNICEF) reported in 2004 that the ratio of trained doctors to the general population in Liberia is one doctor for every 10,000 people (UNICEF, 2004). The ratio of trained registered nurses to overall population, although higher than the availability ratio for doctors, is about one for every 5,000 people. The shortage of health care workers, especially nurses, is a global challenge for all countries, including developed ones. In a developed country like the United States, there are more doctors and nurses per population; however, some rural and urban areas do experience health care workers shortage. There are an insufficient number of proper training facilities for health care workers in Liberia. Existing training facilities lack the infrastructure and materials needed to train future health care workers adequately and properly. With a limited number of available training institutions, it is nearly impossible to train the large number of health and allied health care professionals needed in the new Liberia.

Medical and nursing education in Liberia is largely based on the Western model of health care delivery. In general, training programs based on a Western model are flawed in a number of ways: They are unsuited for responding adequately to local health conditions, they fail to take into account many of the traditional values and belief systems that impact health in local communities, there is inadequate cooperation between the various stakeholders because they are not invested in utilizing the Western model, and they contribute to a "brain drain" because the professionals trained obtain more transferable skills that enable them to emigrate. The loss of staff to opportunities outside Africa puts an extra burden on an already dysfunctional system. The mismatch of training programs to health needs of the local populations diminishes the ability of committed health care workers to effectively tackle many health problems in their work situations.

The government of Liberia will need to organize periodic short-term training programs with emphasis on achieving the goals of health for all. The postsecondary institutions of Liberia should be encouraged to develop in-service training programs in health care delivery with emphasis on how health care workers can address the local diseases and problems impacting the people of Liberia. Such long-term training should be made attractive to health care workers from both urban and rural areas. The lack of qualified, motivated doctors, nurses and other health care workers is not unique to Liberia. The current health worker crisis is also exacerbated by the HIV/AIDS epidemic, which reduces further the availability of trained health care workers due to staff deaths or increased family obligations.

Urban-Rural Imbalance of Health Care Personnel

In some sub-Saharan African countries, governments have made great efforts to reduce the imbalance in the recruitment and distribution of trained health care workers. For instance, in the African countries of Malawi and Tanzania, there is now a better urban-rural balance of health care workers compared to that of the previous decade (USAID, The Health Sector Human Resource Crisis in Africa, 2003). Urban and rural imbalance in the distribution of health care workers continues to persist in many sub-Saharan African countries, including Liberia. Typically, trained health care professionals prefer to live and work in urban settings because of several factors. When health care workers work in urban areas, they have access to more amenities than their rural colleagues: good housing, schooling for their children, electricity, and water. In addition, most tertiary care hospitals are located in urban an setting, which makes it inevitable that most health care workers are going to concentrate in urban areas because there are higher-level job opportunities, as well as supplemental employment opportunities, in their disciplines. Given these factors, it is sometimes difficult to encourage health professionals to work in rural settings.

In Liberia, like most sub-Saharan African countries, trained health professionals are employed by the government, which assigns them to hospitals, health centers and health posts. Mission hospitals and clinics and private-concession hospitals and clinics also serve as venues for employment of health care workers in Liberia. Trained health professionals include physicians, physician assistants, pharmacists, registered nurses, licensed practical nurses, certified midwives, nurse's aides, environmental health technicians, laboratory technicians, X-ray technicians, and other personnel involved in preventive or therapeutic care.

Prewar reports from the MOH&SW documented disproportions in urban-rural staffing, low utilization rates in tertiary hospitals and clinics, and limited outreach of community-based services. This pattern reflects a dysfunctional deployment of health professionals, which is partly a consequence of budget constraints. The situation also reflects the orientation of training health professionals in Liberia, which is tilted more toward a curative system rather than a solid PHC, community based-program. Also, the structure of the Liberian health care system does not provide the structures or incentives for motivating health care workers to work in rural areas.

The uneven distribution of health care workers can also be attributed to their training orientation. In Liberia, future physicians are trained at the sole medical school in the country, the A. M. Dogliotti College of Medicine, at the University of Liberia in Monrovia. The A. M. Dogliotti College of Medicine is oriented to the Western model of medicine. The only place that these doctors can practice the medicine they were trained to deliver is in tertiary care settings, which are in the cities. In a prewar study, reports indicated that approximately 75 percent of Liberia's physicians worked in urban settings, although only 25 percent of the total population lived there (United States Agency for International Development, *Liberian Health Sector Assessment*, 1988). The 25 percent of the physicians trained in the modalities of practicing using a Western biomedical approach must cope with the daily frustration of practicing well below their training threshold.

Although some physicians may elect to practice in rural areas of the country, their function as physicians is often of limited efficiency and value if rural facilities lack supporting health staff (nurses, laboratory technicians, etc.) and diagnostic equipment critical in making a diagnosis. For example, a Liberian doctor trained at A. M. Dogliotti College of Medicine, who received specialty training in cardiology abroad, can end up treating measles and diarrhea cases that could be treated successfully by primary care providers. When a heart case does surface, this cardiologist does not have the equipment, facilities, or human resources to provide the cardiac care he or she is capable of offering. Physicians trained in the Western model function better in an acute or hospital-based setting than a primary health care rural clinic where most of the care is centered on preventive procedures. Doctors trained in the Western model are mostly trained to treat disease rather than prevent illnesses. Liberia's medical college in the postwar era should shift its orientation away from the biomedical treatment model, which emphasizes an acute approach to health care delivery, and toward the PHC model, which embraces community health, public health, disease prevention, and the complex environmental and social context of illness and disease.

In the meantime, because of the flood of internally displaced people in Monrovia and other urban centers, a concentration of doctors in urban areas will be useful until the population shifts back to being rural-centered. Over time, as citizens begin to return to their respective homes and villages in the rural areas, it will also be important to determine how best to motivate and encourage physicians to serve in the rural areas as well. Based on the epidemiological picture of the current health situation in Liberia, the practice of relying more on physicians than other health care workers to deliver health care may not yield most appropriate professional mix to meet health objectives. In terms of communicable disease reduction, provision of prenatal care, environmental sanitation, or development of health services in rural counties, nurses, physician assistants, and community health care workers may be the most cost-effective professionals for delivering health care. The typical biomedical training of physicians does develop the holistic skills necessary to be effective in the social and cultural context of disease in rural communities. Nurses, trained midwives, physician assistants, and environmental health technicians may have a greater impact in working with the patients at the peripheral level before they are referred to physicians at the tertiary level.

The health personnel development process should be reexamined in the postwar era in order to enable it to have major impact on the reduction of primary causes of illness and death in Liberia. Retraining and redeployment of personnel should be geared toward health initiatives that reach the broad community. Historically, there has never been a strategic plan that provides a detailed process for retraining MOH&SW personnel. Introducing new types of health care workers with diverse skills will balance the professional mix and create the opportunity for spreading positive health outcomes across the general population. Many health care delivery systems around the world have considered or implemented the introduction of new groups of health care workers to fill the gaps in their systems or improve the cost-effectiveness of the workforce (Buchan and Dal Poz, 2002). Around the world, some countries have developed new roles that are country-specific and expanded the responsibilities of specialty roles. For instance in the United States, the role of advanced practice nurses (family nurse practitioners, clinical nurse specialists, and clinical nurse midwives) expanded in the 1990s. A review of the literature on the efficiency and cost-effectiveness of nurse practitioners reveals that with proper training, quality of care is improved, while organizational costs are reduced when the roles of advanced-practice nurses are expanded (Buchan and Dal Poz, 2002).

In Mozambique and other sub-Saharan African countries, there has also occurred the birth of new roles, such as surgery technicians, anesthesiology technicians, and clinical officers. Before the civil war in Liberia, the MOH&SW had a successful program in which physician assistants were trained and many of its graduates were dispersed to staff critical areas and/or clinics in the rural settings of Liberia that lacked physicians. The physician assistant program run by the MOH&SW should be revived, and a new cadre of health care workers should be trained to launch the health personnel development process.

To smooth the way for change, professional boundaries of the health professions need to be clarified and respected. Achieving optimal health for the population will be dependent on the degree to which the different health professions can work together to resolve conflicts about professional territory. In some instances, this may mean writing new laws and policies to govern their practices and roles. Many questions must be answered initially. Are workers actually being trained to assume new roles, or are the roles of the existing staff being expanded? The process of establishing a better health professional mix will vary from one African country to another. It will be based on the level of sophistication of their health care systems, cultural factors, and professional factors, and the ability of all health professions to work together as a team.

Prior to the civil war, the Liberian health care system had a sizable health workforce, but it was thwarted in meeting the stated official goals of the MOH&SW by a poor deployment pattern. This pattern was exaggerated by the economic crises of the 1980s, and, more recently, the civil war. The dismal outlook for Liberians' health is a consequence of limited human resource planning to carry out equitable deployment and improved health service utilization. The development of comprehensive strategic planning is essential in the postwar era.

Poor Coordination of the Centralized Ministry of Health and Social Welfare Personnel Management Systems

In many sub-Saharan African countries, the health care system is highly centralized, leading to poor coordination and weak management of existing health care services outside the capital city. As in other sub-Saharan African countries, the coordination and monitoring of Liberian health care workers have been inadequate. For instance, recognition of the contributions that employees make to the system has been limited. Also, disciplining substandard and unethical employees has been ineffective because the system is corrupt. For example, if the village chief complains about the head nurse coming to work late or drunk, it could take up to several months by the MOH&SW central office to investigate this individual or impose some punishment against that person. In the end, no sanctions may be imposed. In many instances, an employee who faces disciplinary actions is usually just assigned to another health post. This obviously sends the wrong signal to the rest of the employees. Instead of tediously working through the centralized structure, it would be more efficient for such an employee to be disciplined by his or her immediate supervisor, who is in a better position to conduct performance evaluations.

The centralized structure of the MOH&SW also poses inherent difficulties for health care personnel in the periphery to communicate with the central authorities in the city. Paramount to inefficiency are the delays in communication and decision making processes. In many rural clinics, there is no electricity and, therefore, telephones, fax machines, two-way radios, or computers are not available. New employees assigned to rural communities often do not have a clear understanding of what their assignments are or how much they will be compensated. Because the MOH&SW does not issue the payroll checks itself, it takes months for the personnel office to forward new employee names to the Ministry of Finance (MOF) and then for the MOF to include the new employee on the payroll. A new employee must wait for about four to six months before receiving his or her first check.

Compounding the problems of centralization are the endemic corruption, tribalism, nepotism, and favoritism in the Liberian political system. The duties of recruitment, assignment, and personnel management for health care personnel are therefore influenced by politics. While most of the health care professionals working for the MOH&SW are able and capable, there are some workers that obtained their positions because of their tribal affiliation, county of origin, or some internal connection. It is customary for politicians to influence the appointments of employees, including position and place of assignment. For instance, a physician assistant assigned to a rural clinic in Liberia may have a politician of influence protecting him or her from being disciplined, even if she or he is guilty of an offense that warrants punishment. This weakens the legitimacy of direct supervisors and undermines their authority. Favoritism also plays a role in who is selected to go abroad for advanced training or in-service programs.

Many health care professionals in sub-Saharan African settings, including Liberia, lack supervision, do not understand their role as health care professionals, and are unsure of expectations about their performance. Many nurses or physician assistants are recruited and assigned to a rural health post but rarely undergo orientation before their departure for their assignments. The role of a supervisor in the African context may have different meanings to different people. While some supervisors may not have the knowledge and training to understand personnel management processes and how to improve organizational performances, in many government agencies, supervisors may be regarded by employees as individuals out to control them and therefore will be viewed at with suspicion. Because written performance evaluations are not necessarily required for promotion in many of these settings, a supervisor may not bother to do a performance appraisal of his or her employees. Personnel appraisal systems in many sub-Saharan African countries tend not to be based on agreed-upon goals but, rather, are based on characteristics over which the employee may have little control, such as tribal affiliation, connection with public officials, or the means to bribe.

In the health care delivery system in sub-Saharan African countries, including Liberia, management information systems are very weak. There is limited information or data on personnel characteristics: availability of health care workers, numbers of employees in specific categories (e.g., physicians, nurses, physician assistants, etc.), and geographic location of employment. While some of this information could be obtained from payroll databases, in many instances, payroll spreadsheets are plagued with names of individuals who cannot be accounted for but are still being paid. These people have never worked for the MOH&SW or were employed at some time and have since then been relieved of their positions. Somebody is pocketing their paychecks. It may be possible to obtain complete information at the county level; however, these data are not integrated into the central MOH&SW personnel database. Therefore, making policies relying solely on this information carries with it some limitation.

Low Salary Scales, Lack of Motivation, and Poor Morale among Health Care Workers

The salaries of health care workers in sub-Saharan Africa have not caught up yet with the inflation experienced by that part of the continent. Health care professionals are paid less compared with workers in other professions, such as engineering and accounting. With the exception of a few countries such as Nigeria, South Africa and Botswana, salaries for health care professionals in other sub-Saharan African countries are dismal. Many of these countries are ill equipped economically to increase employees' salaries commensurate with those in the private sector. As a result, many government employees are less motivated than those employed in the private sector so, as can be expected; many health centers suffer from poor staff morale. Before the Liberian civil war, and even today, a nurse in the country can expect to earn about 40 percent to 50 percent more when she or he elects to work in the private sector. This problem, in fact, was exacerbated during the civil war period. Now that the war is over, employment in the health care sector is mostly provided by nongovernmental organizations (NGOs), private organizations, and United Nations (UN) agencies. These organizations pay employees well and some pay in U.S. dollars, which have a higher market exchange rate. As the Liberian MOH&SW begins to staff its health centers with government health care workers and the role of NGOs in the provision of health care recedes, the salary expectations of health care workers (raised by the NGOs) will have to be matched. As the Liberian government faces budgetary constraints and struggles to rebuild its broken health care system, it will have to grapple with the differences in salary levels between the public and private sectors.

One challenge will center on what to do in order to attract well-trained health care professionals in the public sector, even if government salaries are not comparable with those paid by the NGOs. Little has been done to retain government health care professionals (e.g., pharmacists) who are in greater demand in the private sector. Besides the issue of salaries being at a very low level, government employees' salaries are usually not paid in a timely manner. In prewar days, it was common for health care professionals to face salary arrears of up to six months. The problem of delays in salaries is endemic in Liberia and remains a challenge for postwar health administrators. Employees' disappointment with the MOH&SW not coming through with their meager salaries on time can have negative impacts on the morale of staffers, especially among those individuals who have large families. Ways must be developed to improve the payment processes for employees, especially those working in outlying health care facilities.

In the postwar era, as the Liberian government embarks on reforming the health care delivery system, health professionals must not be ignored. Changes should include paying workers salaries that are commensurate with their training and comparable to those in the private sector; providing promotion incentives for workers to serve in health care deprived remote areas; and improving working conditions through the provision of drugs and medical supplies, as well as medical equipment. Budgets must also be allocated for supervisory activities—especially in the rural health posts of the country. This reform process will include providing money for travel allowances, provision of vehicles, and improvement in communication services.

One of the proposals suggested for the postwar reorganization is to develop a cadre of health care workers who are purposely trained to meet the health care needs of local populations, especially at the primary care level. Before the civil war, the Liberian MOH&SW had an operational network of community health care workers. These individuals played a special role in providing health care to the people of Liberia. For instance, they were instrumental in providing information on family planning, diarrhea prevention, and other local health conditions. Community health workers have been used in various capacities in sub-Saharan Africa for the last several decades with varying success. The limitation of utilizing this category of health care worker is that training, often provided in isolation by the government or an international organization, fails to integrate these workers into the overall health care delivery system. They are rarely paid a regular salary, as compared with other categories of health care workers, and in some cases, they may be provided only a minimal incentive for the work they do. Although the community health workers can be regarded as critical to the overall health care delivery system in many sub-Saharan African countries, their roles and efforts are often unrecognized and undervalued.

Without true compensation, this cadre of workers may lack the motivation to spend more time on health promotion activities that are critical at the peripheral levels of the health care delivery system. As Liberia and other wartorn African countries emerge from civil strife, it will be an opportune time for their governments to examine seriously how community health workers could be trained and effectively integrated into the overall health care delivery system.

Lack of compensation is a human resource crisis that leads to unethical behaviors on the part of health care professionals in order to support the family members that depend on them. These health care professionals are absent from work in order to engage in income-supplementing activities. While complete data may not be available on absenteeism at most health centers in sub-Saharan Africa, McPake, Asiimwe, Mwesigye, et al., (1999), in one study in Uganda, found that many workers spent time engaged in informal activities to generate income that would supplement their salaries when they were expected to be at health posts. In the extreme, this could mean stealing drugs and supplies to sell on the black market.

Patterns of "Brain Drain" among Health Care Workers

Developing countries suffer from the emigration of highly educated and skilled workers to developed countries. Losing skilled professionals to more favorable geographic, economic, or professional environments, i.e. "brain drain," leads to depletion of the intellectual and technical personnel in underdeveloped countries. One reason why African health workers are leaving their countries is because they refuse to practice in dysfunctional health systems with unsafe conditions. They cannot tolerate working in a setting where they are unable to meet the needs of their patients and where their salaries keep them from meeting their own needs.

Although not a new concept, brain drain is a complex phenomenon that takes on many forms. Conceptual categories include (1) intra country brain drain, (2) public sector-private sector brain drain, (3) inter country brain drain, and (4) unstable environments leading to brain drain. The popular notion of brain drain is an international problem, with people wanting to travel abroad to better their lives economically. In developing countries, intracountry brain drain is equally damaging to national human resource development.

Intra Country Brain Drain

In sub-Saharan Africa, brain drain in the health care sector is manifested in the rural-to-urban migration of skilled health care workers. Improving salary scales may help retain health care workers in rural areas. However, some health care workers who want to satisfy their career objectives, not just their financial objectives, may be tempted to move to urban areas after they experience the shortcomings of their rural health care assignments. The failure of countries emerging from civil conflict to retain qualified health care workers in rural health posts should not be blamed entirely on doctors and nurses who are trying to practice their skills to the highest degree. Governments fuel the rural-urban migration of health care professionals by allowing or failing to mitigate the lack of socioeconomic development in rural areas in comparison to that in urban settings.

Health care professionals opting to stay in the cities to work obviously have more professional advantages compared to their rural counterparts. They increase their market value by moonlighting at another job or teaching at a community school; they have access to professional education and medical technology that their rural counterparts can only dream of; there are better schools for their children to attend; and there is better housing and sanitation as well as safe drinking water. Sub-Saharan African governments must employ a variety of strategies to retain professional health care staffers in rural areas. Some of these strategies may include establishing training institutions in rural settings, where future doctors and nurses can do their internships and clinical projects in a rural setting; making rural field clinical experiences mandatory; and recruiting more rural students for urban schools with the hope that they will be motivated to return to their rural communities. A major challenge in postwar African countries, including Liberia, is that the next generation of health care professionals, who grew up in refugee camps and peri urban slums, have no recent experience with rural life. Training them to return to their villages will be challenging.

Public Sector-Private Sector Brain Drain

This process involves highly skilled health care professionals leaving government agencies or other public sector employment. In this process, many of the best nurses and doctors end up in private practice or working for nongovernmental agencies. What first starts as volunteer work or as a part-time job on the weekends to supplement ones salary can quickly become an avenue for professional prestige and career enhancement. Central governments in many sub-Saharan African countries are still the major employers of health care professionals, although they are losing their highest skilled employees and administrators, weakening government-run health care facilities. Some great health care professionals still choose to remain in the public sector to serve their people. But the health of a country should not rely on the altruistic nature of a few; it should depend on sound human resource development.

Over the past two decades, there has been a proliferation of NGOs in Africa playing a role in the provision of health care. While some NGOs train their own health care professionals locally, many NGOs recruit from the already limited pool of skilled health care professionals trained by national governments. As a result, countries in sub-Saharan Africa are beginning to see an exodus of skilled health care professionals from the governmental sectors to work for NGOs. This poaching of trained local health care professionals creates a void in the governmental health care delivery system. Many of these NGOs pay their local employees more than the government pays government health care professionals with similar qualifications. Therefore, in an effort to achieve better quality of life, many health care professionals who once worked in the government sector seek employment in the private sector. In most war-torn countries, NGOs are the fulcrum for the health care system. After war, making the government the fulcrum of the health care system again is a hard transition.

Increasing the salary of the health care workers in the public sector to be commensurate with their private-sector colleagues is a way to shift the balance. Just as incentives are given to health care professionals who elect to work in rural areas, governments may also want to provide some incentives to retain skilled health care workers (especially middle-level managers) in public service. Other incentives to stem the brain drain would be limiting the hours that health care professionals can moonlight or engage in income-generating activities outside their main jobs. In developed countries like the United States, such regulation is referred to as "conflict of interest policy." Many managers and individuals in full-time professional jobs are asked to report any outside income above $10,000 that they earn depending on the guidelines of the primary employer. Lastly, the government or public sector needs to increase partnerships with the many NGOs in African countries to collaborate in implementing health projects and share funding.

Inter Country Brain Drain

Inter country brain drain is not just the loss of skilled health care workers to developed countries; it is also the loss of trained health care workers to other sub-Saharan African countries. This issue has become a very contentious one in today's global economy, because health care skills (e.g., medical or nursing skills) are a valuable commodity that can be transferred successfully to another African environment, creating a void in the emigrant's home culture. In the postwar era of war-torn African countries, inter country brain drain within Africa is an issue for concern and must be addressed because pulling human resources from one country to another to fill a void destabilizes the health care system of all of Africa in the long run. Epidemic outbreaks know no boundaries, and any lack of health care personnel in a given country to contain a disease outbreak will eventually affect other countries as people travel, carrying the disease. In the West African country of Nigeria, the stance by Kano State indigenous leaders against WHO campaign to immunize for polio led to a polio outbreak that spread to the neighboring countries of Benin and Togo. Pressures from the international health community persuaded chiefs and other local leaders to eventually endorse the campaign, but not before many children were afflicted with polio in Nigeria and surrounding countries.

In many African countries, the emigration of health care workers has adversely affected the supply of trained individuals able to provide health care to their people. For instance, in the southern and eastern regions of

Africa, health care workers from poorer countries, such as Kenya, Malawi, and Zimbabwe, migrate to South Africa and Botswana in search of better jobs. While health care workers from poorer African countries are migrating to South Africa, Botswana, or Nigeria, health care workers from these countries are also emigrating abroad, to the developed countries of Europe and North America. Unlike those who engage in inter-African migration, in which health care workers move from one country to another yet still make a contribution to the improvement of health on the African continent, African health care workers who emigrate to Western countries have less opportunity to be involved directly in improving health care in Africa itself.

Two critical health professions where the impact of brain drain is felt most are in the disciplines of medicine and nursing. In some African countries (e.g., Swaziland), there may not be a medical college. African countries with medical schools, including South Africa, meanwhile reportedly lose more home grown physician graduates than they are able to replace from abroad. In a recent study, Physicians for Human Rights, a nonprofit organization based in Cambridge, Massachusetts, reported that African health care workers are leaving their countries because they are discouraged and frustrated from practicing in an underfunded and dysfunctional health care system. They burn out from practicing in unsafe conditions where they cannot begin to meet the needs of their patients and where their salaries cannot meet their own needs (Physicians for Human Rights, July 2004). More studies are needed to understand the depth of the health care worker brain drain phenomenon as well as to determine potential solutions to resolve both intra country and inter country brain drains.

How should inter country brain drain be resolved? It must be recognized that for some African health care workers, it is only a dream to receive advanced health care training in a developed country. When the opportunity to train abroad presents itself, it is too tempting to resist. Training abroad increases a health professional's skills and market value in the public and private sectors and enables that person to emigrate abroad and find gainful employment. For several decades, international agencies such as the United States Agency for International Development (USAID), the World Bank, and WHO have recognized the problem, but many trainees may not want to return to their home countries after advanced training abroad. These agencies are committed to human resource development in health care in sub-Saharan Africa. These agencies recruit the best health care workers in a developing country who have the potential to contribute to the health care system. They invest in their training and education abroad with the expectation that this new cadre of advanced trained health care workers will return to their respective home countries and make enormous contributions to the health care system there. But if these professionals do not return, the international agencies are more reluctant to invest in the next wave of trainees. Departing trainees leave a vacuum in their home countries and short-circuit the plans for training new local health care workers upon their return. The intention was for this investment in education to have far-reaching effects. In an effort to reduce this brain drain, international agencies recommend ways to discourage people from staying in the country of their advanced training. Individuals sent abroad for advanced training should be required to return home to serve their country for a specified time. If they do not return, they should be required to pay back the monies spent on them during the training process.

In 2004, Physicians for Human Rights released a report entitled, "An Action Plan to Prevent Brain Drain: Building Equitable Health Systems in Africa," that addresses this problem and offers a series of recommendations on the brain drain issue while meeting health care needs of the people in Africa. The areas emphasized in this report are improvements in African countries' health infrastructures, implementation of higher salaries and benefits for health workers, increased investment in local institutions of higher learning, reduced recruitment by wealthy nation, and focus on capacity building for human resources management in individual countries.

Unstable Environment Leading to Brain Drain

Health care professionals are usually regarded as neutral in many civil crises. In the war-torn countries of Liberia and Sierra Leone, members of both government and rebel factions all needed health care. Health care workers must care for everyone, regardless of the fact that some of their own family members or tribal groups may have been harassed, abused, and in some instances even killed by warring factions. Health care professionals can act out of altruism and provide health care to all parties involved in the conflict. Because health care workers have high credibility, an altruistic approach can set the tone for peace. Many organizations, notably Médecins Sans Frontières (MSF) or Doctors Without

Borders, have been highly visible because they work without ethnic prejudice in many areas torn by conflict by providing health care to all people. It is because of the presence of doctors and nurses working for such
notable organizations such as MSF that true suffering of local populations have often been brought to light before the world.

The irony is that even though health care professionals are regarded
as credible individuals during warfare, they are still at risk for being
abused and in some instances killed in many conflict zones. In conflicts
throughout Africa, (including the ones in Liberia and Sierra Leone),
health care professionals were targeted for several reasons: (1) They
were thought to be reporting human rights abuses to the international
community, (2) they were thought to have material goods that could be
sold on the black market; and (3) they were thought to have vehicles the
rebels could steal for increased mobility.

In the Liberian situation, there have been reports of nurses and doctors being shot in hospital settings while caring for individuals from another rebel group. This breakdown in law and order creates an opportunity for rebels to loot the hospitals. Local health professionals were especially vulnerable compared to their international colleagues practicing at
these same health facilities because of their tribal affiliations or previous
relationships with the rebel groups. Because many trained Liberian
health care workers fled to neighboring African countries and to the
West, the postwar era will require the development of more trained
health care professionals to replace the ones that may be reluctant to return to their homeland and abandon the life they have created for themselves in exile.

Impact of the HIV Epidemic on the Health Care Delivery System, the Health Care Workforce, and the Development of New Health Care Professionals

In the HIV/AIDS literature on sub-Saharan Africa, there are increasing references to the impact of the disease on the general population, the
health care delivery systems, and the depletion of scarce resources for
health care delivery (Minnaar, 2005; Marchal, et al., 2005). For instance,
there are documented reports of increased pressure on hospitals and other
health care centers to divert resources from the treatment and prevention
of other conditions to treatment for those afflicted with HIV/AIDS. The

rapidly increasing number of HIV-infected patients also threatens the normal functioning of many health care facilities. Before the epidemic, sub-Saharan African governments were already straining to provide comprehensive health care to their populations. The high rate of HIV infection is now straining these health care systems to the breaking point.

There are increasing concerns regarding the impact of HIV/AIDS on the health care workforce in sub-Saharan Africa. If more doctors and nurses are affected by HIV, what does this mean for many of the health care systems that already lack the skilled workforce needed to care for the general population? Ncayiyana, in a short article, "Doctors and nurses with HIV and AIDS in sub-Saharan Africa," (2004) stressed that the HIV/AIDS epidemic will have an adverse effect on the health care delivery system in countries that already have low health care workforce. Many of these countries are already experiencing the loss of skilled health care staffers due to absenteeism, low staff morale, and burnout from the burden of increased patient workload. Ncayiyana suggests that the impact is already being felt in the discipline of nursing, where many nurses are contracting HIV infection also.

In war-torn African countries, the impact of HIV/AIDS on the health care system and the health care workforce is exacerbated. The fact that many skilled workers fled the country during wartime places added demands for knowledge and skills to manage the HIV/AIDS epidemic, both at the micro and macro levels. During wartime, even health care workers who remained did not have the opportunity to keep their skills updated in the area of HIV/AIDS. Specific skills are needed to be proficient in working with individuals infected with HIV: counseling, management of comorbidities, use of antiretroviral therapy, and home-based care. MOH&SW officials in the new Liberia will have to allocate some resources into these areas.

Because AIDS is a disease that is fatal, it will require nurses to have training and expertise in the care of terminally ill clients. Care for individuals in their last days can be emotionally draining for most health care workers. Additionally, doctors and nurses live in communities where relatives and friends may also be infected with HIV, which compounds their professional burden of caring. They may have to provide home care or attend the funerals of relatives and friends who have died from AIDS. All this can lead to absenteeism and burnout. With high prevalence rates and more HIV patients being admitted to hospitals, there is an increasing chance for health care professionals to contract the infection from their

patients through needle sticks or bodily fluids. If health care professionals risk becoming infected with a deadly virus from their patients, what
are the prospects for recruiting young people to fill the gap involving
health care professionals? Will young people begin to view nursing and
other health care professions as too risky? Given the low ratio of nurses
or doctors to overall population, the HIV epidemic is likely to magnify
the inadequacies of health personnel development in sub-Saharan African countries.

Understanding the multiple factors that tend to limit the optimal performance of the health care workforce, the development of health care
professionals should be paramount in war-torn countries such as Liberia.
There is the need to develop a comprehensive and coordinated approach
to the development of human resources in the health care sector of all
sub-Saharan African countries and, most urgently, in those emerging
from civil war. The policies must include the precautions needed to keep
health care workers from contracting HIV from their clients and the treatment of health care workers already infected with HIV. This process will
help increase health care workers' productivity level while reducing the
attrition rates among skilled health care professionals.

Sub-Saharan Africa bears the brunt of the HIV pandemic. Eighty-
five percent of people living with HIV/AIDS live in sub-Saharan Africa.
. In war-impacted African countries, research suggests that there is a
higher degree of sexual violence among individuals fleeing conflicts and
"survival sexual" activities there than in stable environments. For the
countries of Rwanda, Sierra Leone, and Liberia, there are numerous documented and anecdotal reports of rape during their civil wars. The chaos
of war also damaged the social support systems and formal health infrastructures. Many families and communities were uprooted, causing the
population to be demoralized. While the actual fighting among rebel factions may have ended in these African countries, there still is a breakdown of law and order. Institutional breakdowns make a population more
vulnerable to the multiple risk factors of HIV/AIDS and less capable of
mitigating the adverse consequences to the community.

How individuals, families, and countries emerging from civil conflict
will address the HIV/AIDS epidemic is beyond comprehension at this
time. HIV/AIDS is not just a virus; it is a multifaceted condition that is
woven into the social, economic, and cultural aspects of society. In Africa's ancient civilizations, cultural mores have been carefully handed
down and embraced for countless generations. But that cultural under-

standing may not be adequate to make the abrupt, dramatic cultural changes that are needed to halt the epidemic.

The extent to which each country can develop and implement effective HIV prevention and care programs to reduce the impact on its population is yet to be known. It is clear, however, that in the postwar era, efforts must be geared toward effective leadership, capacity building, and remobilization of the entire population. Caring for those afflicted by the disease, caring for the orphans, and reducing the enormous stigma that accompanies the disease in many African cultures is paramount.

Studying the impact of the HIV epidemic on the general population, researchers point out that no sectors of the population have been spared. Two sectors that the disease has particularly affected are the educational sector and human resource development sector. The extent to which the HIV/AIDS epidemic has affected the educational and workforce development processes in war-torn countries like Liberia is not yet fully measured. Systematic research in this area is relatively absent or limited in war-torn countries. The postwar era in Liberia will be an opportune time to launch activities that will lead to the understanding of the impact of the HIV epidemic on the health care workforce and on the development of human resources. Recognizing the urgency of this problem will lead to the establishment of programs that will create the kind of change that will reverse the negative impact of the disease.

The direct impact of the HIV epidemic on the educational sector of war-torn sub-Saharan African countries is not known. Some studies suggest that the sero-prevalence positive rate of HIV infection among employees in the educational sector in sub-Saharan Africa may be just as high as that for the general adult population (Cohen, 2002). Cohen also reports that countries with high prevalence rates of HIV infection, such as Botswana and Zimbabwe, experience an enormous burden of sickness rates and deaths. Human capital is declining. High morbidity and mortality rates resulting from HIV/AIDS have been found among teachers in sub-Saharan countries, including Malawi, Uganda, Botswana, Kenya, Zambia, and Zimbabwe. The loss of experienced teachers in these countries will lead to prolonged dependence on unqualified people filling in for teachers and increase the demands for new and qualified individuals to fill the gap.

Administrators at all levels of the educational system—national, county, and district, in both private and public sectors—in sub-Saharan Africa are also contracting the disease. The educational infrastructure is crumbling from the loss of such key personnel. The viability of particular institutions, including the precious few institutions of higher learning, is dependent on replacing the personnel lost from HIV/AIDS. In Liberia, as in most sub-Saharan African countries, government-sponsored training programs are the primary channel for producing professionals in health care and other fields. If the staff members of government-sponsored training programs also contract HIV/AIDS, the output of professionals will be drastically reduced, compounding the replacement dilemma.

With many highly skilled Liberians residing abroad because of the civil war in their homeland, the government already faces a shortage of highly skilled professionals in specific areas critical for reviving the economy and launching economic development programs. These include a range of professional areas such as education, health care, law and order, environmental health, telecommunications, and engineering. The lack of well-trained individuals to fill critical positions in the government ministries will make it difficult to develop effective strategic planning that can pull the country out of crisis in the postwar era.

Educational programs provided at all levels (primary through postbaccalaureate) will be crucial in the development of human resources in the long term. Educational programs will be seen as pivotal in transforming child soldiers, empowering women and young girls, and improving both the formal and informal economic sector of the new Liberia. Even before Liberia's civil war, there were disparities in education among various segments of the population, leading to hopelessness and despair. A hopeful sign, however, is that many of the young people who have survived the years of civil war see education as a way out of poverty. A goal, therefore, of any government that comes to power in Liberia will be to raise the skill and educational levels of the general population. Reaching this goal will eventually lead to a rise in the living standard of the country. Direct investment in the educational sector will be an important strategy for the Liberian government to embrace in the postwar era.

Improvement in the educational sector can be seen as an essential avenue for the reduction of the spread of HIV infection in the general population. The educational sector can be used as a forum for understanding the multiple and complex web of factors that puts individuals and communities at risk for contracting HIV infection. In many sub-Saharan African countries, one of the major risk factors that put people at risk for contracting the infection is low literacy among the population. Low literacy levels impede access to accurate information relating to

HIV prevention. Other factors such as the lack of employment opportunities, low levels of formal education, and lack of technical skills to obtain jobs, also put many young people at risk. When youths feel resigned to a future without promise, they may carelessly engage in risky activities that lead to the contracting of HIV infection and other sexually transmitted diseases.

There is unanimous agreement among public health officials in both developed and developing countries that education and health are interrelated. Investment in education will lead to a better-educated population and, in the long-term, assist individuals to become more proactive regarding their own health and that of their communities. As over half of the new cases of HIV infection are found among young people, educating this segment of the population will hopefully lead to reduction in the number of new cases seen in sub-Saharan African countries. Among the general population, improvement in education will mean people will have a greater understanding of the health factors, as well as the environmental factors, that negatively or positively affect their health status. With improvement in education, people will also learn more about basic health issues, better hygiene habits, good nutrition, prevention of common ailments, and ways to access health care services.

It will be important in the postwar era to collect systematic data on the impact of the HIV/AIDS epidemic on the educational sector and human resource development. Health care officials in the countries have serious gaps in their understanding of what is happening in their respective countries involved and regionally across Africa. Some questions data could answer are: How many staff absences result from being sick with HIV infection? Which levels of the educational sector (primary, secondary and postbaccalaureate) are most affect? Do school absences differ among position, e.g., teachers, administrative staff, or school secretaries?

The HIV epidemic and its impact on the development of human capital open up another opportunity for collaboration between the Liberian Ministry of Education (MOE) and the MOH&SW. With all government sectors facing budget constraints, it will be important to help the MOE and MOH&SW understand the gravity of the situation and develop appropriate interventions and policies to help ameliorate the impact of the HIV epidemic on the educational sector.

Opportunities and Challenges: Mitigating the Health Care Human Resources Crises in Postwar Liberia

Promotion of Universal Primary Education (UPE)

Over the last two decades, efforts have been stepped up to make at least primary education universally accessible to all individuals. Despite the efforts from sub-Saharan African governments and NGOs, such as the United Nations Educational, Scientific, and Cultural Organization (UNESCO), universal primary education for young people is still an elusive goal, especially for young girls in sub-Saharan Africa. At the World Education Forum in Dakar, Senegal, in April 2000, reaffirmation was made of the benefits for a broad and comprehensive view of basic education and its critical role in empowering people and transforming societies. The forum's core messages were universal access to learning; focus on equity; emphasis on learning outcomes; broadening the means and the scope of basic education; enhancing the environment for learning; and strengthening partnerships. Many sub-Saharan African countries, including Uganda, Kenya, and Tanzania, have all embraced the concept of UPE and are now beginning to see some positive impact on the literacy levels of their populations.

When experts think about human resource development, the suggestion is made to invest in education and health. The assumption here is that improvement in these two sectors will lay the foundation for other aspects of development. Health and education have been on the bottom of the list of priorities for sub-Saharan African governments. If a country invests in the population's education and health, it is investing in the human capital critical for sustaining economic growth of a country. If individuals are healthy and experience improved standards of living, society as a whole can benefit.

In many of its programs in sub-Saharan Africa, the World Bank has invested in primary education in particular in an effort to boost country's economy. In one of the World Bank's studies, it is noted that the single most important factor in putting developing countries back on the path to sustained economic growth is UPE. Education creates opportunities for people to make better use of technology and to seek and use information while adapting to changes within their environments. In Côte d'Ivoire, research has shown that an extra year of schooling enhanced earnings by

12 percent; in Ghana, an extra year of schooling increased the farmers' output by 5 percent.

Investment in education complements investment in other sectors. For instance, an improvement in the development of human resources in sub-Saharan African countries through the provision of basic education, health care, and nutrition directly improves the quality of life and lessens the vulnerability of populations in the society. Higher education, whether vocational or college, even more dramatically improves a country's productivity levels and decreases the population's dependency level on the government for handouts. UPE is the critical foundation for preparing a cadre of young people to be ready for higher education. In the new Liberia, therefore, it will be prudent to invest in early childhood programs. Investments in early childhood programs enhance the effectiveness of primary and secondary education and will eventually improve health outcomes and income levels. Provision of better health care and nutritional programs also reduces infant death rates, which are very high in sub-Saharan African countries.

Education is also noted as having great impact on women's health, their productivity, and their income levels. World Bank reports indicate that when women are literate, the yields in their gardens can improve by as 15 percent. Women with higher levels of literacy are better able to care for themselves and their families. With education, women can limit the number of children they bear, thereby preserving their own health and the health of their babies. Women who are educated can also become skilled workers and take their rightful place among their male counterparts in the workforce.

In the postwar era of war-torn countries such as Liberia, it will be important for government officials to invest heavily in the area of primary education. While many war- torn countries will face financial and institutional constraints, these countries must begin to ask themselves what their priorities for human resources should be. As in the prewar era, the Liberian government will continue to play the most important role in improving human resource development in the country. However, results will depend on how well resources are used, how successfully programs link to other government sectors, and how sustained is the will of those in leadership to serve the people well. Once an achievement has been made in the area of UPE, the Liberian government should begin to shift its emphasis toward secondary education. Efforts should be made to do this in a cost-effective manner.

Development and Launching of Health Training
Programs for Ex-Combatants

The impact of the civil war on Liberian society has been devastating. Most infrastructures were destroyed, and the formal economy nearly collapsed. Now that the war is over, efforts are being directed toward the promotion of peace and the reintegration of ex-combatants into Liberian society. Reintegrating these individuals into civil society is critical for post-conflict peace building, reviving the country's economy, and sustaining development projects.

If properly planned and managed, the demobilization of former fighters is invaluable in rebuilding societies that are emerging from civil war. The process of demobilization can also be viewed in some instances as a time to launch new development initiatives. However, if the process fails to provide for the social integration of former rebels into society, it poses a potential threat to society through increased political and social instability. For instance, if the ex-fighters in Liberia and other war-torn countries cannot find work to do, the country runs the risk of falling back into chaos. For many young people, the only job skills they have acquired over the years of civil conflicts involve the use of weapons. While the UN has successfully disarmed thousands of young people in Liberia, there are still reports of violent crimes and armed robberies perpetrated by young people. This generation's comfort level with weapons puts the general population at risk. Insurrection, although a remote possibility in a country so thoroughly depleted by civil war, is still a possibility if there continues to be thousands of jobless youths, abandoned and roaming the streets.

The reality is that at the micro level, many of the young people who fought on the sides of various warring factions will face problems in making the transition from rebel life to civilian life. They may not have the skills or experience needed for gainful employment. During the war, many of the warring factions made empty promises to the child soldiers that once they won the war, they would give those youths positions in the national government. The problem is that no one faction won the war, and the peace accords call for all factions to work together. Also, in many rebel groups, military leaders operated in a hierarchical manner and created little room for the creative and lateral thinking required in many sectors of civilian life.

In war-impacted African countries like Liberia and Sierra Leone, former combatants are competing with other citizens for scarce jobs. Former rebels are at a distinct disadvantage. Local industries are suspicious about them and their behavior, especially those who have had a history of engaging in heinous crimes such as decapitation of bodies and systematic rape. It is important in the postwar era that after demobilization, a strong human resource development effort be undertaken to facilitate retraining and skills acquisition for those ex-rebels who are being reintegrated. This training process will help increase their chances of finding employment in the civilian sector. Long-lasting solutions to the Liberian crisis will have to focus on the many prewar factors that led to the civil war including poverty, lack of educational opportunities, and economic inequities among various segments of the population.

One recommendation is to focus on the training of ex-combatants as a new cadre of health care workers given the shortage of health care workers, especially at the lower end of the Liberian health care system. Rebuilding the basic rural education and vocational education sectors is a clear priority. But advocacy for basic education and vocational training must also come with respect for the contribution that young people in Liberia can make in this postwar era. Their roles must also be viewed as relevant to the building of the new Liberia. Ex-combatants can be trained as community health care workers and dispersed across the nation, especially in rural areas. They can provide health education to families on basic ailments that affect their local communities. They can be trained in the areas of HIV/AIDS prevention; home-based care for those afflicted with HIV/AIDS, and prevention of communicable and tropical diseases endemic at participants' assigned posts. This new cadre of workers should be compensated, and their work should be endorsed or recognized by MOH&SW officials. This recommendation is in line with the PHC approach of empowerment as a healing force in society.

Trained ex-combatants could be one of the country's greatest assets in rebuilding a strong national health care delivery system. The process would begin by recruiting a pool of highly motivated men and women who want to become health care workers. The MOH&SW should streamline and standardize the training modules for this new group of health care workers for the sake of efficiency, career opportunities, and job satisfaction. This type of training can be done at any one of the institutions of higher learning in Liberia. In order not to compete with other health programs, it may take special funding from international agencies such as the USAID and the World Bank. The program for training ex-combatants should be designed in a spiral framework so that those ex-combatants who are motivated and want to return to or advance to college can have the opportunity to do so in the future.

Building Partnerships and Expanding Collaboration among Stakeholders for Human Resources Development

Numerous stakeholders and interests become apparent when one reviews the many facets of human resource development. In the new Liberia, there is an urgent need to ensure the relevance of education and training of health professionals to the health needs of the population served. There is also the need to forge new partnerships between the health and education sectors in countries emerging from civil conflicts. Health care professionals, who were trained in the prewar era, will need continuing professional development.

In the prewar era in Liberia and most sub-Saharan African countries, health care sector reform programs that countries undertook had inconsistent results in addressing the complex issues affecting health care workforce development. Paramount among the findings is the fact that health care professionals in most African countries are precluded from or have had little influence in the formulation of health care policies. Additionally, the education and training of health care workers in many of these settings have rarely considered health care sector reforms. The issues of continuing education, including programs to motivate and retain skilled staff, are usually not addressed during the development and implementation phases of programs. Any actions taken in countries like Liberia in reforming the health care sector, the education and training of health care workers, and the deployment and retention of such workers, have occurred largely independently of each other. In this realm, there is an insufficient appreciation of the importance of building partnerships between the education sector and the health care sector in many sub-Saharan African countries. Such partnerships in the postwar era are important and would facilitate meeting dual goals: ensuring the participation of health professionals in the design and implementation of national health care policies and reforming health professional education to be more relevant to the societal needs of the population.

The multiple constraints that hampered the optimum performance of health care workers in prewar Liberia will need to be addressed in the postwar era. There will be the need to design a comprehensive approach to the development of health care human resources to help reduce the unnecessary disease burden and mortality experienced by the people of Liberia. Postwar Liberian government, along with the private sector and the international community, needs to act as quickly as possible. The increased attention of the international community to the development of the health care workforce in Liberia is a reason for optimism. If Liberia or other African countries fail to create an environment conducive to development of the health care workforce, improvements in the health status of the general population in the postwar era will continue to lag.

Note

1. *Freedom and Socialism.* A Selection from Writings & Speeches, 1965-1967, Dar es Salaam: Oxford University Press.

CHAPTER 7

THE ROLE OF TECHNOLOGY AND ESSENTIAL PHARMACEUTICALS IN THE LIBERIAN HEALTH CARE SYSTEM

Science knows no country, because knowledge belongs to humanity, and it is the torch which illuminates the world. Science is the highest personification of the nation because that nation will remain the first which carries the furthest the works of thought and intelligence.[1]

—Louis Pasteur, French biologist & bacteriologist (1822 - 1895)

The Global Burden of Infectious Diseases in Sub-Saharan Africa

Pharmaceuticals are probably the most important component of the health care delivery system in any country. In sub-Saharan African countries, where the brunts of infectious and communicable diseases are borne, large segments of the population lack access to basic pharmaceuticals for endemic conditions. While every country and region of the world suffers from multiple health conditions, there is nowhere on this planet that experiences a greater burden of illness than sub-Saharan Africa. But the intangible burden of global health disparities can also have a ripple effect on developed countries because we live in an increasingly global economy. A small economic example that illustrates this point is that if cocoa and coffee farmers in Côte d'Ivoire fall ill due to malaria, tuberculosis, or HIV infection, the price of coffee, and chocolate in the global market will rise. The increase in price will be felt especially in the developed world, where consumption of these products is prevalent.

The benefits of globalization, like its burdens, are not equally distributed around the world. In the last half of the 20th century, we have witnessed enormous advancement in medical science and technology. These advancements have led to reduction in infant mortality rates; reduction in maternal mortality; discoveries and development of new treatment remedies; and an increase in life expectancy. Despite these advancements, a healthy life is difficult to sustain for millions of people in sub-Saharan Africa. Disparities in health by all indicators exist between rich and poor nations. Disparities exist among countries in sub-Saharan Africa, and within countries between rich and poor or different geographic locations. Professionals in health care, working for the common good within the context of globalization, have the potential to create a global community.

Reports from several international agencies—the World Bank, the World Health Organization (WHO), and other United Nations (UN) agencies involved in health care—continue to sound the alarm of the inequalities in health that exist in the world today. In developed countries, widespread access to an array of effective drugs and vaccines has led to a decrease in infectious diseases. Yet, in the poorest countries of the world, including most countries in sub-Saharan Africa, six in 10 individuals still die of infectious diseases, according to WHO. Many of these deaths could be prevented if people had access to simple pharmaceuticals, such as antibiotics, that are widely available in developed countries.

In sub-Saharan Africa, preventable diseases continue to kill millions of people. Diarrhea, often contracted from unclean drinking water, continues to be the major cause of mortality in Africa for infants and children under 5 years of age. Over 4 billion acute cases of diarrheal diseases occur every year, primarily among children in developing countries, according to WHO. The United Nations Children's Fund (UNICEF), the UN agency that focuses on children, also reports that 2 million children die annually from diarrhea. Lower respiratory infections, such as pneumonia, are another condition that adversely affects children. Every year, millions of people die of lower respiratory infections in sub-Saharan Africa; many of the children are under 5 years of age. Malaria, eradicated in most developed countries, remains a leading cause of death in sub-Saharan Africa, where 90 percent of the world's cases occur. Rarely does one hear of a child dying of measles in developed countries like the United States. However, in sub-Saharan Africa, measles is still a major childhood illness that kills 700,000 children annually—even though it can be prevented with a cheap and effective vaccine. This figure could be decreased drastically by availability and access to childhood immunizations.

The disparities in health conditions and the lack of access to life-saving medications are far-reaching. For instance, tuberculosis claims 2 million lives annually, with 90 percent of these deaths occurring in developing countries where distribution of drugs and monitoring of health programs is limited. Today, the HIV/AIDS pandemic is another condition that threatens the progress being made in the health care delivery systems of most sub-Saharan countries. According to the UN's AIDS Program, more than 44 million people globally are infected with HIV/AIDS (United Nations AIDS Program Annual Report, 2005). About 85 percent to 90 percent of those infections occur in sub-Saharan Africa, where millions of individuals still do not have access to new life-saving antiretroviral medications. While many individuals infected with HIV/AIDS in the West have longer and improved quality of life due to new therapeutics, contracting HIV/AIDS infection in many sub-Saharan African countries is like a death sentence.

Disparities in Pharmaceutical Health Services Research on Neglected Endemic Diseases

Disparities in pharmaceuticals are not only visible in the area of access to needed medications; there are inequities in how research is done and how new medications are developed. According to the Global Forum for Health Research, every year, more than $70 billion is spent worldwide on health research and development by the public and private sectors (Global Forum for Health Research, 2002). However, only an estimated 10 percent of this funding is used for research into 90 percent of the world's health problems. This disparity is referred to in the international community as "the 10/90 gap" (Global Forum for Health Research, 2002). The development of a new medication is a risky process because a company could invest and lose millions of dollars seeking a product that would not be profitable on the market. Therefore, many pharmaceutical companies are inclined to pursue research and development of medications that would generate more profit for them.

Today, the "blockbuster" medications are for cholesterol, diabetes, and arthritis conditions that are more prevalent in developed countries, where the population would be willing to pay high prices for the medications. According to Médecins Sans Frontières (MSF), also known as Doctors Without Borders, of the 1,393 new drugs approved for use between 1970 to 2000, just 13 drugs—barely 1 percent—were for infectious diseases that disproportionately affect the developing world (Médecins Sans Frontières, 2001). The consequences are that diseases that are endemic to developing countries in sub-Saharan Africa— diseases that may be easy to treat or eradicate—may continue to adversely impact the health status of those countries, since no one is researching in these areas. Since pharmaceutical companies are part of Western health care systems that are based on the market approach, they, too, are influenced by profit, just like every other sector of the system. It is not foreseeable in the immediate future how populations of developing countries will benefit from research innovations.

Some of the conditions endemic to sub-Saharan Africa that have received little attentions are Chagas disease, Leishmaniasis, and trypanosomiasis. Chagas disease is the world's third most prevalent parasitic disease, infecting between 16 million and 18 million people per year. It kills an estimated 45,000 people a year. Leishmaniasis is a parasitic illness that afflicts some 1.5 million people and, if left untreated, has a 90 percent fatality rate. African trypanosomiasis, (sleeping sickness) is a parasitic disease that infects half a million people worldwide and causes 50,000 deaths annually. Although drugs have been developed to treat trypanosomiasis, many patients are becoming resistant to the treatment, rendering ineffective the medication currently in use. From the market perspectives, pharmaceutical companies have little commercial interest in researching and developing new pharmaceutical alternatives for diseases that mainly affect people in poor countries. One of the main reasons for such lack of interest is that once such medications are developed, poor individuals in these countries may not be able to pay for such medications and companies may be unable to reap their profits.

Today, the scientific community may be technically equipped to take on the challenge of controlling infectious diseases in the global community, but is it altruistically inclined to do so? The knowledge, expertise, and tools exist to save lives on a grand scale, but the diffusion of health care technology and pharmaceuticals to developing countries requires a paradigm shift from profit making to community partnerships. The control of infectious diseases cannot rely solely on technology; it requires an understanding of sociocultural factors and how these factors fit into disease transmission, treatment, and care. A concerted global effort that is community-based, combining cultural and technological approaches to disease control, could dramatically reduce excess morbidity and mortality burdens on children, women, and other vulnerable populations.

HIV/AIDS in Sub-Saharan Africa and the Pharmaceutical Industry

The HIV/AIDS pandemic is one of the health conditions that bring to light the global disparities in access to pharmaceuticals. Although pharmaceutical companies have lowered their market price for many of the medications used in treating HIV/AIDS in developing countries, medications are out of reach for millions of people living with HIV/AIDS. Medications for HIV/AIDS include antiretroviral agents, antibiotics, anti-cancer drugs, and palliative medications to relieve pain. With over 85 percent of HIV/AIDS cases located in sub-Saharan Africa, it is important to note that the annual per-capita expenditure for health care in this region ranges from $10 to $200, and therefore many of these countries will need help from the international community. Many families in the region survive on approximately $1 a day, making it impossible for them to pay for these medications.

An efficient health care system, integrated with other sectors of society, is paramount to reducing not only the spread of HIV/AIDS, but also improving the quality of lives for those individuals already infected with the HIV virus. While there is a call for free medications at both the local and international levels, creating access to these medications is not enough. Even with free pharmaceuticals, many of the health care systems in sub-Saharan Africa may lack the necessary infrastructure to support monitoring the use of these pharmaceuticals at the patient and system levels. The interrelated processes of prevention, treatment, surveillance, and care require a well-developed infrastructure staffed by trained health care professionals and a strong link between primary and tertiary services. Because the treatment regimens require appropriate support and periodic evaluation of those taking the treatments, health care workers are key to helping stem the spread of HIV/AIDS. Indeed, research reports suggest that improper usage of the medications may result in the mutation of an HIV strain that becomes resistant to currently available medications.

Several broad strategies have been proposed to fund the availability of HIV medications for those in need in sub-Saharan Africa as well as to provide training for health care professionals. Such strategies range from increasing loans for African countries, providing debt relief, and increasing the collaboration between the private sector (pharmaceutical companies and Non-Governmental Organizations [NGOs]) and the public sector (African governments) to create a sustained program to provide medications for those infected. These public-private partnerships have led to pharmaceutical companies lowering their medication prices.

Some pharmaceutical companies, however, have met with criticism from governments as well as from NGOs for refusing to lower prices of life-saving medications that would improve the quality of life for millions of people around the world. It is important to put this in perspective. The pharmaceutical companies' primary aim is to generate return on the investment made in discovering a new product. Their shareholders expect a profit on their market shares, and as a result, the industry has argued that although it remains committed to research and development of new drugs, it must be able to reap what it has already invested in current products. So, while there is a push for allowing the production of generic drugs—which could be distributed more cheaply—this alternative has not been embraced by the pharmaceutical industry because it is still trying to reap the dividends from its more expensive brand-name medications.

The Pharmaceutical Industry's Contributions to Improving the Health Care of Countries Emerging from Civil Conflicts in Sub-Saharan Africa

The 20th century brought to bear the application of science to disease prevention and treatment. During this period, many vaccines and antibiotics were discovered. Today, in fact, antibiotics continue to be used in the treatment of infections, many of which would lead to death without proper pharmaceutical intervention. Immunizations save millions of lives every year from diseases such as measles and whooping cough.

On an altruistic level, we must do everything we have the power to do to save lives in jeopardy. From the standpoint of self-interest, the health status of individuals around the world is interrelated. We are all in this boat together. Poor health in one sub-Saharan African country may directly and indirect impact the health of neighboring countries. There's a Liberian proverb that says, "Disease and disaster come and go like rain, but health is like the sun that illuminates the entire village." We must recognize our need to work together for the betterment of all peoples. What good is it for the pharmaceutical company to develop a life-saving medication for a disease, but price it so high that vulnerable populations which are more affected cannot afford such medication?

There is no ideal time to intervene in global health concerns. Whether a country is emerging from civil crisis or is highly corrupt, isolated, or has an unfriendly political ideology or deeply flawed leaders, the international community still needs to act in addressing the health care needs of that country. Opportunity to tackle many of the conditions that plague sub-Saharan Africa and states like Liberia and other countries that are emerging from civil crisis now exist. The sooner we strategically apply our best health care approaches, the better chance we have of eliminating or eradicating disease agents. For example, over the last decade, there have been reports of a rise in drug-resistant organisms, including those that cause malaria, tuberculosis, and, more recently, HIV infection. This should teach us that medications don't remain effective forever. Had anti-tuberculosis medications been administered and monitored more widely, for instance, we might not be facing the global threat of drug-resistant tuberculosis today.

There is yet another reason for urgency. Disease threats are constantly changing. Over the past two decades, multiple new human illnesses have emerged or reemerged. Each could tip the balance of power in our effort to combat infectious disease. The smallpox eradication campaign has allowed us to see how nations could collaborate in large-scale health initiatives. Smallpox affected both developed and developing countries. In response, the developed countries used their scientific abilities to produce the vaccine and the eradication methodology that they shared with the developing countries. While the U.S. and other developed countries in the past have been able to control the spread of some infectious diseases within their national boundaries, they still need to be concerned about those diseases in other countries, where there is a lack of the infrastructure to control them.

Today, public health experts and politicians are optimistic and determined to find solutions to limit the transmission of and expand the treatment for many diseases. For example, in recent years, under President George W. Bush's administration, the United States' contribution to the global fund for HIV/AIDS prevention and treatment has increased substantially. Besides governmental efforts, numerous non-governmental efforts have created coalitions of individuals and organizations devoted to global health. Not-for-profit organizations, large philanthropic foundations, and even pharmaceutical companies are beginning to work together to resolve global health crises. Increasing public-private partnerships with governments around the world is a cost-effective way to bring better health outcomes to needy populations. Despite the launching of these good-faith efforts, widespread sustained benefits have not yet accrued. It remains to be seen if these efforts will translate into benefits for individuals at the lower end of the economic ladder in sub-Saharan Africa. Global health has taken on a new urgency, given the emergence and reemergence of infectious diseases. UN related organizations such as WHO and UNICEF continue to be at the forefront of global health issues. We have also seen the expanded efforts of several philanthropic groups, including the Bill and Melinda Gates Foundation, the Carter Center, Rotary International, and the Program for Appropriate Technology in Health (PATH). All of these organizations share a common perspective that an investment in the health of a people will have a great impact on socioeconomic development.

These organizations have renewed their commitment to global health, as it becomes more evident that the health and welfare of the people in developing countries are intricately linked to the health and welfare of the people in more affluent nations. As advancements in transportation technology make it feasible for more people to travel, it becomes even more difficult to contain a disease within a given geographic area. A virus or bacterium arising in one corner of the world can rapidly spread across national boundaries. We have seen this process occur with several conditions, including sub-acute respiratory syndrome (SARS) and H5N1 avian flu. Although these conditions were first observed in Southeast Asia, they soon began to spread to other parts of the world. As the global community acknowledges that every human life matters, momentum is building to make health care accessible and affordable to everyone, including those who are vulnerable and less able to purchase health care services for themselves and their families.

Traditional Healing Practices and Remedies: An Ecological Perspective

Traditional Healing and Liberian Belief Systems about Health and Health Care

In planning how to reform the Liberian health care system, it is important to understand that traditional healing practices exist alongside modern medical health care services. In fact, traditional healing practices are more accessible to the general population because they are socioculturally acceptable and relatively cheaper. Therefore, refining and incorporating some of the positive aspects of the traditional healing services in postwar Liberia will definitely serve the interests of the Liberian people, especially when a foremost concern for many people is to simply access health care—any health care—no matter the source. As officials of Liberia's Ministry of Health and Social Welfare (MOH&SW) concentrate their efforts in overhauling the modern health services systems, it would be advantageous to simultaneously seize the opportunity to conduct unbiased studies about traditional medicine: examining the materials, methodology, and procedures utilized by traditional healers, including the dispensing of herbs and other pharmaceuticals. A more comprehensive understanding of the role of traditional healers in prevention and treatment of endemic diseases—as well as maintenance of quality of life for all sectors of the population—should be a noble goal of health-sector reforms.

Traditional healing practices have supported the health of the people in sub-Saharan Africa longer than modern or biomedical practices. In present-day Liberia, people use both modern and traditional medical practitioners. In traditional healing, healers use diverse remedies: tree bark, leaves, nuts, fruit juices, roots, and parts of domestic and bush animals. In Liberia, there is a wide variety of different types of traditional healers who specialize in different ailments and cures: *zoes*, juju healers, diviners, herbalists, witch doctors, and the like. While the limitations of some traditional healers are scrutinized with skepticism, other healers have been lauded by educated and uneducated Liberians alike for their ability to provide successful remedies for many ailments and conditions. Stories of successful traditional healing remedies include treatment for deadly poisonous snakebites, respiratory ailments, abdominal pains, and menstrual cramps. In many local villages, mothers would seek out traditional healers to provide them with treatment for children with high fevers arising from malaria and other diseases. The bark of a native tree, kojolubo, has been used for constipation or to cleanse the intestines of impacted fecal matter. Traditional birth attendants (TBAs) have also been known to use extracts from the bark of certain trees to increase uterine contractions for pregnant women in prolonged labor.

All of these reports suggest that traditional healing practices have a practical use that is interwoven into Liberian culture. Osujih (1993) suggests that traditional healing practices incorporate a more person-centered approach than do many modern health care institutions. Western medicine has realized these limitations and is now struggling to provide holistic care in a system that was not designed with the patient at the center of the system. New MOH&SW officials may want to incorporate the positive aspects of traditional healing practices in Liberia's new health care system. A complementary health care system that integrates both traditional and biomedical approaches would stand a better chance of being accepted by the general population.

The Liberian view on health and illness is complex and sometimes difficult for the outsiders and privileged Liberians to understand. The population of Liberia is made up of numerous tribal groups that have deeply embedded belief systems that have been maintained for centuries. As is the case in most cultures, many of these belief systems center on the causes of illness, healing practices, marriage ceremonies, social status, and the hierarchy of power. Although the belief systems of each tribe have unique characteristics, there are some common aspects that span all tribal groups—for example, the belief that one's well-being reflects the strength and quality of one's connections to ancestral spirits. It would be too simplistic to suggest that there is one "Liberian world view" representative of all tribal groups, but it would be too complex, on the other hand, to detail the micro-differences of each tribal belief system when designing a countrywide approach to health care. A balance between respecting tribal differences and recognizing commonalities is essential for efficiently addressing the health care needs of a tribal people whose tribal lineage has been decimated by prolonged civil war.

For centuries in Liberia, traditional healers in rural areas passed on their healing practices to the next generation through apprenticeships. This apprentice system has been disrupted by the civil war. Today, over half of the Liberian population consists of youths less than 18 years of age who likely grew up in a refugee camp within Liberia or in another

African country. In addition, during this postwar era, a large segment of the formerly rural population is now living in urban settings. Globalization has exposed these young people to Western perspectives that underestimate or devalue the essence of the traditional system in Liberia. The current socio demographic changes and trends in urbanization create additional challenges in identifying the health belief systems of Liberians.

Contrasting Traditional Healers with Biomedical Approaches

Regardless of the perceived benefits of traditional medicine, the efficacy of remedies is questioned by medical science. One way to understand unexplained benefits is to understand the health care provider-patient relationships that are central to traditional medicine and modern medicine. Modern medical practitioners who are trained at universities in Liberia or abroad may no longer appreciate the diverse cultural beliefs of the Liberian people and how such beliefs influences health. In urban centers in Liberia, the outpatient waiting halls in hospitals are overcrowded with individuals wishing to obtain modern health care services, attesting to the fact that the regard for western medicine in Liberia is increasing. However, the inability of many individuals to pay for needed services, as well as time considerations and the compartmentalization of medical care services makes it difficult or impossible to build strong health care provider-patient communication and relationships.

In the modern health care system, health care providers rarely spend the time needed to understand the psychosocial aspects related to the problems of the patient that led to his or her condition. This problem, in its broader context, involves a cultural process that is germane to trust building for Liberians. Traditional healers, in most instances, are directly involved in the production of healing compounds. In fact, their patients might even participate in gathering some of the raw materials used. For many Liberians, the transparency of this process legitimizes their treatment. In contrast, biomedical health care providers practicing within the modern health care sector are far removed from the development of the pharmaceuticals they give their patients and are unlikely to spend time explaining drug composition. Scientific validity and reliability may be insufficient reassurance to a patient who has depended on a hands-on connection to treatment.

A biomedical health care provider may become first acquainted with a pharmaceutical product at the point of distribution and have no first hand experience in its development to share with a skeptical patient. Medical and pharmacy schools, nursing schools, and other health care educational institutions need to teach future health care workers how to communicate effectively to patients that the pharmaceuticals they are offering in treatment are developed with a process that is in a way similar to the one their traditional healers use. For example, a patient who trusts the use of boiled tree bark to offset the symptoms of malaria because the traditional healer involves him or her in the process may be reluctant to take the prescribed anti malarial pills, chloroquine, because he or she doesn't know the source of the medication. A culturally sensitive healthcare provider will know that it is critical to fill the patient in on the provenance of the medicine.

Many researchers suggest that Western approaches to health care could benefit from examining how traditional healing practices function in a culture. Western approaches to health care delivery are grounded in the scientific approach and are therefore highly valued within the scientific sector; other practices, not following a biomedical approach, are usually regarded as "quackery" by that sector (Liverpool, et al., 2004). In the Western framework, the relationship between the patient and provider is regarded as private, aimed at helping the individual patient become well or adapt to his or her illness. Health care providers operating within the biomedical approach concentrate mostly on what is happening to the patient; thus under this approach, typical questions asked of patients seeking care at a hospital include, "Why are you here?" or "What is happening to you?" The health professional is also fixed on arriving at a diagnosis, including checking the individual for natural factors such as bacteria or viruses. Science, not superstition, is used to explain the cause of illness. Attempts are made to assess the patient and arrive at a diagnosis. Sometimes pharmaceuticals are dispensed, and the patient is told, "Take these medications for two weeks and make an appointment to see me again." In the modern health care system, the boundaries for visits are restricted, and monitoring of treatment regimens is done by the patients themselves or by relatives and significant others. For Liberians, a major problem with this approach is that in many settings, trained health care workers may not always be available to monitor treatment regimens, and patients must rely on their own resources.

In the African traditional healing approach used by zoes in a typical Liberian village, a practical mutual relationship is first developed; instead of keeping the healing process private, it becomes a communal interaction for everyone in the village. The healer deals with both supernatural and natural forces and her or his focus during the patient's visit are centered on "Who caused the illness?" For instance, has the individual angered the spirits or ancestors? What sort of social upheaval exists in the village or in the household of the client? Unlike the Western-trained healer, the African traditional healer is usually the one who tells the patient why he or she has come for help. Being able to describe accurately the patient's experience before he or she even begins to describe it builds trust and credibility for the healer.

Herbs or other pharmaceuticals are incorporated, and strict rituals are spelled out for the individual to follow. Sometimes, traditional treatment regimens are even more rigid than those used in the modern health care system. The burden of compliance is on the whole community; everyone related to the patient has a stake in supporting the patient in complying with the treatment regimen. Lacking the formal boundaries set by Western medicine, the traditional healer-patient relationship is fluid, and a patient can visit a healer as often as she or he wants need. In fact, it is common for traditional healers to request that the patients live with them in their houses while undergoing therapies. Unlike a modern health care provider with access to X-ray machines, microscopes, or CT scans to aid in the diagnostic process; the traditional healer relies on indigenous techniques to mediate between his patient and the ancestral spirits. Techniques may include augury using bones, sticks, smells, dream interpretation, or channeling sounds from animals. In essence, most traditional medical practices in Liberia and other sub-Saharan African countries synthesize social, cultural, and religious components into a holistic practice.

Creating a Paradigm Shift: Integrating Traditional Healers into the Modern Health Care System in Postwar Liberia

Integrating the traditional healing practices of Liberia into a modern health care system will be paramount to preventing and treating diseases. In revitalizing the system, health planners should consider multilevel comprehensive approaches to health care delivery that include the traditional healing networks that span urban and rural areas. An important first step is for formal health care officials to convene conferences in all counties to assess needs, confer on critical health issues, and elicit community input and support for new programs. Because traditional healers in Liberia are an integral and recognized sector of health care in the lives of the majority of Liberians, their participation in developing new health care forums will be critical. While the Liberian government has the noble goal of providing health care to all citizens, the people interacting with their families and communities will help to sustain new health programs. Therefore, the voice of the common person should not be left out of the health planning process. Traditional healers hold high status in communities and have access to wide segments of the general population; they should be involved in the planning stages of any health program, as they could serve as advocates for the people. Officials in the formal health care setting interested in implementing prevention and health promotion messages can tap into their popularity and trust. Because of the absence of 24-hour access to modern health care, traditional healers—with training—could serve as an on-the-ground access point for programs dealing with HIV/AIDS, sexually transmitted infections (STIs), and diarrheal control.

Building an ongoing dialogue between biomedically, trained individuals and traditional healers would decrease the mistrust between both groups and lead to the creation of a coordinated approach to controlling common illnesses. A strong relationship with biomedical health professionals will encourage traditional healers to refer patients to secondary and tertiary care facilities when they know a condition is beyond their scope of practice. In this postwar era, there must be political recognition of Liberian traditional medicine, as well as the formulation of policy, regulatory, and legal frameworks to reduce the friction between the two systems. Western countries, including the United States, are achieving this balance from the other direction, having become dependent on compartmentalized biomedical approaches, only to have the general population yearn for holistic care. As a result, in 1999, the U.S. National Institutes of Health established the Center for Complementary and Alternative Medicine (CAM) in an effort to study the efficacy of holistic regimens. Liberia could collaborate with other African countries (e.g., Ghana, Nigeria, and other nations that may have better equipped laboratories) to study some of the remedies, pharmaceuticals, and traditional practices used in West Africa.

Proposals for Pharmaceutical Reforms in Postwar Liberia

In developing countries, medicines offer a simple, cost-effective answer to many health problems, provided they are available, accessible, affordable, and properly used (World Bank, Better Health in Africa, 1994). In Africa, the reliance on medicines could be regarded as one of the most visible symbols of quality health care. For instance, the World Bank reported that in Senegal, between 1981 and 1989, household expenditures for pharmaceuticals accounted for half of all health expenditures (World Bank, Better Health in Africa, 1994).

Like other African countries, Liberia regards a regular supply of pharmaceuticals as a fundamental component of a well-functioning health care system. The percentage of the health care budget allocated to pharmaceuticals by the Ministry of Health is unclear and is destined to change during the rebuilding process. Because Liberia does not have its own pharmaceutical industry, pharmaceuticals are largely imported from abroad at great expense. According to the World Bank (1992), pharmaceutical expenditures typically make up 20 percent to 30 percent of total recurrent costs at public and private health facilities in Africa. They also represent a sizable share of per-capita expenditures on health.

Health care workers are frustrated that treatment plans are limited by the lack of pharmaceuticals. In a developing country like Liberia, the importance of pharmaceuticals to the general population is illustrated by what happens when medicines are unavailable—visits to health centers and clinics decline dramatically. Anecdotal accounts of the experience of Liberian health care professionals confirm that when health facilities run out of commonly used drugs, visits by patients drop.

Because pharmaceuticals are a highly marketable commodity and a vital component of health care worldwide, it is difficult for most sub-Saharan African countries to compete for and maintain a constant imported supply of pharmaceuticals because of the complications inherent in the currency exchange and importation process. The aim of the government of Liberia is to make sure that the pharmaceuticals used in the country are high quality and are purchased at the lowest possible cost.

Prior to the civil war, the Liberian government formulated national drug policies, created a list of essential drugs as suggested by WHO, and created the National Medical Supply Depot (NMSD) for government health facilities. Although the NMSD existed for the purchase of drugs for government facilities, it had large uncollectible accounts receivable from outlying health clinics and could not replenish drug stocks. This created a situation where government hospitals and clinics had no drugs or medical supplies to treat patients. In an effort to alleviate this situation, the NSMD was dissolved and the National Drug Service (NDS) was established. This service procures drugs through the International Dispensary Association (IDA) and other budget suppliers of bulk drugs and supplies the drugs to government clinics. The NDS has the responsibility of assuring the continuous availability of high-quality drugs and medical supplies at low cost to the entire public health system. The previous system was laden with inefficiencies and waste in the management of pharmaceuticals because it was a top-heavy hierarchy. Post-war reconstruction could benefit from a more efficient, equitable, and sustainable pharmaceutical system.

Review of the African Pharmaceutical Markets

Essential health care is one of the tenets of primary health care. In many African countries, a large percentage of the population has no regular access to "essential drugs." WHO lists several categories of drugs that are essential for treating common illness (e.g., antimalarials, antibiotics, vitamins, antipyretics, anti-diarrheals, and the like). The lack of essential drugs leads to an increase in complications and deaths from illnesses that could have been treated. Shortages of appropriate pharmaceuticals affect every level of health care delivery in many African countries, including at primary care levels where the spread of common illnesses could be brought under control before they become epidemics. The paucity of pharmaceuticals due to management, logistical, and financial problems has been widely documented, especially in peri-urban and rural areas. In Liberia, drug shortages and absences are frequent, even at major public hospitals in larger cities.

Nonprofit facilities in Africa such as mission hospitals, experience fewer problems with keeping pharmaceuticals in stock because of their connections with international philanthropic groups that can quickly respond to needs. Hospitals that are established for a particular multinational company's employees, such as for those of the Firestone Rubber Plantations Company, have the means to connect with the international pharmaceutical market. Private, for-profit hospitals have the funds and foreign exchange capacity to buy drugs for their limited patients despite the high costs on the market, because their clients tend to be from upper-income households in urban areas.

In Liberia, as in other African countries, trained pharmacists are few, and they generally prefer to open retail stores in urban areas and to trade largely in Western specialty drugs. Wholesalers and representatives of industrialized countries reinforce this urban-rural disparity because they prefer to work with the private pharmacies in large cities. In the postwar era, it will be important to determine how best to support pharmacists in rural areas by creating incentives and a cost-effective and efficient distribution system for pharmaceuticals.

Because health delivery in the private sector appears more organized than it seems to be in government facilities, there is widespread belief that its pharmaceuticals are superior and thus worth a much higher price. A common misconception among consumers (as well as some health care providers) is that generic or low-cost drugs supplied through public agencies are inferior to those sold in the private sector. This is not necessarily the case, but the misconception often leads to wasteful drug decisions. In Kenya, for example, it has been found that some patients traded in their free generic drugs at pharmacies to buy identical specialty drugs, which they believed were better (World Bank, Better Health in Africa, 1994).

Without pharmaceuticals being widely accessible to the general public, residents of peri-urban and rural areas generally find private suppliers are more accessible sources of drugs, albeit irregularly and offering pharmaceuticals of questionable quality. There are also reports that some of the drugs sold by these suppliers may be stolen from the public sector, further jeopardizing the continuity of needed pharmaceuticals in the larger system. Other suppliers may import pharmaceuticals from neighboring countries where quality control is often absent (Whyte, 1990).

The logistical process of obtaining the drugs, including funding, is not the only problem. Another problem is that the prescription process in sub-Saharan Africa is not sufficiently standardized and regulated to prevent misuse of pharmaceuticals. Medicines that do reach their destinations are often inappropriately dispensed. In one study, Foster (1990) it was found that in Mali, the average prescription called for 10 drugs, sometimes including duplication of the same drug under different names. Foster points out that in many cases, it is likely that one or two drugs would have sufficed. This simplistic pattern of "more is better" is not unique to Mali and perhaps would be found in Liberia and other sub-Saharan African countries if similar studies were conducted.

In yet another study, done in Nigeria, researchers observed that diarrhea (the major cause of mortality for most sub-Saharan African children under five years of age) was often treated with antibiotics more potent than necessary (Isenalumhe and Ovbiawe, 1986). Finally, many patients who visit a health center for ailments such as malaria request injections instead of pills because they are perceived to be more potent. In another study, researchers in Ghana point out that although injectable medications were the standard treatment for only a minority of patients, they found that 96 percent of the patients were given at least one injection and then were given prescriptions that called, on average, for use of four different drugs (Dabis, Roisin, and Breman, 1988). In many of these settings, the so-called "essential drugs" are often misused because limited understanding leads to poor compliance with prescribed regimens (Foster, 1990). Using more drugs than are necessary leads to drug resistance, alters standards of care, inflates the expectation of the patient in terms of adequate treatment, and exacerbates drug shortages.

Major constraints impacting any health care system, not only in a developing country like Liberia but also in developed countries, are family income, price setting, disease patterns in local communities, and the educational levels of the patients. In Liberia, many families have low incomes, cannot afford the price of drugs, and have high illiteracy levels influencing how well they comprehend and follow treatment regimens. These constraints, however, could point to opportunities for improving the pharmaceutical and health care delivery programs of Liberia. In view of the high levels of illiteracy and traditional cultural belief systems that impact health decision making in Liberia, especially among the rural and female populations, it seems clear that additional information, education, and communication programs could make an immense contribution to more efficient drug use.

The Essential Pharmaceuticals Problem and Overcoming Obstacles

The reality in many African countries is that pharmaceutical markets within countries and among sub-Saharan African countries are not currently efficient, equitable, or sustainable. Commitments to primary health care are futile if reliable supplies of pharmaceuticals are not made easily

available in peri-urban and rural areas. This disparity prompts households to buy medicines from unregulated dispensers or to bypass local
primary health care facilities and travel long distances to secondary care
facilities and hospitals, where a wider range of pharmaceuticals is available. Cost-effective care is further compromised; endemic illnesses are
not treated by relatively simple regimens of essential drugs dispensed by
health care providers at the ideal point of entry into the health care system, i.e. at the primary health care level (World Bank, Better Health in
Africa, 1994).

Because of the inefficiencies and waste in the procurement and dis-
pensation of pharmaceuticals in a precarious health care system, the government is paying a higher price for pharmaceuticals than is necessary.
The health care systems in African countries emerging from civil conflicts will need more funding to procure essential pharmaceuticals for
populations experiencing the greater health burden that is associated with
civil war. To administer these funds responsibly, it will be important to
make effective use of existing resources by training health care professionals in management and organizational skills as well as in health care.
Efforts must be made to sustain pharmaceutical programs over the long
term. One aspect of sustainability involves recouping the revenues that
are expended for pharmaceutical products, particularly those used in the
government-run sector of health care providers, and ensuring that a designated reserve of foreign exchange is available to pay for imports. The
World Bank has been instrumental in suggesting relevant solutions to the
problem of drug distribution. The World Bank suggests that countries
purchase their supplies and medications by prepackaged kits assembled
by wholesalers. The contents of the kits are determined by average patterns of use. The kits would eliminate some of the managerial inefficiencies that now afflict centralized distribution systems. Care is also needed
to make sure that the kits take into account differential patterns of morbidity by region.

Another method suggested by the World Bank for reducing drug distribution problems is the estimation of the quantities of basic
pharmaceuticals needed at different levels of the referral system. According to Brudon-Jakobowicz (1987), primary health care centers could
meet most of the needs of the population with only 20 to 40 pharmaceutical items. To figure out which pharmaceuticals are needed in each geographic region, epidemiological studies need to be conducted at the actual practice sites. This assessment process would involve looking at

morbidity and mortality rates at major hospitals and primary care centers. Prescription practices should also be guided by standard treatment protocols to achieve optimal outcomes from the available pharmaceuticals.

The popular community-based programs for financing pharmaceuticals called revolving drug funds (RDF) are a way to bolster the availability of pharmaceuticals for disadvantaged populations in sub-Saharan Africa. In the past, RDF programs began with an initial stock of drugs donated by the community, the government, or some other donor. The drugs were then sold to community members at prices that allowed for the replenishment of stock. RDFs can be operated in the public or private sectors, on either a for-profit or not-for-profit basis. A RDF program was successfully introduced into several Liberian counties in the 1980s, but the impact of the civil war decimated the health systems in those counties, leaving the RDF program, as well as all the other facets of the health care system.

The postwar Liberia and other sub-Saharan African countries emerging from civil conflicts could benefit from following some of the recommendations of the World Bank concerning the use of RDFs (World Bank, 1987). These recommendations include the following:

Gradual Price Increases

Sharp price increases should be avoided, especially in areas where the population is not accustomed to paying for public-sector services (Blakney, Litvak, and Quick, 1989). Blakney, Litvak, and Quick suggest that gradual increases over time, accompanied by service improvements, will be more successful. With poverty and unemployment at all-time highs in postwar Liberia, and with many Liberians disconnected from traditional ways to supplement income, MOH&SW officials will have to balance payment for pharmaceuticals with the ability to pay. A sliding fee scale could be negotiated on a family-by-family basis. When the economy begins to improve in the next decade, then the RDF program can be revisited and new requirements for accessing the program can be instituted.

Realistic Revolving Drug Fund (RDF) Programs

A few RDFs, in countries like Senegal, Mali, and Niger, ran into some problems because the amount the patients were asked to pay was insufficient to maintain the programs' momentum (Cross et al., 1986; World Bank, 1992). In Liberia, it was noted in a joint report completed by the MOH&SW and the United States Agency for International Development (USAID) that a major problem was that due to lack of training in program management, strict implementation of the process became too cumbersome for some members (USAID, Liberian Health Sector Assessment, 1988). These problems are symbolic of the failure of MOH&SW to establish an effective procedure for the collection of payments from those who have the ability to pay while still providing for indigent sectors of the population. Because the process was new, it was naively embraced as a way to solve all the pharmaceutical procurement and distribution problems at once. The RDF program was overly ambitious and introduced without a period of testing through small pilot projects. This postwar era is an opportune time to do a retrospective analysis of previous RDF programs to gather information on a productive way to move forward.

Uniform Standards for Operating RDF

Cost recovery programs based on the amount of drugs sold may create incentives for over prescribing and using pharmaceuticals inappropriately to treat illnesses. Standard treatment protocols, external supervision, and payment by illness episode can help reduce these incentives (McPake et al., 1992). A fee-per-service system creates a disincentive for controlling costs and, rather, induces providers to order non-essential procedures and pharmaceuticals. A fee-per-visit system creates an incentive for the health care provider to use the most cost-effective measures to treat an illness. If the MOH&SW launches RDFs in the postwar era, establishing uniform standards of care will be critical to ensuring the proper prescribing of pharmaceuticals to achieve optimal health for the population.

While it is clear that modern pharmaceuticals will be essential for the health outcomes of the people of Liberia, there are significant challenges: the lack of consistent information; the separation of financers of the health care system from policy makers and decision makers; and poor management of drug supplies. At present, these challenges render pharmaceutical markets in Liberia ineffective. Because the situation is already dire, there is great potential for well-thought-out programs to increase the drug coverage in Liberia while reducing costs. Based on research done by the World Bank, it is within the reach of sub-Saharan African countries to provide essential pharmaceuticals to their populations if these countries are stable and managed by altruistic leaders with the vision to improve the health and quality of life of their people. The hope for Liberia, as it emerges from civil war, is that new leaders will view the health of the population as a priority. It will be important for any postwar Liberian government to recognize that a healthy population will spur economic development at every level. In Liberia, where agriculture is the bedrock of the economy and requires manual labor, healthy people are essential to rebuilding the country.

The MOH&SW is going in the right direction by assigning the public policy responsibility for drug management to the National Drug Service. However, operational responsibilities for wholesale drug purchase and distribution need to be increasingly assigned to the private sector because it has already established connections to the international market. To help facilitate this process, the government of Liberia should foster the development of the private commercial and noncommercial drug sectors. Reinvigorating public-sector distribution and promoting cost-effective means of supplying essential drugs will make them affordable and available to the poorest groups in Liberian society.

Note

1. World Health Organization (2004). *World report on knowledge for better health: Strengthening health systems* (pp.97). World Health Organization: Geneva.

CHAPTER 8

REVIVING THE INTELLECTUAL CAPITAL OF LIBERIA TO INFORM THE REBUILDING PROCESS

Health systems should nurture a stronger culture of learning and problem-solving to tackle the major challenges of our times. This could be achieved through a greater understanding of how the diverse elements within a health care system interact with each other, and by finding innovative ways to solve complex problems.[1]

—Tim Evans

Introduction and Brief Overview

There was significant intellectual capital in Liberia before the civil war. Students learned at two major universities that included medical colleges and nursing programs, several community colleges, a number of teacher-training institutes, vocational schools, and hospital-based health professional training programs in Liberia. Others attended institutions of higher learning in other sub-Saharan African countries and abroad. The standard of education at institutions of higher learning was rigorous, as evidenced by the number of Liberians who obtained competitive scholarships and fellowships to study abroad for advanced degrees.

Some of the rigor stemmed from the collaboration with noted international agencies involved in global education, including the Council for International Exchange of Scholars (which administers the Fulbright Scholar Program), the Ford Foundation, the United States Agency for International Development (USAID), and others. Students at the university level, as well as at the vocational level, benefited from distinguished teachers with advanced degrees who created an intellectual environment that prepared students for a competitive local and international work environment.

This vibrant intellectual community was all but destroyed during the civil war and will need to be rebuilt from the ground up. Sadly, many of the intellectuals who were the backbone of Liberia's institutions of higher learning were killed during the civil war; others fled the country to avoid death. A healthy layer of intellectual capital serves important functions in a country, especially a developing country: envisioning a future, creating initiatives, critiquing national and local developments, and serving as a voice of reason in the face of corruption and upheaval. This intellectual layer has the potential to endow its country with a gift that is critical to all other development: empowering people in all sectors of society to be involved in their own destiny. The members of the educated segment of society are indebted to the educators and other intellectuals who embraced them and helped them develop their talents. They also owe loyalty to the less privileged members of society who suffer from the lack of opportunities that they themselves have enjoyed.

Reassembling Liberia's intellectual capital is paramount to rebuilding the country. In order to build credibility and vital connections in the international community, Liberia needs to show the world that it has the thinkers needed to skillfully create an economic and health infrastructure that resonates with the new sociopolitical climate in the country as it emerges from civil war. First, the country needs to tap into the surviving intellectuals who were internally displaced. Reintegrating teachers and other professionals will require a series of steps: offering a job guarantee; providing resources for relocation; providing housing; creating an adequate compensation package; assuring security for teachers and their families; and providing the training necessary to enable teachers to adapt to a profoundly altered learning environment and a traumatized student population. To lure back the intellectuals who emigrated to neighboring countries, Liberia will need to appeal to their loyalty as well as provide a resettlement package that will make it feasible to move an extended family back. Those intellectuals, who emigrated farther abroad, to Western countries, will need even more incentive to move back, much of it intangible.

In addition to the necessary compensation package, Liberia's leaders will have to appeal to the exiled Liberians in a number of ways: nationalistic pride and altruism; creating a feeling of safety and security; a promise of escape from government harassment; and support in the face of reentry cultural shock that they will experience, possibly including a lukewarm reception from fellow Liberians who were unable to escape the traumas of the war. An unintended consequence of the civil war was that many Liberian exiles took advantage of educational opportunities during their exile. The new postwar governments must appeal to the professional pride of Liberian exiles, because if they return, they will be the most highly skilled professionals in the country. These professionals are culturally competent, a criterion that will be essential in developing and instituting new programs. No matter how entrenched they are in their host countries, the pull of their birth country are impossible to extinguish. This is an opportune time for many Liberians who felt helpless to contribute before and during the civil war—except within their family networks—to contribute on a societal scale.

There is a need for the international community to contribute its professional skills, but its contribution will be magnified if it works alongside Liberians with the same level of professional training, as well as cultural competence. The members of the international community who participate in rebuilding countries emerging from civil conflict contribute not only their professional skills, but also their network of expertise and resources around the world. The model of international collaboration in rebuilding war-ravaged Liberia can present a positive precedent for replication in other sub-Saharan African countries emerging from civil conflict.

There are international organizations whose mission includes improving literacy in sub-Saharan Africa. It would be fruitful for the Liberian government to reinvigorate its relationship with these agencies. Many of these agencies pulled out of the country years ago, during the heat of the war. As these agencies revisit their former plans for helping Liberia improve the education of its citizens, they will have to create and pursue strategies to adapt their programs to meet the needs of an even more challenging educational environment.

Global technology has created educational venues that did not exist before Liberia's civil war. Even in institutions of higher learning, the primary route of learning was through lectures in a classroom setting. Many of these institutions had meager libraries, and blackboards were the extent of teaching technology. Computers were barely beginning to be used in the administrative areas of these institutions, and had not yet been used as a teaching tool. Many academic buildings and science laboratories were destroyed during the war. As these institutions are rebuilt from the ground up, now is the time to design and incorporate a technology infrastructure. This technology infrastructure will enable the on-line delivery of courses to students in remote regions. Satellite computer centers established by institutions of higher learning can serve as outlying classrooms to serve a much broader student body. On-line educational opportunities—especially when offered in rural areas—could serve as an incentive for some of the internally displaced people now living in periurban ghettos to return to rebuild their villages. As Liberia works to get its colleges and universities up and running again, these courses could be broadcast from institutions of higher learning in neighboring countries.

The advent of rebuilding Liberia could serve as a catalyst for creating a virtual educational consortium of colleges and universities in the western belt of Africa. Having on-line educational offerings could speed up recapturing the lost generation of Liberian youth that missed out on an education. A technologically oriented classroom might appeal more to youths who have been jaded by war and are skeptical of the old ways of doing things. This virtual consortium will also offer some educational stability in the western belt, despite future civil conflict. In addition to the virtual educational route, technology on campus can be used in other significant ways: for updating teaching faculty and staff on new ideas, upgrading their skills, and connecting them to colleagues in their fields around the world; in the classroom, technology can be used to enhance instruction by supplementing lectures with multimedia presentations; students can use technology for research and assessment, as well as connecting with peers in other institutions around the world; and administratively, computers can be used in running the rebuilding institutions more efficiently and effectively.

In the new era of higher education in Liberia, colleges and universities cannot afford to isolate themselves and be regarded by the populace as elitist institutions working in an ivory tower, out of touch with the realities of the common people. Colleges and universities need to reposition themselves to create better partnerships with local communities. The first step here would be for institutions to look at how their mission aligns with the rebuilding process of the country. Each university, be it private or public, is part of a local community, whether the institution acknowledges it or not. It thus behooves these institutions to take responsibility in catering to the needs of the immediate environments in which they are located, as well as in having a broader vision of responding to national needs for education. They have a responsibility to work on both a micro and macro level in influencing government policy on education, health, agriculture, and other areas that will influence the well-being of the general citizenry.

Many colleges incorporate service learning as a significant part of learning in all the disciplines, including health care. A fruitful experiential learning initiative would be to expand outreach and community health programs so they would be relevant to student learning and the practices in which graduates will eventually find themselves. Many of the endemic diseases could be prevented if local populations were aware of how to practice disease prevention and health promotion behaviors. For example, diarrhea-related diseases—one of the major causes of death among children under the age of 5 years in Liberia—could be prevented if people were aware that they need to boil their water, wash their hands, and maintain other good sanitary habits. Students learning in community-based settings have the opportunity to serve as pivotal sources of information and are in place to be influential in health behavior change. As Liberia emerges from civil conflict and struggles to rebuild its health infrastructure, its institutions of higher learning will need to react to health crises as well as be proactive in preventing the unnecessary loss of life from diseases that could be prevented through simple, proven methods.

Liberians have a long history of helping one another survive during tough times, but generally, assistance is directed toward their own family structures or villages. The safety net of the traditional family and village, however, has been unraveled. Liberians now need to expand their circle of concern beyond their own families to include the welfare of the broader society. Because the new government will be handicapped financially well into the future, private citizens will need to create a new ethos of volunteerism, a concept that may be alien to many Liberians. A cadre of students at the secondary and university levels could form the first wave of volunteerism. These students could volunteer in the community for educational credit in lieu of payment. Once this service learning process is broadly under way, the hope is that the students of this new generation will develop altruistic motives as they advance in their careers. These students will also serve as role models for other segments of the population.

As the new government becomes more established, it can seek out funding that could be earmarked specifically to stimulate community service in the general population. Community service is a productive way to develop job readiness and update skills. But participants must be able to meet basic needs during this transition period. A culturally astute, wraparound job readiness program could meet the complex needs of young people who have been shaped by their participation in and victimization from the civil war.

As universities move into local communities through service learning, they could seize the opportunity to conduct research on the effectiveness of outreach efforts. The research programs that are developed in universities should mirror the concerns of the local communities. Collaboration with scholars throughout Africa and internationally will enable knowledge to flow both ways. Liberian universities could benefit from international funding; the international community could gain insights into global health disparities; developed countries could increase understanding of the health belief systems of their ever-growing immigrant populations.

The Internet is an ideal tool in the exchange of knowledge and in initiating partnerships with countries like Liberia that are perceived to be unsafe. Without being physically present, the most expert health professionals around the world could serve as consultants to the administrators of massive health-related programs. For example, many programs in postwar Liberia will require expertise in design, implementation, and evaluation. Health program evaluation, in particular, requires highly specialized skills in research methodology. Many of the professionals in Liberia who had those skills are gone. Those remaining may have lagged in keeping up with recent advancements, and hence, they need international consultants to bring them up to speed quickly. For example, international experts could conduct short Internet courses in epidemiology, biostatistics, and sampling methodology for staff members of Liberia's Ministry of Health and Social Welfare (MOH&SW) involved in implementing health-related programs.

Prior to the civil war, the Bureau of Planning and Development at the MOH&SW was responsible for identifying health problems and formulating programs and projects that would benefit the Liberian people. The prewar objectives included the coordination of bilateral programs and resources within the ministry to strengthen and provide institutional services for medical, mental health, and rehabilitative programs. The bureau's prewar goals also included promoting research and personnel development and increasing accessibility of health care to the people of Liberia. The lengthy civil war in Liberia decimated the whole mode of health care organization and delivery. In this postwar era, comprehensive needs assessment must be conducted in order to get a realistic picture of current health care needs in vastly altered local community systems. For example, health-related programs that depended on the endorsement of local tribal chiefs may now need to function through less formalized, more volatile, and even fragile hierarchies that were created during the civil war. Tribal chiefs may have been killed or displaced or may not carry the same authoritative stature that chiefs had in the prewar era. New influencers in various communities need to be identified to serve as liaisons to the formal health care structure at the MOH&SW.

Western Influence on Health Knowledge in Liberia

While a range of research previously conducted in Liberia produced new health knowledge, it is evident that most of the scientific knowledge being applied in Liberia's modern health service sector has been inherited from the global health community. With the immigration of Westerners to Liberia—ranging from employees of multinational companies to missionaries—Liberia has eagerly sought to embrace advancements in medicine and other scientific fields. But now, all of these advancements are relevant to the daily lives of people in Liberia. For instance, at Liberian universities, curricula may overemphasize Western chronic diseases that have low incidence rates in Liberia. It would be more practical at this point in Liberia's history to teach students about diseases that they will actually encounter in their practices.

Increasing dispersion of scientific medical knowledge has been aided by the Internet and is becoming more accessible to developing countries. The World Health Organization (WHO) and other international organizations have been instrumental in disseminating health research knowledge to developing countries. But a distinction must be made between bio-medical knowledge, which is universally valid everywhere in the world, and social applications of health knowledge, which must be adjusted to the spectrum of cultural and health needs in each country. Biomedical knowledge is being used to great advantage in Liberia. The social application of health knowledge requires informed decision making by Liberian health leaders if it is to have the most beneficial impact.

Dissemination of Health Knowledge in Liberia

Research has been conducted in Liberia that provides vital information on disease processes and prevention (e.g., malaria, schistosomiasis, diarrhea, etc.). The irony is that Liberia lacks the infrastructure to use this research and build on it. Research institutions were limited; there was a medical school at the University of Liberia and an undergraduate-nursing program at Cutting University College. The country's other institutions, more vocational in nature, provided practical training in health-related disciplines rather than an appreciation for research and its application. Based on the disease patterns in Liberia, what is probably needed are more programs for training primary health care workers and middle-level health managers. But in the postwar era, as energy is directed toward the practicalities of improving the immediate health status of the people as a whole, it will be important not to lose sight of developing an environment of research that supports the goals of higher education, which include fostering inquiry and setting in motion the innovations of the future while developing the intellectual capital of the country.

Institutions of higher education can create new, innovative channels for generating and utilizing research that extend beyond the traditional classroom: conferences, symposia, books, journals, Internet methods, small group training networks, professional associations, mentoring, and apprenticeships. As in other sub-Saharan African countries, however, the health facilities in Liberia are not well equipped with a flow of medical literature, making it difficult for health professionals to implement more effective treatment plans. In rural settings and public institutions, it becomes difficult for health practitioners whose continuing education has been limited to collaborate with their private-sector colleagues. New MOH&SW administrators during this postwar era should attempt to improve continuing education as a means of continuous quality improvement. Allocating funds to this purpose will prove to be cost-effective in the long run, because it will pave the way for creating a uniform standard of care in all public health institutions.

The Role of Liberian Institutions of Higher Learning in the Reorganization of the Health Care Delivery System

The period after a war is an era of unprecedented challenge and change within the health sector, but it is also a time for seizing opportunities for creative interaction among different disciplines within health care: medicine, nursing, pharmacy, midwifery, and traditional medical practices. It is also an opportune time for the health care sector to collaborate with other government and quasi-government sectors that influence health: agriculture, housing, urban planning, rural development, transportation, utility and sewer services, and education.

Modern universities the world over are the institutions where intellectual capital is produced, individual human potential is developed, intellectual freedom is exercised, and knowledge is systematically disseminated. Intellectuals in the postwar era cannot isolate themselves from the ills of the people; they must strive to be a force for social change. A lesson to draw on would be to allow intellectuals to freely practice analysis and critique without fear of prosecution from postwar governments that may feel threatened.

Universities are very interesting places. They do not exist in a vacuum. They influence their communities, and their communities influence them. There is often a conflict of interest, clash of values, or misunderstanding of roles. Universities are good at plans, protocols, and standards; whereas, in the community, it is action that is valued. Many of the decisions that community members make about health care are based on previous experience with health care professionals and with government. Universities must gain a good grasp of the belief systems operating in a community. While university intellectuals have been socialized to think abstractly, local community people measure the value of an idea or a program by its impact on their quality of life.

The process of redefining the mission of universities in a developing society like Liberia's, handicapped by the chaos of war, will lead them to their true social meaning. According to a WHO document, *the role of universities in the strategies for health for all* (1984), universities are established by society to deal with the problems of the extension and dissemination of knowledge. The redefined mission of postwar universities in Liberia should put university-community collaboration at the center of universities' intellectual activities. University officials must be cognizant of the fact that veering too much into the community's value system may compromise academic cultures that exist to foster intellectualism. Universities in postwar sub-Saharan African countries must be willing to take a risk to move out of their "comfort zone" to address these issues, even if it means compromising some of the traditional bounds of academia in order to accommodate the needs of communities and their people.

WHO suggests five ways in which the modern university can provide community service (*the role of universities in the strategies for health for all* [1984]) as follows:

Sharing Technology and Resources

A conservative step a university can take toward community service is to put existing equipment, infrastructure, and human resources at the disposal of the community. This step could neither require an obligation to be involved in the community nor forge a new function for the university. For example, university conference rooms could be used by the community for forums on health; the kitchen could be used for nutrition demonstrations for health promotion programs during school breaks; the library could be made accessible to community groups involved with literacy programs; the residential halls could house youth during prolonged youth leadership development programs; and Internet service could be shared with community leaders for communication purposes.

Sharing Expertise

The community comes to the university with specific requests for expertise in the areas of education, research, cultural activities, etc. Such service does not change the university, which carries on its traditional functions without interruption. All that is required from the university is that it should be competent, available, efficient, and less expensive than other competing organizations. For example: the community could request research on what it can do to prevent its children from dying from a specific disease; the community may request that the university establish an oral history archive on traditional healing practices so that they can be handed down from one generation to the next; the community may also request translation of medical information into its ethnic language or into visual communication for non-English readers.

Conducting Community-relevant Research

In most university settings, in both developed and developing countries, research needs are not always congruent with the needs of the community. When there is a national crisis, such as recovery from war, the university needs to broaden its research goals beyond the building of abstract new knowledge that enriches intellectual capacity and eventually sifts down into the community. That momentum for discovering new knowledge needs to continue to keep higher education robust, but community relevance also needs to be of high priority. This direction presupposes community acceptance of the university's capacity to conduct research and suggest solutions without being bound by prior options of the community.

The university, in this postwar setting, needs to make adjustments in how it operates, including the embracing of community participation in the analysis of problems and in the definition of demand. This presupposes that the university is prepared to make adjustments in its own structures, research agenda, and teaching methods. For example, promoting participatory research in postwar Liberia could help mitigate suffering from communicable and infectious diseases. The long-term goal in postwar years will be to understand how universities can translate knowledge from research into practical use in local communities so people can improve their own well-being.

Facilitating Community-Based Solutions to Problems

In this approach, the university participates, at the community's request, not only in analyzing problems but also in putting forward possible solutions. Autonomy and intellectual integrity are essential if the university is to provide service of the quality expected of it. It is useful for the university to help communities to develop health programs, but communities need to evolve to the point where they become better problem solvers and find solutions to their own problems. For example, a university can teach a community about the infectious diseases that result from improper garbage disposal, but the community itself may decide how and where the garbage will be disposed of and what sanctions will be invoked against community members who fail to follow prescribed procedures. The village elders would impose penalties upon violators, and those penalties could involve working on clean-up details doing such tasks as clearing paths to water sources or constructing log bridges across creeks, because such efforts would be meaningful to that community.

Participating in the Implementation and Evaluation of Programs

Implementation, a stage of problem solving, is a phase that universities are often not fully involved in as they try to stay true to their organizational objectives of intellectual pursuits. However, due to the postwar shortage of skilled and professional workforce members, universities in countries emerging from civil conflicts will need to be involved in implementation if purposeful change is going to occur. For example, a faculty member could design a course on the development and implementation of immunization programs that includes an outreach component. As students study the science behind immunization and theoretical approaches to community-based programs, they could also participate directly in actual health campaigns that would involve the administration of immunizations. The research program of faculty members could entail the evaluation of the effectiveness of these programs and explore what would lead to the program sustainability.

As Liberia emerges from civil war, pursuing a combination of all five of these approaches will make higher education relevant to reconstruction. If higher education does not try to be more relevant, it will not garner the community support and interest it needs to flourish. The relevance of the university to reconstruction, the development of a participatory infrastructure, and the creation of a new Liberian mindset are all important to a viable future for Liberia. Otherwise, Liberia faces the danger of going back to the former status quo.

This is an unusual time. The protracted civil war has disrupted the continuity of generations of intellectuals engaged in planning the future of the country. Liberia's institutions of higher learning should have a new role that transforms them from being passive servants of elite elements of Liberian society into active institutional participants in planning for their country's postwar reconstruction.

The health of the country cannot be dependent on building a health system that caters only to the needs of small, privileged elite. The university, therefore, is a place to begin thinking about an egalitarian approach to all aspects of society and must be in the forefront of efforts to make such an approach reality. The university also serves as a check and balance because, traditionally, it has been the intellectuals that challenge any government that does not have the welfare of all the people in mind. Universities need to operate in an egalitarian manner themselves, recruiting students from all layers of society. The university can lead the way in the move away from tribalism toward a truly national identity by creating a student body and faculty-staff-administration group that reflect the ethnic and socioeconomic diversity of the country. This would be another way of creating geographic dispersion of the skills and knowledge needed for reconstruction because many students return to serve their communities after graduation. This will have an impact on health disparities among ethnic, rural, and urban populations. This implies profound changes in purpose and thought as well as institutional and individual behavior.

The Role of Liberian Institutions of Higher Learning in Developing Specific Health and Development Programs

It has been said that the health of the people is the foundation upon which all their happiness and all their powers as a state depend (Grosse and Auffrey, 1989). WHO's mission of advocating for health for all has brought a more profound dimension to how the concept of health is perceived and operationalized. WHO's definition is broadened and includes programs that focus on individuals as well as populations, the maintenance and promotion of well-being, the prevention of illness, the treatment of disease, and the rehabilitation of the disabled. The enhanced definition of WHO advocates that communities should become self-reliant in achieving optimal health.

In Liberia, development, economics, culture, education, and other systems necessary for the growth of a country were stymied by the protracted civil war. Rebuilding the country means reviving and moving all these sectors forward because society is an intricate interdependence. There is a bivariate relationship between the functioning of these systems and the health of the nation as Liberia moves toward the ideals of social equity and justice. Postwar leaders will have to recognize that Liberia is a developing country, whose health care needs is somewhat different from those of developed nations. Therefore, international funding should be funneled toward resolving those pressing socioeconomic and health needs, as opposed to building massive health institutions too unwieldy to address community-based problems.

The MOH&SW and the private sector will have to place more emphasis on the primary health care level, which will address issues related to high infant mortality rates, immunization coverage, maternal morbidity rates, and availability of safe water and good sanitation. Producing more medical doctors is a long-term goal, but producing more middle-level health care professionals who can address these critical health care issues is the key to immediate resuscitation of the Liberian health care system. Universities could play a role in improving basic literacy through adult education programs. An improvement in community members' literacy levels would lead to their being able to make informed decisions about the health of themselves and their families.

Liberian universities are well placed to understand the factors that support or undermine health in relation to human development, and they can monitor how such development programs can be utilized to enhance the quality of life of the Liberian people. Experts can bring intellectual talent to bear upon the various aspects of development beyond the immediate purview of health itself. This can be achieved as a contribution to the total national effort for development without compromising their established autonomy. For these universities to play this new role adequately, it is vital that they create a new equilibrium between education, research, and service and define new strategies for assisting Liberian society in addressing other urgent problems.

For example, the universities can establish certificate, undergraduate, and graduate programs in education, the social sciences, health, agriculture, computer science, architecture, engineering, and urban-rural and environmental studies, which have relevance to the reconstruction of the country. Through collaboration with other institutions, government, the private sector, and local communities, universities can assist in developing a national agenda of health care reform.

Finally, in this regard, it is fundamentally vital that the universities and the MOH&SW in postwar Liberia find ways of interacting effectively. Without policy-level access to educators who produce human resources or to research workers who can answer questions about health service problems, health decision makers are deprived of information critical to their making sound decisions. On the other hand, university leaders with effective access to the health care system where their graduates will work have inadequate guidelines (quantitatively and qualitatively) for prudent planning of human resource training and distribution. The interaction of the university and the Ministry should be seen as an example of constructive interdependence, the lack of which leads to waste, unnecessary duplication, and general ineffectiveness. Postwar Liberian universities should step out of their "ivory towers" and be willing to conduct participatory community-based research where the universities themselves, as well as communities, will benefit from joint ventures and alliances that will complement and expand their own bases of responsibility for the health of Liberia's general population.

Note

1. World Health Organization (2004). *World report on knowledge for better health: Strengthening health systems* (pp.97). World Health Organization: Geneva.

CHAPTER 9

LIBERIA'S HEALTH CARE SYSTEM: A FRAMEWORK FOR REFORM IN THE POSTWAR ERA

Knowledge is not a commodity—it does not flow down a gradient from researchers to decision-makers. Using a soccer metaphor, management of knowledge is not about keeping an eye on the ball but on the goal, and being sensitive to the nature and vagaries of the playing field. Knowledge is not the ball but what goes on between the players who share a belief and a common purpose—to score the goal.[1]

—Ariel Pablos-Mendez M.D., M.P.H., Professor,
   Columbia University of Mailman,
   School of Public Health

The Search for Concepts and Strategies

Achievement of health in Liberia depends on a shared vision of a future that is not stumbled into, but deliberately designed. This must be a far-reaching vision, chosen not just because it seeks to make life better for Liberians today, but also because it forces Liberians to carry out their collective responsibility to ensure the welfare of future generations. Liberians need to move beyond dependency on their neighbors and the international community to self-reliance in resolving many of the problems that face their country in the postwar era, such as problems in education; transportation; water, utilities, and sanitation; and health care.

Strategic health care planning should be based upon a broad health vision grounded in the social fabric of Liberian society. A healthy future for Liberia cannot be measured merely by how many modern health care facilities the country has, how many trained health care professionals there are, or how many dollars are allocated to pharmaceuticals. One way it is going to be measured will be by the health outcomes for all the people, no matter their status in society. The issue of accountability will be a new measurement to be reckoned with in postwar Liberia in terms of health care. Previously, there had been a breakdown in accountability between the leaders and the people due to the lack of participatory governance. A government that decides not to be accountable to its citizens will become an obstacle to achieving optimal health for the people. A health care system that caters primarily to an affluent minority will be a skewed health care system that will generate an imbalance in health outcomes across the population; an inclusive health care system that fosters a participatory approach to the design of health programs will achieve better health levels and higher satisfaction with health care services. It is not enough for the health policy makers in postwar Liberia to endorse the World Health Organization (WHO) notion of "health for all"; rather, they must try to develop practical, customized, prudent health policies that will make profound differences in the lives of all Liberia's people.

Globally, health care delivery is experiencing evolutionary—and even revolutionary—changes due to technological advances and a growing sense of social consciousness. The health care system in Liberia stagnated during the civil conflict that left the country devastated. Reviving the system will require becoming up-to-date with advances in health care and igniting a sense of social responsibility. Policy makers have the opportunity to lead the country into a new era of altruism and advancement.

Citizens have the opportunity to elect officials who are responsible to them and their welfare and are capable of moving the country along to meet its strategic objectives. That requires the general population to be well informed on the issues and the stands that politicians take on those issues. Citizens need to exercise their rights by voting in every election—at the local, county, and national levels. Illiteracy is not an excuse to not take part in the democratic process. Voter education can be adapted to the literacy levels of the people. Those who are educated are morally and ethically responsible for helping other citizens to gain access to balanced information and for assisting them in accurately casting their ballots. During political campaigns, it will be important for citizens to demand that politicians articulate their health care platforms. Once politicians are elected, citizens need to keep them accountable to their campaign promises, especially in areas that affect the complicated, interrelated factors affecting their health and well-being.

There should be no illusion on the part of health care officials about the ease of reviving the health care system and promoting good health for the general population. Restructuring a healthcare system of a failed state is monumental task. This rebuilding process will involve every sector of postwar society and will require the infusion of substantial resources. Because of the war, health officials will be faced with such complicated issues as post-traumatic stress syndrome among combatants, many of whom were children during the war. It is realistic to expect increased antisocial and violent behavior among not only adults, but children as well. The question remains: How can any postwar government adequately deal with poverty, poor housing conditions, sanitation, and nutrition? Health officials also must cope with population growth when extended family structures are barely functioning and struggle with absorbing the needs of new family members. Ever-present infectious and communicable diseases such as malaria will be yet other conditions to reckon with.

The emergence of new diseases, including HIV/AIDS, further erodes the extended family structure, strains family resources, and requires brand-new ways of accessing and providing complex therapies. Other sub-Saharan countries that have been spared the setback of war have enjoyed a window of opportunity to develop programs that influenced risk-taking behavior. The efforts by these stable countries eventually led to some decline in the incidence and prevalence of HIV infection. On the other hand, war-impacted countries like Liberia sustained social disorder of such a magnitude that it will require even more comprehensive and major resources to catch up with other countries. It is important to the health of all the people in sub-Saharan Africa for unstable states to address immediately the issue of how to reverse the acceleration of new cases of HIV, due to the intercontinental migrations of people. All these factors will make planning of health care in the new Liberia more difficult.

A Realistic Appraisal of the Current Health Care System

Past practices have left Liberia with a health care system characterized by erosion of infrastructure, declining access to health care services, and inadequate supply of essential pharmaceuticals. These constraints lead to poor health outcomes, including increased malnutrition in children, unusually high maternal mortality, and increased infant mortality. Efforts at reform have been frustrated in the past by poor funding of the system, corruption and greed at all levels, misguided policies, and failure to utilize available expertise and experience to the fullest. These structural issues are amplified by poor staff morale, leading to an exodus of trained health care professionals. The common practice of problem solving before one really understands the problem should become a practice of the past. Postwar health officials will have to take the time to understand the interconnected relationships between problems before moving to the planning stage of problem solving. If planning is done without any vision for the future, it will become difficult to achieve optimal health for the nation.

In order to enhance the health status of the people of Liberia, a visionary, innovative, and egalitarian approach to health care delivery is necessary. Poverty is a major factor in poor health outcomes. The difference between being rich and ill and poor and ill can be life and death. A rich individual living in a village—farming cash crops and owning a vehicle—has the means to transport his wife during labor to deliver in a hospital, minimizing complications, while a subsistence farmer who travels by foot has no alternative but to trust in a traditional birth attendant (TBA) from the village. If the pregnancy is a risky one involving prolonged labor, the TBA may be unequipped or lack the skills to perform a complicated delivery, thereby putting the mother and the fetus at risk. Since most Liberians are desperately poor, they are relegated to making similar forced choices.

Rather than seeing poor people as dependent victims, a fresh approach would be to view them as valuable resources in rebuilding countries emerging from civil conflict. Although vulnerable, in order to survive, poor people rely on resilience, resourcefulness, and optimism. Their inner drive to survive and prosper is the very spirit a country needs to revitalize its economy and health. Some of the beckoning questions that Liberian officials must face in the postwar era include: How can poor people's lives become more secure so that they have a foothold to step out of poverty? How can poor people gain access to economic opportunities? How can they receive ongoing health care to sustain their daily efforts to improve their lives? In developing countries and countries emerging from civil war, poverty could be conceptualized on two fronts: poverty of information and poverty of material goods. Each requires a different macro strategy; however, it is important to remember that these issues are merged within a person's life.

Reducing informational poverty is the key to reducing material poverty. Informational and material poverty both have an impact on health. For example, if efforts are directed toward improving informational poverty by such methods as teaching basic sanitation, nutritional awareness, breast-feeding practices, and family planning, then families can optimize their resources. The rural poor especially need access to information.

In countries plagued by civil war in which there is limited order afterward, social disruption leads to poverty. Many individuals experience lasting psychological trauma that impairs their ability to lift themselves up from poverty. Some effort has to be made to pay particular attention to that vulnerable group. Helping poor people find their voice is the foundational strategy for elevating the status and living conditions of the poor. Poor people, organized in groups and using their voice, can make an impact on policy making and, thus, the value of citizen participation. Contrary to conventional attitudes, poor people provide strength to a country because they possess latent energy and resilience once given the opportunity to improve their lives. Liberian policy makers must realize that improving the lives of poor people will mean addressing both informational and material poverty at national, regional, and local levels.

The postwar era in countries emerging from civil conflicts is an opportune time for developing visionary plans that would be used to reform the health care system and that would address the needs of all people. These strategies will include the goal of trying to achieve the following: (1) creating a societal consensus on future directions in health care; (2) endorsing a broader approach to health care that emphasizes health and wellness; (3) using low-tech, cost-effective technology to implement care; (4) responding to changing sociodemographic, political, economic, and cultural milieus; and (5) basing health care reforms and policy decision-making on projections of long-term impacts on the health of the people.

Even before the civil war, the Liberian health care system had developed over the years essentially as a system that focused primarily on treating illness rather than on emphasizing health promotion activities, a focus that is typical of most sub-Saharan African countries. The services provided, including education, research, planning, and data collection, are all focused on illness and disease. The orientation toward sickness is coupled with a disregard of alternative practices and approaches in favor of a few high-level institutions in a misguided attempt to prove that their health care delivery system has achieved some level of sophistication. This type of approach is typical of developing countries that are trying to embrace the global perspective on what defines good health care delivery. Although the leading causes of morbidity and mortality in Liberia for all age groups are still preventable in nature, the medical education system for physicians and nurses appears to produce practitioners who look only at disease processes and not the wider concept of health.

Overall, levels of financial support for health promotion and illness prevention have characteristically been too low and have not matched disease patterns. In the postwar era, there will be a constant need to develop innovative ideas for disease prevention programs that will have an impact on the population. In previous administrations, the community health intervention approach that would be most relevant to disease prevention has been hampered from taking on major initiatives for various reasons: poor leadership, limited resources, inadequate legislated powers, weak management, and the lack of grassroots participation. Besides these administrative problems, the health care delivery system has not interacted and collaborated enough with other systems at the policy and program levels. For example, Liberia's ministries of finance, education, rural development, and agriculture could work with MOH&SW in developing joint programs that would holistically meet the health care needs of the people. Optimal health and well-being is not isolated from other aspects of human life; it is integrated into socioeconomic, religious, cultural, and environmental aspects of life. When the efforts of government ministries are compartmentalized, it is harder for them to have a long-lasting effect on society.

During a prewar administration, the Liberian government established a National Primary Health Care (PHC) Program, financed under the National Socioeconomic Development Plan with the assistance of collaborating agencies and other governments. The civil war halted all PHC programs. As a starting point, it would be important to revisit the PHC plan, regardless of how it will be conceptualized in the future. There needs to be recognition of who owns the program and is responsible for establishing clarity of purpose and comprehensive implementation. The Liberian people, in the postwar era, will also have to assume some responsibility for their own health. Past neglect in building citizens' responsibility for their health and the lack of reinforcing discipline among medical professionals in management and leadership led to the failure of past health initiatives. Liberia needs a system that fosters collaboration among all stakeholders in key decision-making; this suggests an interdisciplinary approach that includes professionals from other relevant disciplines at top management levels, including health economists, health policy analysts, anthropologists, sociologists, epidemiologists, demographers, and communication specialists.

Because officials at the MOH&SW are in appointed positions, serving at the pleasure of the administration, they may be handicapped in being able to push for health-related legislative reforms. If any plans are developed in the postwar years, the government should endorse them so that such plans are legitimized and funded. The legislative role in health care delivery in postwar Liberia must be transparent and consistent with a clear vision for improving the health of the population. In the absence of effective legislation supporting health reforms that benefit the people, public decision-making and programs will be developed on the basis of institutional aspirations or professional demands rather than on the needs of the community. Cost and quality are two important factors to consider when reforming the system. Given the fact that Liberia has limited resources, political decisions have to be made to ensure quality care while containing costs and recovering some of the expenses. Cost recovery was one of the weak areas in prewar administrations.

This is a new era for sub-Saharan African countries seeking funding to support health care and social service systems. During the cold war between the West and the Soviet bloc, it was easy to receive handouts from either side because African countries were being played as pawns. During that time, there was a scramble for exploiting Africa's natural resources (diamonds, gold, iron ore, rubber, and timber). African countries have already been compensated for the rights to some of these resources, and there is no more revenue to be gained. Other resources have been depleted, and as for some of those resources that are still being mined, they have lost their value on the global market. International companies that were giving back to the community through tax revenues and altruistic donations have pulled out of Liberia and moved to other parts of the world.

Globally, developed countries themselves are faced with their own economic crises and are donating and loaning less money to developing countries, even though the need is still pressing. Countries that have been critical in the development of Liberia in the past have diverted their resources to other developing countries that have avoided civil war and to other competing needs. The ideology of what constitutes development has changed over the years in terms of time and perspective. It has shifted from looking for long-term, subtle changes to using measurable objectives that have been formulated by bureaucrats. Leaders at the forefront of health care reforms in postwar Liberia must be cognizant of these global changes which may adversely impact local health care policies.

As a start, the government of Liberia could institute a health tax based on income, so that the wealthier segment of society helps support the health care infrastructure. Further, the fee-for-service system that was sporadically implemented in the past, particularly in private rural health care institutions, was seen to be oriented toward the provision of "cures" rather than health promotion and illness prevention. This inevitably encouraged the greater use of acute care and hospital-based services. If the fee-for-service program is revived in the postwar era, two factors need to be considered: equity in service provision and cost recovery. In this postwar era, Liberian politicians and health care leaders will need to develop a new paradigm that embraces both health care delivery and economic development.

Before the civil war, it was clear that increased demands for new and expensive technologies in Liberia's health care system were made with little or no assessment of efficacy in the Liberian context and the cost-benefit ratio. For example, poor policies and procedures for maintenance of equipment in government hospitals and health centers, coupled with unskilled use, have led to a waste of useful technology. Moreover, continued dependence on high-tech solutions rather than appropriate technology reinforces the bias toward the biomedical model and promotes the overspecialization of professionals. Skewing the health care delivery system toward a biomedical, high-tech approach creates a bias against the conservative tenets of primary health care. This type of structure also leads to an emphasis on training health care workers to use advanced technology and creates a milieu of dependence on technology in settings where the highest need is for simpler disease prevention and health promotion measures. Before the civil conflict, many skilled health care professionals in Liberian hospitals (especially physicians who had specialized training) drifted away to "greener pastures" as soon as they completed their training abroad because they could not practice their high-tech expertise in hospitals that did not have sophisticated equipment. There is a need to define a basic package of essential health care services. The high cost associated with technological solutions results in a shift of resources away from community-focused caring programs.

Over the years, bureaucratic inertia in the MOH&SW and other sectors of the government made it difficult, if not impossible, to achieve change, whether politically inspired or scientifically correct. Consequently, new health initiatives received little encouragement from MOH&SW officials. The lack of fiscal policy caused various community support services to suffer. Inefficient administration of MOH&SW funds damaged credibility and made it impossible to carry out reforms. The result was that the benefits and the ease of implementation of proposed economic and health reforms were exaggerated to make them acceptable. In this case, the process of change was unpredictable, as was the impact of programs on the health of the population.

Defining a Strategic Vision for Health Care Delivery in Postwar Liberia: Understanding Structural Barriers

Underlying any proposed reform of postwar Liberia's health care system should be a clear and holistic definition of health. While WHO espouses universal access to health care, achieving optimal health is dependent on the environment in which people live. Aspirations for health in countries emerging from civil conflict will obviously differ from those in countries that enjoy stability and economic growth. In a postwar era, enormous work needs to be done to help citizens cope with their stressful and unhealthy environment, as well as the frustrations of dealing with a dysfunctional health care delivery system. For many of these individuals, it may just be matters of helping them meet their daily needs. It may also mean helping them recapture personal resources that helped them survive before the war, such as access to safe drinking water and vegetable gardens. Optimal health is a positive concept, emphasizing social and personal resources as well as physical capacity. A noble effort would be helping improve the quality of life for individuals emerging from civil conflicts, as they define it. This could mean securing physical safety, rebuilding of their familial and social networks, reclamation of their previous identities, and opening up sustainable economic opportunities.

The postwar governments of Liberia, through the MOH&SW, should become more committed to the provision of quality health care for all people and the management of the health care delivery system. These goals should be achieved through establishing a blueprint for transforming the Liberian health care system. Postwar health care reform should include infusing significant dollars into the health care system, creating accountability within the system, expanding community-based program design, encouraging personal responsibility for health, and developing a new cadre of health care professionals that will create a stronger, more diverse team in both clinical and public health settings.

One concept that should be elaborated upon is the issue of equity of health policies. Defining equity in health is somewhat different than defining equity in terms of economic goods. Equity in health means that everyone should at least be able to receive basic primary health care services at an affordable cost. In order to create this equity for all, higher-income individuals or privately insured individuals may have to pay for these services at a higher rate.

Conceptualizing Institutional and Structural Reforms

In order to understand how to initiate organizational change, it is important to understand how Liberians relate to organizations and how their social networks and affiliations influence their decision-making. Individuals who become part of organizations generally come from the educated and professionalized segment of society. This sets up a barrier between the professionals and their constituents. Most of the organizations are based on Western models of how people should effectively work together to achieve organizational goals. The Liberians who have advanced in these organizations are often the ones who could most easily adapt to these models. One approach would be to find change agents who are adaptable to both the Western culture these organizations represent and the Liberian culture they serve. The ideal approach for countries emerging from civil conflict might be to introduce new organizational models that are a hybrid of Western and Liberian organizational perspectives.

The "village" concept of equity and shared responsibility for the good of all would be an important place to start in reforming the system or creating a new model. The African tenet of teamwork—where each member of the team works to the best of his or her ability and is valued for her or his effort—highlights that employees are the critical assets in system building. Patience, endurance, and resiliency are indigenous characteristics that can support or obstruct organizational change, depending on the urgency of the issue at hand. Slowing down the approval process in order to gain communal "buy-in" may ultimately speed up the implementation phase, but this is useful only if there is enough time. The perspective that many Liberians have on illness or health is that members of a person's network will do their share to take care of that person if that person does his or her share to get well.

Patience is a virtue in the health care profession. For example, it takes time and trial and error to conceptualize a health program and see it through to the achievement of outcomes. However, complacency is a dangerous state of mind for health care planners and a dangerous situation for health care systems. Liberians in the prewar era—at both the personal level and the health systems level—have been too complacent when it comes to facing the changing world. Because of the endemic nature of disease and the lack of health resources, sub-Saharan Africans as well as individuals in other developing countries have developed too high a tolerance for morbidity and mortality. This unfortunate tolerance has been built over the years as a survival mechanism; people adapt to the conditions that are beyond their control.

In a war-torn country like Liberia, people have adapted to daily violence, the fear of being raped, and bare minimums of food, inadequate shelter, overcrowded and unsanitary conditions, and disease outbreaks. This defeatist attitude, feeling of apathy and fatalistic outlook on life constitute a barrier to changing people's health behaviors or willingness to access health care. This same kind of complacency seen on a personal level with the general population is also evident in the health care providers who interact with the population and are responsible for dispensing health care services. Just because they are professionals does not mean they can escape personal feelings of defeatism, apathy, and fatalism. In fact, as the front line against excess burdens of disease and mortality, they may be even more vulnerable because they see these things on a bigger scale and regularly encounter crisis in their daily practice.

Research conducted locally that illustrates the benefits of health care programs will be instrumental in counteracting negative attitudes and instilling hope in the public. An important systemic change for countries emerging from civil war is for their ministries of health to regard public health information as a tool for changing the public's knowledge, attitudes, and beliefs about health. Outcomes of programs should not be kept within the system but should be widely disseminated for public use. Recognition of the progress being made in reducing mortality and morbidity is crucial for a country that is trying to reform a health care system that has been decimated from civil conflict. It creates solidarity between the government and the people; it makes reform transparent; it instills trust in the efficacy of health programs; and it creates a climate of proactive health behavior. Health programming is one of those realms by which unity and nationalism can be fostered; typically, illness and disease cross the boundaries of ethnocentrism. The desire for health is a universal quest. Working for the greater good in health care is a powerful effort that a government can make as it rebuilds its country.

Working toward the greater good of society is an ongoing effort. For instance, health care professionals should continue to teach prevention to families that have escaped health crises as well as to families that have experienced illness and death. All families need to sustain faith in the health care system, despite its shortcomings. This is where, in the postwar era, Liberia's government will have to be frank with the public about realistic health objectives in reasonable time frames; there should be no place for grandiose promises to curry political favor. Even when the government cannot reach a health goal—which will happen because some disease patterns are unpredictable—health professionals need to clarify the situation to the public. Although some Liberians may be resistant to facing difficult truths, there still should be an effort to strive for honesty. In the end, people want to know where they stand, especially about something as important as their health.

Sufficient political commitment is needed to support change in the health care system because otherwise, change will be disconnected from reform in other sectors. Postwar MOH&SW officials need commitment from legislators as well as the executive branch in order for health care reform to take hold. Liberians must not be afraid of change; some degree of risk is important to institutional reform. Good governance reduces the risk over time, as change becomes part of the system. A proactive stance in health planning and delivery also reduces risk because the system will be prepared to better handle unforeseen catastrophes. A system that strives for honesty and rewards employees for contribution to the common good will yield a better outcome and will be able to sustain itself in the future.

The most empowering approach for Liberians to conceptualize institutional and structural reforms would be to combine a Liberian sensibility of human interaction in a cultural context with a Western understanding of organizational change. Change is conceptualized differently in a sub-Saharan African country than in a Western country. In the Western world, change often feeds a desire for a sense of control; in a developing country, a person might feel more in control if she or he resists change and tries to maintain the status quo, even if that status quo may be perceived by others as undesirable. In order to support systemic change, people have to be made to see that there are better alternatives that are achievable through a combination of self-determination and collectivism. This happens both within the system and among the public.

Changing dysfunctional bureaucracies is going to be one of the paramount tasks in the postwar area. No matter how the Liberian government is reorganized, there will still be a need for a central agency responsible for health care. A centralized structure needs to be operating at optimal efficiency and with integrity in order for the localized programs to work. Integrating national and local aspects of the system will ensure the functionality of both.

The major thrust of health reforms should be devoted to the MOH&SW functions of planning, management, service delivery, funding/resource allocation, and revenue generation. Reforms in these areas should be complemented by strategic reforms to foster strong commitment from the central government and others already involved with clearly written goals and objectives as well as clear definitions of roles and responsibilities, backed by a legislative agenda and corporate planning. In addition, issues such as gender and health, human resource development, the role of nongovernmental organizations (NGOs) and donor coordination should be addressed.

Reforming Organizational Structure

The central focus of reform should be decentralization of the health care system so that counties and major hospitals can have discretionary authority over personnel recruitment, the assignment of tasks, and the allocation of resources. This process should include the setting up of suitable structures for community participation in decision-making, quality control, and financial accountability. As decentralization gets under way, the primary agency responsible for health care organization and delivery, the MOH&SW, needs to increase its capacity for monitoring and consultation.

The role of the primary health agency in sub-Saharan African countries, usually located in the capital city, should evolve into one where the agency sees itself as a central agency whose objective is to build its capacity to provide leadership, resources, and a national agenda for the implementation of health care for all citizens. A centralized pool of expertise in the major departments of health planning and management could efficiently supply the logistical and technical support and expertise to address critical health issues at local levels. A complementary goal of the central health agency would be to help local communities to build capacities for management initiatives in district-based health care.

This structure will ensure the ability to monitor the quality of health care on a national level. National coordination of disease control is necessary because people are mobile, so it would be difficult to restrict diseases by geographic area. In addition, concurrent health programs can benefit from collaboration in terms of educational campaigns, purchasing medical supplies in bulk, and having a national framework for evaluating outcomes. Improved financing for the health sector can result when funding is lobbied for on a national level. When the central health planning agencies in sub-Saharan African governments are viewed by other governmental sectors as being critical to the overall development of their respective nations, they will be considered key stakeholders in the decision-making process for issues that impact the health of the population.

The proposed new central structure clarifies the collaborative relationship among legislators, the heads of various governmental agencies, and the professional/technical operational leaders of the central health care agency. Other responsibilities of a centralized administration include the setting of policies and national guidelines, the coordination of research and provision of information on health issues, and the coordination of donor contributions to the health care sector. An immediate critical function of the centralized health-governing agency will be to assist local communities in seeking out necessary funding to fill the gaps that limited national resources cannot provide in the postwar era.

Out of necessity, in any country emerging from civil conflict, the national government will need to set policy priorities because it has to address the needs of the country as a whole and because the community-based health networks have been shattered by war. As the national government works to revive community-based health networks, the centralized health-governing agency can rely on these networks to give accurate information about community needs and to participate in implementation of health programs. It should be the eventual aim of the health care reform process that communities provide plans—conceived at the local level—for incorporation into a national health plan.

The reform process should be designed so that health programs and projects can be evaluated impartially. Before any program is implemented on a large scale, base-line data must be gathered and a pilot study should be conducted to ensure feasibility. The successful implementation of a reform process depends on the appropriate training of all stakeholders. If the central health-governing agency does not have the expertise to train stakeholders adequately regarding programmatic issues, it may want to tap into the private sector for consultants. Along with program design and implementation components, the central health-governing agency also needs to institute reforms in the health care financing sector.

Reforming the Financing of Health Care

Financing is the lifeblood of any health care delivery system. If the health care system is poorly financed, undesirable health effects could result. Financing of health care is a major problem in sub-Saharan African countries. New health policies in countries emerging from civil conflict will call for initiatives in the area of cost containment and sourcing of revenue. For instance, effective cost containment requires a budget structure that would make possible the most effective provision of health services to populations most in need. Proposals for raising more resources for the health care sector should be an important part of any reform plan. Some options suggested by the World Bank that are applicable are compulsory or private insurance; user charges (cost recovery and cost sharing); and community financing.

Cost sharing in the provision of health care could be a viable option for a country emerging from a civil war because it allows the cost to be spread across the consumers and the national government. It allows consumers to become more aware of the true cost of health care so that they are more proactive in their own health care and more prudent about accessing and using health care in an effort not to spend their personal funds unnecessarily for services that may not be needed. It also helps citizens gain an appreciation for the investment that the government is or is not making in health care.

No government in sub-Saharan Africa has infinite resources to spend on providing health care to its people. Therefore, there has to be a way to distribute health care equitably that will not put the financial stability of the country in jeopardy as the country also focuses on reforming other crucial sectors. For cost sharing to be an ethically sound approach in a country whose health care system has been shattered by war, there must be the recognition that many individuals will not be able to afford even the minimum fee that will be asked of them. Hence, the government will have to find a way to take care of those vulnerable people without destroying their dignity. Compassionate cost sharing is a way to help people recover their dignity and feel empowered to more self-sufficiency again. International donors are persuaded to give by the degree to which local programs have the potential to become self-staining, and cost sharing is one indicator that self-sufficiency will eventually be possible.

Reforming the financing of health care is a long-range proposition for countries emerging from civil conflict. Because the infrastructure of the country is dysfunctional in profound ways, reform will require infusion of capital and the lending of expertise in planning, finance, and management. Experts from these fields could include Liberians who were studying or practicing abroad during the civil conflict; experts from other countries, both sub-Saharan and beyond; and experts operating beyond borders in international health-related organizations. During the first phase of reform, leaders need to articulate a strategic vision for rethinking the organization and financing of the health care sector. Critical to this phase will be the identification of key stakeholders in the process.

Consensus building among stakeholders is a key component to reform because stakeholders need to embrace the broader view if they are going to champion change at the community level. The international community should seize this opportunity to support peace in Liberia by helping to revive the country's health care system. If the devastated health care system does not become functional, in time it will indirectly create an environment that could lead to further instability in the country. The general population will question why postwar governments have not taken the steps to provide basic health care for its members. In addition to support from international philanthropic networks, multinational companies operating within the borders of Liberia will also have to contribute their fair share to rebuilding. Multinational companies need to examine their role in health care reform as it contributes to rebuilding the country. Liberians who came of age during the civil conflict will not have the same threshold as others might for tolerating exploitation by outside companies seeking to make a profit at the expense of the Liberian people. On the one hand, Liberia needs multinational companies to boost its economic system; on the other hand, these companies will be held to a high standard of practice that includes giving back to the community.

While the international community is contributing capital and human resources to rebuilding the health care system, the next phase will be for Liberians to find significant ways to help themselves. There is a common Liberian saying that when someone is washing the back of a sick person, the sick person needs to be washing his or her own chest. Independence, autonomy, and sustainability of successful health care programs are the ultimate goals. To achieve these goals, the Liberian people must take a proactive role in their nation's health care system, as well as in their personal health. The issue of community involvement in health care reform is compounded by the heterogeneity of the Liberian community (culturally, economically, educationally, and geographically). All of the diverse segments of Liberian society must be considered when developing or designing future health programs.

The new approach to health care in Liberia should be goal-oriented rather than simply crisis-reactive. Health initiatives should center on understanding the determinants of health and on developing responsive programs. Liberia, as a tropical country, is faced with many endemic conditions that are propagated by the physical environment and climate. Lifestyle is a major determinant of health, no matter where one lives. Physical and social environments, as well as a lack of medical care, influence choices that may negatively impact health. An environment like Liberia's, decimated by civil conflict, precludes some of the traditional health-supporting choices that the general population followed prior to the civil war: gardening, subsistence farming, walking as transportation, unpolluted air, clean water, adequate outhouses for sanitation, and effective garbage disposal. The country's internally displaced individuals live in overcrowded conditions that serve as a medium of ill health and perpetuate poor health choices, such as eating processed foods, drinking pol-

luted water, inhaling smoke from burning garbage, and becoming sedentary. Before the civil conflict, people lived in a comforting social network; during the civil war, they lived in social isolation and fear that has
carried over to postwar years. Resolving some of the physical health crises might be easier than resolving the psychological and social crises of
war that may linger for decades.

In a society where people have differing attitudes toward and approaches to health, there is a need for tolerance and for mechanisms to
limit conflict. Groups with differing views, such as traditional healers
and private physicians, should be able to interact through local structures.
In a developing country, the decision to diversify choice and potential in
health should be made against the background of a community-based
approach of providing health care for the collective good of society. The
new approach to health in Liberia should also stress cooperation rather
than competition among the stakeholders.

In the past, health care planners have neglected to involve other sectors of the government that impact health care delivery. A collaborative
attitude promotes a freer exchange of information, the opportunity for
dialogue, the formulation of shared values and ideas, and the consideration of joint solutions to shared problems. Liberia's ministries of education, agriculture, and health could work together using scarce resources
to achieve such goals as optimal health for primary-school children. For
example, there could be joint efforts by these different sectors to establish feeding programs in the schools.

Minimizing Corruption Within the Health Care System in the Postwar Era

In both developed and developing countries, corruption always exists
in health care systems to some degree. The existence of corruption is due
to both structural and personal factors. Structural factors include system
wide variables such as the complex organizational layers of health care
delivery; the fluidity and variability of payment methods; and the hierarchy of power in health care professions and among professionals. In most
countries, the delivery and utilization of health care occur under imperfect market conditions; patients have limited information about the availability of services as well as the prices charged by and the quality of providers. Patients also do not bear the true cost of services, as a third-party
payer, such as an insurance company or the government, is involved.

Other factors contributing to the possibility of corruption within the health care system of many sub-Saharan African countries stems from the practice of modern medicine in a setting that is still traditional. The biomedical approach relies heavily on the dispensing of pharmaceuticals; patients expect to be treated with pharmaceuticals; and pharmaceuticals are the fastest-growing segment of most health care delivery systems. Developing countries have a greater reliance on pharmaceutical companies outside their borders, which creates more opportunities for corruption. Where pharmaceuticals are a scarce and valuable commodity, a black market in pharmaceuticals will flourish.

Poverty and a low literacy rate are personal factors that breed corruption in the health care system. The crisis nature of illness also makes patients vulnerable to inappropriate and inadequate treatment because they are seeking an immediate resolution as opposed to navigating the system to seek the best value. Limited access in terms of availability and affordability of health care puts patients at risk for exploitation or could make them prone to engaging in minor forms of corruption. Because of the desperate nature of life in a developing country—and the concomitant struggles to survive during civil conflict—the general population in countries emerging from civil war may have developed too high a tolerance for corruption. People in war-impacted countries survived through acts of corruption, so corruption become a way of life. Add to this tragic history an unrelenting community and family pressure to provide for and rescue extended family and community members, and there exist the ingredients for corruption in health care professionals. A lack of checks and balances in health care governance, a reluctance to make organizational processes transparent, and a sense of entitlement among the elite leaders that disenfranchises the common people all lead to fissures of corruption in the health care system. The progress that health care professionals and communities make toward eliminating corruption in the health care system can inspire other sectors that are undertaking reform.

Paying health care professionals a decent wage commensurate with their skills and paying them in a timely manner would be the first major step in creating a disincentive for corrupt actions. Developing a national code of ethics for the health care system is a visible and useful tool for creating a climate of integrity among health care professionals. It can be part of the training process as well as an integral part of practice. Many developed countries have created mechanisms by which patients can become aware of their rights in the health care system and of avenues for lodging grievances if they are dissatisfied with their care and services received.

In many sub-Saharan African countries, patients are passive when dealing with the health care system. As the system in the postwar era is being redesigned, it will be important to educate patients to develop a more proactive stance in advocating for their rights to optimal care and to be treated with dignity and respect. Corruption interrupts the normal operational processes on every level. In order to navigate the system, desperately poor people feel compelled to use their scarce resources to "tip" the receptionist, the triage nurse, the lab and X-ray technicians, and the pharmacist. Grossly underpaid health care professionals feel compelled to accept tips in order to raise their low wages to a subsistence level.

Along with strategies for preventing corruption—such as a transparent organizational system, reasonable wages paid on time, a clear understanding of professional ethics, and a patients' bill of rights—specific individuals involved in corrupt activities will need to be prosecuted. Within health ministries, anti-corruption bodies should be set up to help reduce the entrenched corruption in these settings. Such bodies should be responsible for fair hearings and appropriate treatment, undertaken with sensitivity to cultural norms that have evolved over time. Comprehending the underlying motives for corruption may reveal real barriers to accessing health care that need to be resolved before the issue of corruption within the system can be addressed. For example, there may be a conflict of interest between health care professionals and the cultural value system within which they live. A health care professional may be encouraged to exercise loyalty to members of his or her village over the system. Because there are so few professionals who have been generated from local communities, the ones who succeed often carry the burden of responding to all the health care needs of their respective villages. Making good in response to community members' requests for preferential treatment may not necessarily be perceived as corruption within the value system of many sub-Saharan African countries. A noble goal would be to unravel corruption while teaching villagers how to be their own advocates for health care. This would relieve the pressure on health care professionals who believe that they owe loyalty only to their home villages.

There are many triumphs of human will in sub-Saharan Africa today; the majority of the continent's people are coping with crises such as drought, famine, endemic infectious diseases, poverty, illiteracy, and intertribal conflict. No matter the hardship, the will to survive with dignity is omnipresent. In many sub-Saharan African countries, civil conflict, however, tests the human capacity for economic and cultural survival. War exacts tangible and intangible costs that cause countries to lag behind in progress—economically, educationally, and in the general health status of the population.

When these civil conflicts end, there should be an opportunity to rise above the destruction and build on the positive attributes of the people. Citizens who have lived through a war have a chance to heal their emotional wounds if their country learns from the tragic mistakes that led to the war. Communal efforts in renewal can be a healing process. As is the case of other failed states, the world's attention will be focused on Liberia for only a short period after the war. This is the time for hope to be rekindled in everyone.

Delivering health care is a hopeful endeavor that can bring unity to a country. Health is at the core of the well being of the general population. In turn, such well-being helps jump-start other national and local development initiatives. Restructuring the agencies responsible for the delivery of health care (for example, the MOH&SW in Liberia) should be of paramount importance. The previously centralized, bureaucratic structure may need to be reformed in order to smooth the way for launching postwar health initiatives. Optimal health is a universal right for all people, not just for people of influence. The ill health of one sector of the population has an adverse impact on the entire population.

The power base needs to be decentralized to allow for greater public participation and greater local control over the outcomes of health initiatives. The need for continuous quality improvement is critical in health care reform. There is a need to periodically revise the vision of the future that guides planning processes. Policy leaders in Liberia must be ready to learn from their past mistakes. Such humility will increase their credibility with the people.

Authoritarian and nonparticipatory bureaucracies will not create or foster community ownership in health initiatives. An important task in Liberia during this postwar era will be to tap into the skills of local health care professionals, the international community, and government services to resolve health care problems. There will be numerous stakeholders working together in the postwar era, so there is bound to be some intergroup conflict over how certain programs are developed and implemented. It will be important for each group to respect the others. Only through this mutual respect can nationalism triumph over tribalism.

Over the next decade, the people of Liberia will measure the progress of any postwar government in their country by improvements in the health status of the general population; in the number of children in school and the quality of their education; in access to and availability of basic amenities, including water and electricity in towns and villages; and in citizens' general perceptions of happiness and of their ability to determine their own destinies.

Notes

1. World Health Organization (2004). *World report on knowledge for better health: Strengthening health systems* (pp.97). World Health Organization: Geneva.

CHAPTER 10

EPILOGUE

The test of our progress is not whether we add more to the abundance of those who have much; it is whether we provide enough for those who have too little.[1]

—Franklin D. Roosevelt, president of the United States of America, second inaugural address, 1937

Rising to the Challenges of Rebuilding the Liberian Health Care Infrastructure

Liberia is rich with natural and human resources, as well as diverse sociocultural assets. These assets were not fully embraced and utilized in prewar Liberia. The nation's previous leaders did not consider the health of the people as a priority area or appreciate its intricate linkage with economic development. As a result, numerous economic development strategies—even before the civil war—were sometimes misguided and failed to yield optimal results for the funds invested. The protracted civil war has also led to near destruction of the Liberian health care delivery infrastructure, and it will take years to create a new, fully functioning system. A major consequence of the civil war is that progress made in improving health outcomes for the people in the 1970s and

1980s has all but vanished, and Liberia has since fallen behind other sub-Saharan African countries in meeting major health indicators.

The excess disease burden borne especially by vulnerable populations must matter in the reconstruction of postwar Liberia. Ecologically, a setting that breeds poverty also leads to poor health of populations. When the health of populations is compromised, economic development stagnates. Poor health in Liberian households can translate into decreased productivity at the national level. In one of his many writings on health and sustainable development, Amartya Sen eloquently emphasizes that "health is among the most important conditions of human life and a significant constituent of human capabilities which we have reason to value" (Sen, 1999). Especially in the 21st century, the health of the general population is an intricate manifestation of a country's ingenuity and its ability to develop new knowledge and progress.

As Liberia emerges from its civil conflict, it faces the public health challenges of high infant, child, and maternal mortality rates. Previous governments lacked the capacity in health policymaking and were unresponsive to the inequities in the health care system. Because the fighting halted subsistence farming and the majority of the population was internally displaced to urban centers, food has become scarce and prohibitively expensive for many. The current public health infrastructure is weak; health care facilities are variable in quantity and quality and are not adequately responsive to the needs of the population. The postwar Liberian government has made health care one of its priorities; the Liberian people aspire to make progress in improving their health and must be empowered to bring about change. A major challenge in the postwar era, therefore, will be to examine the internal and external impediments to development and health reforms in Liberia.

Enhancing the Health System and the Health of the Liberian People in the Postwar Era

In my preface to this book, I told the story of Lorpu and Na Korto, which revealed the interconnectedness of health with socioeconomic development. At the end of this book, I return to this all-important story. I would like the reader to think once again about Lorpu's sad demise, a common occurrence for many Liberians. What might have been written on the charts of patients like Lorpu as the cause of death? The doctors would probably write, "Patient died from obstetrics complications."

Studies on causes of maternal deaths in sub-Saharan African countries have found the following obstetrical complications recorded: prolonged labor, anemia, postpartum hemorrhage, retained placenta, pre-eclampsia, and miscarriage. But these medical diagnoses do not tell the whole story. Clearly, Lorpu's death from obstetrical complications was only the final link in a long chain of interconnected factors: the physical, biological, sociocultural, economic, and political factors related to health and health care delivery in a developing country. Despite their tremendous efforts, Na Korto and her family, along with her fellow villagers and the traditional birth attendant, were unable to save Lorpu's life. There were multiple factors that rendered their efforts powerless, some of which are culturally related and others that reflect structural flaws in the health care system. What health care professionals might conclude in retrospect was that Lorpu's death could have been prevented by access to prenatal care and early medical intervention during the tenure of her pregnancy and labor period.

Because of their training in the biomedical model, the doctors and nurses on duty the night that Lorpu was admitted to the hospital would probably define her problem as a biomedical one. Because of the narrow viewpoint used under the biomedical model in addressing many of the endemic health problems involved, these doctors and nurses might underestimate their ability to create the kind of societal change that could prevent a death like Lorpu's. The biomedical approach fails to fully consider and appreciate the critical sociocultural and economic factors that fed into the chain of events. All parties involved in this story quietly accepted Lorpu's death. Life goes on.

But health care researchers interested in understanding these dynamics more deeply and in creating change that will save lives are conducting studies in sub-Saharan African countries. They want to identify and understand barriers to the use of antenatal and obstetric care. Adamu and Salihu (2002), in a study in rural Kano, Nigeria, listed the following reasons why women do not access prenatal care: (1) financial constraints; (2) resignation to God's will; (3) husband refusal for woman to travel to another village for care; (4) ignorance; and (5) distance. In probing further, Adamu and Salihu, in the same study, found related reasons why women in the Kano region preferred home deliveries: (1) deliveries are easier at home; (2) resignation to God's will; (3) precipitate labor; (4) financial constraints; (5) husband's preference; and (6) distance.

Lorpu's story documents the need for health planners in sub-Saharan African countries, as well as international organizations working in the region, to look more deeply at the underlying causes of poor health and premature mortality. Whether pregnancy-related or not, many of the ailments that health care professionals will see in their practices are linked to multidimensional cultural factors. These factors may be unclear or overlooked by health care professionals. Even Liberian health care professionals, trained locally in Western health care models, could fail to incorporate cultural insights into their practices. For example, Lorpu's mother and the traditional midwife who brought her to the hospital were scolded by the doctor for not bringing her in sooner. A more effective approach would have been to use this opportune time for some health teaching in an effort to address some of the cultural factors that led to Lorpu's death. There is no need to humiliate a mother whose decisions every step of the way were influenced by sociocultural norms and economic factors. Na Korto had younger sons at home and would most likely interact with the formal health care system. She needed to be empowered to access the health care system in the future. A positive interaction at a health care center would build her trust in the system and pave the way for timely reentry. This kind of interchange between a mother and health care providers could save the lives of Na Korto's other children, whose lives could yet be cut short by, for example, treatable diarrheal-related diseases.

Millions of people in sub-Saharan Africa fall prey to infectious diseases (e.g., malaria or worm infestations) because they are already poor and suffer from malnutrition. Many of these helminthic infestations are treatable, but the lack of access to clean water and to adequate nutrition as well as poor sanitation leads to reinfection. For many in Africa, the cycle of endemic medical problems is only the "tip of the iceberg" that leads to perpetuating downward spirals of adverse health effects and excess mortality. Many sub-Saharan Africans are caught up in a vicious interlocking web of poverty and disease.

Because of their vulnerability and lack of a political voice, poor people are usually an invisible group. Poverty can be viewed as a multidimensional construct in which poor health status is regarded as one of the consequences. Lorpu and her family, like other poor people in sub-Saharan Africa and around the world, are not familiar with the many health and economic declarations that have been promulgated by United Nations (UN) agencies since the international organization's inception. In light of the realization that the health of populations is critical to the development of any nation, nearly 60 years ago, the UN's Universal Declaration of Human Rights was passed. According to this declaration, "[e]veryone has the right to a standard of living adequate for the health and well being of him (her) self and his (her) family, including food, clothing, housing and medical care" (United Nations, 1948). The point of this document demonstrates that the right to health is dependent upon the realization of other human rights, including economic and other sociopolitical rights. For example, young girls in sub-Saharan Africa will be unable to fully protect themselves from sexually transmitted disease and HIV/AIDS unless they have the right to information about STD and HIV transmission and that information is disseminated to them.

Is Achievement of Optimal Health Possible in Sub-Saharan African Countries Emerging from Civil Conflicts?

For many in sub-Saharan Africa, optimal health is an elusive goal, especially in the midst of ever-changing environmental forces on the subcontinent that entail exposure to new risks. Increasing and sustaining economic development will have a positive effect on the entire continent. We must be mindful, however, that the desire for better lives and futures has driven rural people in Liberia to migrate to urban areas, but they find only that it is still immensely difficult to better their lives. In fact, in every sub-Saharan African country, people are migrating to the cities and periurban areas in search of jobs. Their failure to find jobs and the difficulty of acculturating to urban life also has negative effects on their physical and mental health status. The endemic web of poverty continues to ensnare all sub-Saharan African countries. Because African governments are indebted to international lending institutions (e.g., the International Monetary Fund and the World Bank), governments must yield to the demands of the lending institutions to use the monies involved wisely to better the lives of their people. Unfortunately, when governments show restraint with their budgets, they misguidedly reduce health care and social programs.

Low-tech solutions currently exist to provide simple, primary-level, cost-effective health care that would save millions of lives, but disparities exist as to the availability of these life-saving treatments in many sub-Saharan African countries. The reasons for health disparities can be a function of internal and external forces. Creating a climate of accountability to the people and the international community is an important step for transformation of the system.

In 2000, the member states of the UN deliberated and passed a landmark document referred to as the UN Millennium Development Goals; 189 countries signed this document. This framework for improving health globally lists eight goals to be achieved by 2015: (1) the eradication of extreme poverty and hunger; (2) the achievement of universal education; (3) the promotion of gender equality and empowerment of women; (4) reduction in child mortality; (5) improvement of maternal health; (6) the combating of HIV/AIDS, malaria, and other communicable diseases; (7) the ensuring of environmental sustainability; and (8) the development of a global partnership for development (International Monetary Fund, 2004).

These are noble goals. The problem is that studies are now reporting that many countries may not be able to achieve these goals by 2015 unless there is more economic investment and commitment to implementing the programs needed to achieve the goals (Nullis-Kapp, 2004). Achieving these goals may be even more difficult and challenging in sub-Saharan African countries like Liberia. Because countries like Liberia are emerging from civil conflicts and are economically, socially, and politically unstable, it's ability to achieve these goals is at best tenuous. Unless a country can achieve the first goal of eradicating extreme poverty and hunger, health goals will be hard to reach.

Expectations, both in Liberia and internationally, are high for democratically elected leaders to unite postwar Liberia. To resuscitate Liberia is an enormous task. Liberia's infrastructures—economic, educational, natural resource, and health systems—were all destroyed during the civil conflicts and will therefore need a sizable infusion of cash into the systems just to keep them initially afloat. Unfortunately, in countries emerging from civil conflicts, many donors and investors are leery about an all-out investment in a setting that is still fragile and whose future is uncertain. The very nature of countries emerging from civil conflicts with little or no functional health infrastructure makes it difficult to provide health to the people or persuade international health agencies to work in these countries. From the market perspective, no matter how much funding is available, or how morally justified such programs may be, every investment must yield a return. The delivery of health care, however, is one of those areas that could serve as the fulcrum for bringing the population together while launching other development initiatives. For example, a maternal/child health program that is geared toward reducing maternal and child mortality may be less political or antagonistic to the diverse ethnic groups and former warring factions than, say, signing a contract with a multinational company to have the rights to mine iron ore in Liberia.

Creating an Environment for Change and Moving Forward

Proposals for improving the health status of people in developing countries emphasize the importance of public health approaches, including community-based participatory health prevention and promotion programs. These types of health care programs require integration of health services, institutional capacity, and embracing of locally acceptable reforms of the health care sector (World Health Organization, 2004). However, public health actions cannot totally be separated from the economy of the country and from political sectors. Some of the postwar health-related or social problems in Liberia can be prevented through political interventions; for example, the rise in domestic violence and rape could be curtailed by stronger policies that protect women's rights.

Liberia faces enormous challenges today as it emerges from a civil war that decimated its health care system. However, Liberian leaders, as well as the international community, cannot lose sight of the people's potential to embrace change. In both local and émigré Liberian communities, people are expressing their desire for change to occur in all sectors. They are becoming more vocal in advocating how health care could be efficiently organized and delivered. In this postwar era, open forums are needed to debate and discuss the priorities and scope of health care systems reform and the approaches that would be critical for improving health and enhancing development. Liberians are capable people, and Liberians with expertise in health-related disciplines exist, both in the country and abroad. What is needed in postwar Liberia is a vision for the future that would consider the complexities of a fragile postwar society, the intricacies of a modern health care system, and current epidemiological patterns of disease and poor conditions that impair health. Every stakeholder, including postwar governments, needs to admit there are no easy solutions or quick fixes. Policy makers need to make concerted efforts to propose realistic programs.

The following factors   critical to health care reforms in postwar Liberia should be considered:

Involvement of the Liberian People in Designing and Implementing Health Care Programs

In postwar Liberia, self-determination for health and economic achievement should be the goal of all people. One of the tenets of an adequate primary health care program is community involvement. Even in high-functioning, developed countries, privileged with more stable funding for health programs, community involvement is crucial in designing and implementing health projects. Public health experts have learned over the years that neglecting to gain the endorsement of communities in critical health programs lead to failure. All Liberians should be regarded as stewards of their own health, regardless of their literacy levels or contexts for understanding. The role of health providers is to empower people by communicating health information in an accessible and acceptable manner. For example, officials of Liberia's Ministry of Health and Social Welfare (MOH&SW) will become successful in developing, implementing, and evaluating a diarrheal control program in a rural village in Liberia if the local people are regarded as partners in health. New strategies should promote and stress the ethos of collective responsibility for health. If more of the Liberian population begins to embrace the notion of collective action, Liberia will be on its way to achieving improvement in its population's health and well-being. When implementing health initiatives in postwar Liberia, officials should be keen to understand whether such initiatives lead the people to greater control of the health and lives.

Increasing Cooperation among Sub-Saharan African Countries for the Promotion of Health

Many sub-Saharan African countries lag far behind other developing countries on fundamental health indices, including infant and maternal mortality rates, as well as life expectancy (Ncayiyana, 2002). Because these countries also have inadequate health delivery systems, many international experts wonder if the subcontinent can address its own health problems. Ncayiyana (2002), however, posits that while African countries may not be able to resolve all their health crises alone, they could enhance the health of their own peoples if they reprioritize their goals and became committed to redistributing their limited resources. In the same work, Ncayiyana argues that African leaders are also to blame for their failure to create the optimal living conditions that would lead to better health for their people: safe water and sanitation, adequate supply of food, and improved literacy levels. Accordingly, as Ncayiyana writes, "[m]any countries have seen both opportunity and resources squandered on political adventurism, civil wars, misguided macro economic policies, and greed," (p. 688). These are not just African occurrences. Some Latin American countries (El Salvador, Colombia) have also faced similar problems during protracted civil wars. Sub-Saharan African countries can learn from developing countries on other continents that have pulled themselves out of a period of self-destruction.

The civil war in Liberia spilled over into many neighboring countries, including Sierra Leone, Côte d'Ivoire, and Guinea. The adverse effect of the civil conflict was felt not only by Liberians, but also the entire West African Belt. The displacement of populations within the region creates difficulties in controlling diseases and compromises the ability of countries to provide adequate health care for their own peoples. The challenges of disease control and prevention are an opportunity for collaboration. Combined efforts are especially critical in the control of infectious outbreaks, since boundaries in Africa are porous. Improvement in the health of the peoples of Liberia and other sub-Saharan African countries warrants intercountry collaboration on health and other social issues that affect the health of all peoples.

Conclusion

The commitment of African leaders to improve the living standards of the people will also improve their health. Poverty is a serious barrier to health care and overall life satisfaction. People in many sub-Saharan African countries are desperately poor and thus cannot afford adequate housing, and subsequently, are exposed to the microorganisms that cause waterborne illness, malaria, tuberculosis, and the like. Also, because these people are generally poor, they lack access to health care and sometimes cannot afford even simple life-saving remedies. Along with growing the economy, Liberia, in the postwar era, will also need to figure out ways to distribute health care resources equitably to all its citizens, regardless of socioeconomic status, geographic location, or tribal affiliation. Studies now suggest that accumulation of wealth alone may not be a sine qua non for optimal health. Rather, there are complex interrelated factors, ecological and material, that support or undermine one's health status (Hertzman, 2001; Daniels, Kennedy, and Kawachi, 2000). Hertzman (2001) raises a poignant question in his research that is very relevant to Liberia and other sub-Saharan African countries emerging from civil conflicts: "To what extent do the institutions of civil society, as they are encountered on a daily basis, buffer or exacerbate the stresses of daily living, and promote or undermine living conditions that, over the long-term, are compatible with health and well-being?" For many Liberians, health expectations are, for the most part, low on their list of priorities, and they are more concerned about their immediate daily living needs. All that many Liberians ask for is for their government to assist them to meet their basic needs: clean water, good sanitation, education, and access to basic health care. Trust in good governance will be essential to progress. Postwar governments will have greater impact on the people and gain their trust if they make limited promises on what they can do and follow through on such promises.

Finally, along with the proposal for broad representation of all stakeholders in reforming the health care system in Liberia, the following priority categories are proposed for the improvement of the public's health: (1) concerted efforts to reduce health disparities by focusing on vulnerable populations (women, children, war orphans, etc.); (2) creation of an environment for participatory governance in which Liberians can become more involved in their own destinies; (3) revitalizing, reorganizing, and strengthening existing health care institutions, with emphasis on the primary health care level; and (4) development of an agenda to support grassroots health prevention and promotion activities. MOH&SW officials should revisit the possibility of reallocating funds from expensive curative services to priority public health agendas. This would lessen the burden on the use of secondary and tertiary care services for conditions that could have been prevented or treated with early intervention at the primary care level. With effective health reform strategies, I am optimistic as to the possibility that Liberia can once again stand as a proud nation capable of caring for its people.

Notes

1. Roosevelt, Franklin D. (1937). "Second inaugural address." January 20th, Washington D.C. *[http://www.bartleby.com/124/press50.html]*.

BIBLIOGRAPHY

Adamu, Y.M. and H.M. Salihu. "Barriers to use of antenatal and obstetric care services in rural Kano, Nigeria." *Journal of Obstetrics and Gynaecology* 22, (6) (2002): 600–603.

Appiah, K.A., and H.L Gates. *Africana: The encyclopedia of the African and African American experience.* New York, New York: Basic Covitas Books, 1999.

Becker, G.S. *Human capital: A theoretical and empirical analysis with special reference to education.* Second edition. New York: National Bureau of Economic Research, 1975.

Blakney, R.B., J.I. Litvack, and J.D. Quick. "Financing health care: Experiences in pharmaceutical cost recovery." Report by the Pritech Committee. Boston, Massachusetts: Management Sciences for Health, 1989.

Brownlee, A.T. *Community, culture, and care: A cross-cultural guide for health workers.* St. Louis, Missouri: The Mosby Company, 1978.

Brundon-Jakobowic, P. "Evaluation et monitoring dans le contex du programme d'action pour les medicaments et vaccins essentials. In le medicament essential dans les pays en development." Comptes Rendus du Symposium International, Ministere de la Cooperation. Paris, France, May 19-20, 1987.

Buchan, J., and M.R. Dal Poz. "Skill mix in the health care workforce: Reviewing the evidence." *Bulletin of World Health Organization* 80, (7) (2002): 575–80.

Bureau of Statistics, Ministry of Planning and Economic Affairs, Liberia. *Liberian Demographic and Health Survey.* Monrovia, Liberia: Bureau of Statistics, Ministry of Planning and Economic Affairs, Liberia, 1986.

Centers for Disease Control and Prevention, United States of America. "The Impact of Malaria, a Leading Cause of Death Worldwide." <*http://www.cdc.gov/malaria/impact/*> (September 19, 2004).

Centers for Disease Control and Prevention, United States of America, Division of Bacterial and Mycotic Diseases. "Cholera." <*http://www.cdc.gov/ncidod/ dbmd/diseaseinfo/cholera_g.htm*> (April 3, 2006).

Chieh-Johnson, D., A.R. Cross, A.A. Way, and J.M. Sullivan. *Liberia Demographic and Health Survey 1986.* Monrovia, Liberia: Bureau of Statistics, Ministry of Planning and Economic Affairs, and Columbia, Maryland: Institute for Resource Development, Westinghouse, 1986.

Chima, R.I., C.A. Goodman, and A. Mills. "The economic impact of malaria in Africa: a critical review of the evidence." *Health Policy* 63, (1) (2003): 17–36.

Cohen, D. "Human capital and the HIV epidemic in sub-Saharan Africa." International Labour Organization Programme on HIV/AIDS and the World Bank, Working Paper, Geneva, Switzerland, June 2002.

Crisp, B.R., H. Swerissen, and S.J. Duckett. "Four approaches to capacity building in health: Consequences for management and accountability." *Health Promotion International* 15 (2000): 99–107.

Cross, P.N., M.A. Huff, J.D. Quick, and J.A. Bates. "Revolving drug funds: Conducting business in public sector." *Social Science and Medicine* 22 (3), (1986): 335–43.

Dabis, F., A. Roisin, and J.G. Breman. "Improper practices for diarrhea treatment in Africa." *Transaction of Royal Society of Medicine and Hygiene* 82, (6) (1988): 935–36.

Daniels, N., B. Kennedy, and I. Kawachi. *Is inequality bad for our health?* Boston, Massachusetts: Beacon Press, 2000.

Fiscella, K., P. Franks, M. Gold, and C.M. Clancy. "Inequality in quality: addressing socioeconomic, racial, and ethnic disparities in health care." *Journal of the American Medical Association* 283 (2000): 2579–84.

Foster, S.D. "Improving the supply and use of essential drugs in Sub-Saharan Africa." Working paper 456. Washington, D.C.: World Bank Population and Human Resources Department, 1990.

Fox, M.P., S. Rosen, W.B. Macleod, M. Wasunna, M. Bii, G. Foglia, and J.L. Simon. "The Impact of HIV/AIDS on labour productivity in Kenya." *Tropical Medicine International Health* 9 (3) (2004): 318–24.

Global Forum for Health Research. *Monitoring financial flows for health research.* Geneva, Switzerland: Global Forum for Health Research, 2002.

Grassly, N.C., K. Desai, E. Pegurri, A. Sikazwe, I. Malambo, C. Siamatowe, and D. Bundy. "The economic impact of HIV/AIDS on the education sector in Zambia." *AIDS* 17 (7) (2003): 1039–44.

Green, A. *An introduction to health planning in developing countries.* New York, New York: Oxford University Press, 1994.

Grosse, R.N., and C. Auffrey. "Literacy and health status in developing countries." *Annual Review of Public Health* 10 (1989): 281–97.

Guinness, L., D. Walker, P. Ndubani, J. Jama, and P. Kelly. "Surviving the impact of HIV-related illness in the Zimbabwean sector." *AIDS Patient Care STDs* 17 (7) (2003): 353–63.

Habte, D., G. Dussault, and D. Dovlo. "Challenges confronting the health workforce in sub-Saharan Africa." *World Hospital Health Service* 40 (2) (2004): 23–26.

Hertzman, C. "Health and human society: Wealthier nations are not always healthier, and efforts to improve health can be swamped by the effects of inequality and conflict." *American Scientist* 89 (6) (2001): 538–43.

International Development Research Centre. "New Wireless Network for Uganda's Health Care Workers." <*http://www.idrc.ca/en/ev-47580-201-1-DO_TOPIC.html*> (April 1, 2006).

International Monetary Fund. *Health and development: Why investing in health is critical for achieving economic development goals.* Washington, D.C.: International Monetary Fund http://www.imf.org/external/pubs/ft/health/eng/hdwi/hdwi.pdf> (2004).

Isenalumhe, A.E. and O. Oviawe. "The changing pattern of post-partum sexual abstinence in a Nigerian rural community." *Social Science and Medicine* 23 (7) (1986): 683–86.

Jackson, T. "On the limitations of health promotion." *Community Health Studies* 9 (1985): 1–6.

Kelly, K. *Out of control: The new biology of machines, social systems and the economic world.* New York, N.Y.: Perseus Books Group, 1995.

Leeder, S.R. "Health promoting environments: the role of public policy." *Australian and New Zealand Journal of Public Health* 21 (1997): 413–14.

Liberia Demographic and Health Survey, 1999/2000. Monrovia, Liberia: Ministry of Planning and Economic Affairs; University of Liberia; United Nations Population Fund. <*http://www.stanford.edu/~karenf/blog/archives/2006/01/african_documen_3.html*> (June 30, 2006)

Liverpool, J., R. Alexander, M. Johnson, E.K. Ebba, S. Francis, and C. Liverpool. "Western medicine and traditional healers: Partners in the fight against HIV/AIDS." *Journal of the National Medical Association* 96 (6) (2004): 822–25.

Marchal, B., V. De Brouwere, and G. Kegels. "Viewpoint: HIV/AIDS and the health workforce crisis: what are the next steps? *Tropical Medicine International Health* 10 (4) (2005): 300–304.

McElmurry, B.J., C.G. Park, and A.G. Buseh. "The nurse-community health advocate team for urban immigrant primary health care." Journal of Nursing Scholarship 35 (3) (2003):275–81.

McPake, B. *Experience to date of implementing the Bamako initiative: A review and five country case studies.* London. Health Economics and Financing Program, London School of Tropical Medicine, 1992.

McPake, B., D. Asiimwe, F. Mwesigye, M. Ofumbi, L. Ortenblad, P. Streefland, and A. Turinde. "Informal economic activities of public health workers in Uganda: implications for quality and accessibility of care." *Social Science and Medicine* 49 (7) (1999): 849–65.

Meade, M.S., J.W. Florin, and W.M. Gesler. *Medical Geography.* New York, New York: The Guilford Press, 1988.

Médecins Sans Frontières. "Fatal Imbalance: The Crisis in Research and Development for Drugs for Neglected Diseases." 2001. <*http://www.accessmed-msf.org*> (April 13, 2006).

Miller, I. "Executive leadership, community action, and the habits of health care politics." *Health Care Management Review* 17 (1) (1992): 81–84.

Milton, R. "Financing of health services: Proceeding of a World Health Organization Interregional Workshop, Mexico, November 26-30, 1979." Geneva, Switzerland: World Health Organization, SHS/SPM/80.3 (1979): 31–39.

Minnaar, A. "HIV/AIDS issues in the workplace of nurses." *Curationis* 28 (3) (2005): 31–38.

Ministry of Health and Social Welfare, Liberia. *Annual Report.* Monrovia, Liberia: Liberian Ministry of Health and Social Welfare, 1988.

Ministry of Health and Social Welfare, Liberia. *Annual Report.* Monrovia, Liberia: Liberian Ministry of Health and Social Welfare, 1991.

Musgrove, P. "Measurement of equity in health." *World Health Statistics Quarterly* 39 (4) (1986): 325–35.

Ncayiyana, D.J. "Doctors and nurses with HIV and AIDS in sub-Saharan Africa." *British Medical Journal* 329 (2004): 600–601.

————. "Africa can solve its own health problems: But first, the continent must reorder its priorities and commit to distributive justice." *British Medical Journal* 324 (2002): 688–89.

Nemcek, M.A., and R. Sabatier. "State of evaluation: community health workers." Public Health Nursing 20 (4) (July-August 2003): 260–70.

Nkrumah, Kwame. *Africa must unite,* quoted in *Axioms of Kwame Nkrumah* (Freedom Fighters' Edition). London, Great Britain: Panaf Books Ltd., 1977.

Nullis-Kapp, C. "The knowledge is there to achieve development goals, but is the will?" *Bulletin of the World Health Organization* 82 (10) (2004): 804–806.

Nutbeam, D. "Creating health promoting environments: overcoming barriers to action." *Australian and New Zealand Journal of Public Health* 1 (1997): 355–59.

Organization of African Unity and the United Nations Children's Fund. *Africa's children, Africa's future: Human investment priorities for the 1990s.* Addis Ababa, Ethiopia: Organization of African Unity, 1992.

Osuji, M. "Exploration of the frontiers of tradomedical practices: basis for development of alternative medical healthcare services in developing countries." *Journal of Royal Society of Health* 113 (4) (1993): 190–94.

Peden, M., R. Scurfield, D. Sleet, D. Mohan, A.A. Hyder, E. Jarawan, and C. Mathers. *World Report on Road Traffic Injury Prevention.* Geneva, Switzerland: World Health Organization, 2004.

Physicians for Human Rights. *An Action Plan to Prevent Brain Drain: Building Equitable Health Systems in Africa.* Cambridge, Massachusetts: Physicians for Human Rights, July 2004.

Rappaport, J. "Empowerment meets narrative: listening to stories and creating settings." *American Journal of Community Psychology* 23 (1995): 795–807.

Rodriguez, V.M., T.L. Conway, S.I. Woodruff, and C.C. Edwards. "Pilot test of an assessment instrument for Latina community health advisors conducting an ETS intervention." *Journal of Immigrant Health* 5 (3) (July 2003): 129–37.

Roosevelt, Franklin D. "Second inaugural address." January 20, 1937. <*http://www.bartleby.com/124/pres50.html*> (June 30, 2006).

Rotberg, R.I. *When states failed: causes and consequences.* Princeton, New Jersey: Princeton University Press, 2004.

Russell, S.S., and J. Reynolds. *Community financing.* PRICOR Monography Series: Issues Paper 1 Bethesda, MD: Center for Human Services), 1987.

Rustein, S.O. "Factors associated with trends in infant and child mortality in developing countries during the 1990s." *Bulletin of World Health Organization* 78 (10) (2000): 1256–70.

Sen, A. *Development as freedom.* Oxford, England: Oxford University Press, 1999.

Shediac-Rizkallah, M.C., and L.R. Bone. "Planning for the sustainability of community-based health programs: Conceptual frameworks and future directions for research, practice and policy." *Health Education Research* 13 (1998): 87–108.

Shi, L. and D.A. Singh. *Delivering health care in America: a systems approach.* Third Edition, Boston, MA: Jones and Bartlett Publishers, 2005.

Shick, T.W. *Behold the Promised Land: The history of Afro-American settler society in nineteenth-century Liberia.* Baltimore, Maryland: The Johns Hopkins University Press, 1980.

Smith, J.W. *Sojourners in search of freedom: The settlement of Liberia of Black Americans.* Lanham, MD: University Press of America, 1987.

Swerissen, H., and B.R. Crisp. "The sustainability of health promotion interventions for different levels of social organization." *Health Promotion International* 19 (1) (2004): 123–30.

Swiss, S., P.J. Jennings, G.V. Aryee, G.H. Brown, R.M. Jappah-Samukai, M.S. Kamara, R.D. Schaack, and R.S. Turay-Kanneh. "Prevalence of war-related sexual violence and other human rights abuses among internally displaced persons in Sierra Leone." *Journal of the American Medical Association* 287 (4) (1998): 513–21.

UNICEF. *State of the World's Children*. New York, New York: Oxford University Press, 1990.

_____. *State of the World's Children*. New York, New York: Oxford University Press, 2004.

_____. *State of the World's Children*. New York, New York: Oxford University Press, 2005.

United Nations. Universal declaration of human rights. 1948. <*http://www.un.org/overview/rights.html*> (March 31, 2006).

_____. *United Nations Millennium Development Goals*. 2006. <*http://www.un.org/millenniumgoals.html*> (April 13, 2006).

United Nations AIDS Programme. "AIDS epidemic update December 2005." 2005. <*http://www.unaids.org/epi/2005*> (April 13, 2006).

United Nations Conference on the Environment and Development (UNCED). *The global partnership for environment and development: A guide to Agenda 21*. Geneva, Switzerland: United Nations Conference on the Environment and Development (UNCED), 1992.

United Nations Development Programme. *National human development report 1999*. Monrovia, Liberia: United Nations Development Programme, 2000.

_____. *Human Development Report*. New York, New York: Oxford University Press, 2003.

_____. *Human development reports: Liberia*. 2006. <*http://hdr.undp.org/reports/detail_reports.cfm?view=991*> (April 13, 2006).

United States Agency for International Development. *Liberian Health Sector Assessment*. Falls Church, Virginia: The PRAGMA Corporation, 1988.

United States Agency for International Development. *The health sector human resource crisis in Africa: An issues paper*. Washington, D.C.: Academy for Educational Development, February 2003.

Walt, G., and L. Gildon. "Reforming the health sector in developing countries: The central role of policy analysis." *Health Policy and Planning* 9 (4) (1994): 344–53.

Whitehead, M. "The concepts and principles of equity and health." *International Journal of Health Services* 22 (3) (1992): 429–45.

Whyte, S.R. "The consumers' use of pharmaceuticals: A case from Uganda." Paper presented to the World Bank/DANIDA Seminar on Economics and

Policy Choices of Pharmaceuticals in Developing Countries, Copenhagen, Denmark, 1990.

World Bank. *Financing health services in developing countries: An agenda for reform.* Washington, D.C.: The World Bank, 1987.

_____. "Pharmaceutical expenditures and cost recovery schemes in Sub-Saharan Africa." Technical working paper 4. Washington, D.C.: The World Bank, Africa Technical Department, Population, Health, and Nutrition Division, 1992.

_____. *World Development Report: Investing in Health, World Development Indicators.* New York, New York: Oxford University Press, 1993.

_____. *Better health in Africa: Experience and lessons learned.* Washington, D.C.: The World Bank, 1994.

World Health Organization. *Alma-Ata—Primary health care.* Health for All Series, No. 1. Geneva,   Switzerland: World Health Organization, 1978.

_____. *Declaration of Alma-Ata. International Conference on Primary Health Care, Alma-Ata, USSR, September 6-12, 1978.* 1978. <*http://www.who. int/hpr/NPH/docs/declaration_almaata.pdf*> (March 31, 2006).

_____. *The role of universities in the strategies for health for all: A social contribution to human development and social justice.* Geneva, Switzerland: World Health Organization, 1984.

_____. *Evaluation of the strategy for health for all by the year 2000.* Vol. 2, *Seventh report of the world health situation.* Brazzaville, Congo: World Health Organization, 1987.

_____. "Lassa fever." Fact sheet No. 179. April 2000. <*http://www.who.int/ mediacentre/factsheets/ fs179/en/*> (September 19, 2004).

_____. *The world health report 2000: Health systems: improving performance.* Geneva, Switzerland: World Health Organization, 2000.

_____. *World health report on knowledge for better health: Strengthening health systems.* Geneva, Switzerland: World Health Organization, 2004.

_____. *Malaria vector control and personal protection. WHO technical report series: no. 936,* Geneva: Switzerland, 2006.

World Health Organization World Mental Health Survey Consortium. "Prevalence, severity, and unmet need for treatment of mental disorders in the World Health Organization world mental health surveys." *Journal of the American Medical Association* 291 (2004): 2581–90.

SUBJECT INDEX

A

A. M. Dogliotti College of Medicine, 157
Abortions, 37–38
Access to immunizations and nutrition, 118, 167, 185, 188
African pharmaceutical markets review, 198–200
African tenant of teamwork, 231
African trypanosomiasis (sleeping sickness), 186
African Union (AU), 3, 110
Agriculture and health plan development, 120, 123
Alma Ata Declaration (1978), 18, 20n3, 124, 130, 155
Altruism in health care, 93–95
Anemia, 38
Avian flu (H5N1), 190

B

Bill and Melinda Gates Foundation, 190
Biomedicine
  failure of its approach to illness, 245
  as opposed to conservative primary health care, 228–29
  versus traditional healing, 193–95
Bong Mining Companies, 27, 86
Botswana, 168
"Brain drain"
  "An Action Plan to Prevent Brain Drain: Building a Durable Health Systems in Africa" (2004), 169
  defined, 165

inter county, 167–69
intra country, 165–66
public/private sector, 166–67
Bribery/corruption and health care, 238–42
  factors contributing to, 238–39
  in Liberia, 12–14
  Liberian émigrés and, 10
  national code of ethics and, 239
  patients' rights and, 239–40
  strategies for preventing, 239–40
  in the United States, 12
  wages and, 239
Bribery/corruption (institutional)
  bribery defined, 10
  corruption defined, 10
  effects of, 12–13
  in electoral processes, 11
  in Liberian government, 10–11
  as systematic, 11
  tribal favoritism and, 13
  William Tolbert's work against, 13
Brownlee, A. T., 33
Bureaucratic inefficiencies in health care, 128–30

C

Carter Center, 190
Categories for improvement of public's health, 252
Catherine Mills Rehabilitation Center, 64, 65
Center for Complementary and Alternative Medicine (CAM), 196
Central African Republic, 146

AUTHOR INDEX

A

Adamu, Y.M., and H.N. Salihu
   (2002), 241, 249
Appiah, K.A., and H.L. Gates
   (1999), 22, 249

B

Becker, G. S. (1993), 149, 249
Blakney, R.B., J.I. Litvack, and
   J.D. Quick (1989), 198, 249
Brownlee, A. T. (1978), 33, 249
Brundon-Jakobowicz, P. (1987),
   197, 249
Buchan, J., and M.R. Dal Poz
   (2002), 156, 157, 249
Bureau of Statistics, Ministry of
   Planning and Economic Af-
   fairs, Liberia (1986), 249

C

Centers for Disease Control and
   Prevention, U.S.A. (2004),
   48, 250
Centers for Disease Control and
   Prevention, U.S.A., Div. of
   Bacterial and Mycotic Dis-
   eases (2006), 51, 250
Chieh-Johnson, D., A.R. Cross,
   A.A. Way, and J. M.
   Sullivan (2003), 42, 250
Chima, R.I., C. A. Goodman, and
   A. Mills (2003), 49, 250
Cohen, D. (2002), 171, 250
Crisp, B. R., H. Swerissen, and S.J.
   Duckett (2000), 146, 250
Cross, P. N., M. A. Huff, J.D.
   Quick, and J. A. Bates
   (1986), 198, 250

D

Dabris, F., A. Roisin, and J.G.
   Breman (1988), 250
Daniels, N., B. Kennedy, and I.
   Kawachi (2000), 247, 250

F

Fiscella, K., P. Franks, M. Gold,
   and C.M. Clancy (2000), 67,
   250
Foster, S. D. (1990), 195, 196, 250
Fox, M.P., S. Rosen, W. B.
   MacLeod, M. Wasunna, M.
   Bii, G. Foglia, and J. L. Si-
   mon (2004), 55, 250

G

Global Forum for Health Research
   (2002), 181, 250
Grassly, N.C., K. Desai, E. Pegurri,
   A. Sikazwe, I. Malambo, C.
   Simatowe, and D. Bundy
   (2003), 55, 250
Green, A. (1994), 151, 250
Grosse, R.N., and C. Auffrey
   (1989), 213, 251
Guinness, L., D. Walker, P.
   Ndubani, J. Jama, and P.
   Kelly (2003), 55, 251

H

Habte, D., G. Dussault, and D.
   Dovlo (2004), 55, 251
Hertzman, C. (2001), 247, 251

I

International Development Research Centre (2006), 39,
   251

ABOUT THE AUTHOR

An indigenous Liberian now residing in the United States, Dr. Aaron G. Buseh is an associate professor at the University of Wisconsin-Milwaukee College of Nursing. He has over fifteen years of experience in nursing and public health. His instructional concentration is in the area of understanding the organization, financing, and delivery of health care in developed and developing countries.

Dr. Buseh first obtained a bachelor of science degree in nursing from Cuttington University College in Liberia and was awarded an international fellowship by the United States Agency for International Development (USAID) to pursue graduate studies in public health. He completed a master of public health (MPH) degree and a master of science degree in nursing, both from the University of Illinois at Chicago. He subsequently completed his doctor of philosophy (Ph.D.) degree in nursing science from the University of Wisconsin-Milwaukee (UWM).

While enrolled in the doctoral program at UWM, he received the John E. Fogarty International Center, National Institutes of Health Minority International Research Training (MIRT) Fellowship sponsored by the University of Illinois Global Health Leadership Office to complete his doctoral dissertation research in the area of sexual risk behaviors and HIV/AIDS transmission and prevention among adolescents in Swaziland, Southern Africa.

His current research program spans both local and global public health research areas, with a focus on vulnerable populations and health systems research. Dr. Buseh is the author of numerous refereed articles in health-related and social sciences journals. He is a popular lecturer in formal academic settings as well as in local communities on health disparities and sustainable development issues in sub-Saharan Africa.